T3-ATX-531

THE NATURAL FOOD GARDEN

THE NATURAL FOOD
GARDEN

Growing Vegetables and Fruits Chemical-Free

PATRICK LIMA
Photography by JOHN SCANLAN

Prima Publishing
P.O. Box 1260
Rocklin, CA 95677
(916) 786-0426

To Anne Marie Scanlan for her encouragement and appreciation

Like our garden, this book has grown out of the combined efforts of friends. We wish to extend our thanks to Elizabeth Etue for planting the seed thought for the book at the start; Dustin McMullin and Duff Campbell for taking such good care of the garden while we were tapping and snapping; Margaret Dimsdale for some sharp-eyed editing at the dining room table; Mari Bower and Martino Lee for the key to a quiet writing space by the bay; and to all those visitors who shared their gardening secrets with us.

Copyright © 1992 by Patrick Lima and John Scanlan
Photographs and illustrations copyright © 1992 by John Scanlan

All rights reserved. No part of this book may be reproduced or transmitted in any form or by any means, electronic or mechanical, including photocopying, recording, or by information storage or retrieval system without written permission from the copyright holder, except for the inclusion of quotations in a review.

Published by arrangement with Key Porter Books, Canada

Prima Publishing
Rocklin, CA

Library of Congress Cataloging-in-Publication Data
Lima, Patrick.
The natural food garden / Patrick Lima and John Scanlan.
p.   cm.
Includes index.
ISBN 1-55958-202-2 $19.95
1. Vegetable gardening. 2. Organic gardening. 3. Cookery
(Vegetables) 4. Fruit-culture. I. Scanlan, John, 1949–
II. Title.

SB324.3.L55   1992   635'.0484–dc20   91-46243 CIP

Page i:
A sampling of
the garden's seasonal abundance.

Frontispiece:
Lovely to look at and delightful to eat,
French lettuces, such as "Canasta" and "Victoria,"
can be cut at the leafy stage or left to
form dense, compact heads.

Text design: Tania Craan
Typesetting: MacTrix DTP
Printed and bound in Hong Kong

92 93 94 10 9 8 7 6 5 4 3 2 1

CONTENTS

• 1 •
BREAKING NEW GROUND 1

• 2 •
EARTH CARE 7
Creating and Sustaining Lively Soil

• 3 •
BY DESIGN 19
A Kitchen Garden Layout

• 4 •
SPRING STEPS 27

• 5 •
TROUBLE 39
Insects, Weeds, Frost, and Water

• 6 •
SOW COOL 47
Peas, Spinach, Onions, and Leeks

• 7 •
LETTUCE ALONE 57

• 8 •
CULTIVATED COLES 61
Growing Cabbages and Kin

• 9 •
THE ROOT OF THE MATTER 67
Carrots, Parsnips, Beets, Radishes,
and Potatoes

• 10 •
TROPICAL FRUITS 79
Tomatoes, Peppers, and Eggplant

• 11 •
THREE SISTERS OF LIFE 87
Corn, Squash, and Beans

• 12 •
FRUIT OF THE VINE 101
Melons and Cucumbers

• 13 •
SECOND SEASON 109
Midsummer Seeding for Fall Eating

• 14 •
GREEN EXOTICA 117
Arugula, Corn Salad, Florence Fennel,
Mustard Greens, Radicchio, Chicory
and Swiss Chard

• 15 •
ALL ABOUT ALLIUMS 125
Garlic, Shallots, Egyptian Onions,
and Wild Leeks

• 16 •
KITCHEN-GARDEN PERENNIALS 129
Asparagus, Jerusalem Artichokes,
and Sorrel

• 17 •
THE FRUITFUL SEASON 137
Strawberries and Raspberries

APPENDIX 146
Seed Sources

INDEX 151

1

BREAKING
NEW GROUND

FIRST GARDEN

Almost from the moment I set trowel to earth I knew I had found a task I loved to do. Suddenly a world of wonders opened up. It was 1973. My friend John Scanlan and I had access to the garden of a rented city house. Like many other people then — and now — we looked with concern at the array of pesticides routinely used on food plants. A small yard meant that we could grow at least some of our own food free from chemical residues. From the start, it never occurred to us to garden any way other than organically. We knew that freshly picked vegetables and fruits are at their nutritional best, packed with vitamins and minerals. We soon learned how delicious they could be: vine-ripened tomatoes, peas fresh from the pod, a crisp head of cabbage or lettuce mere minutes from garden bed to salad bowl. We also discovered the honest pleasure and satisfaction that come from working with the soil, sowing seeds, tending the garden, bringing in the harvest.

The soil in that first garden was dense and full of cinders. It had probably been the dumping ground for years' worth of coal ashes, but optimistically we dug and planted. Results were mixed. Tomatoes spread into a wild tangle, half their fruit lost under leaves; zucchinis swelled

Larkwhistle, our garden, began as an unpromising plot of land covered with quack grass, and required much work and cultivation in its transformation.

overnight, apparently blown up by some unseen squash fairy. Marigolds bloomed among the vegetables and morning glories crawled over everything. Unwittingly we spread fungus on the Swiss chard by sprinkling every evening. Not knowing better, we transplanted small pea vines from the shade to the sunny front yard. The peas, not knowing that they "resent transplanting," attached themselves to strings and began to climb. Cucumbers soon joined them to veil the front porch in green vines hung with fruit. Squirrels helped themselves. It was not a completely successful garden, but in a season we were smitten. And we had learned the gardener's perennial refrain: "Next year. . . ."

Our homesteading instincts were roused. That winter we pored over copies of *Organic Gardening* magazine in preparation for some "real" gardening next spring. Bags of manure and peat moss arrived from a garden center; seeds came in the mail. We knocked scrap wood together to make shallow boxes for seedlings that sprouted under a bank of florescent lights in the basement. Convinced by garden articles that the key to a healthy natural garden lay in adding as much organic matter to the soil as possible, we scoured the neighborhood for sources.

Coincidentally, this was shortly after the downtown zoo closed. One day, while walking through the deserted zoo, we saw a heap of manure on the other side of a high chain-link fence. The sign on the fence read "Yak," but there was no yak (or any other animal) in sight. Longingly, we looked through the fence. "If we could get in there," John said, "with buckets and bags and a shovel. . . "

Early next morning we were back with two enormous burlap sacks and a spade. Up and over the fence, and in no time, we had two bags full — and heavy. With some effort we hoisted the precious bags over the fence and dragged them to the boulevard. It was going to be a long haul home. There had to be a better way. And there it was, coming down the street. We were soon settled comfortably on the streetcar with our bags of soggy yak dung. It was the first of several excursions to collect what is now sensibly composted and sold as Zoo Poo.

Eager to experiment, we grew a little of almost everything that second season. Adding organic matter to the garden made a noticeable difference. Spaghetti squash trailed along the loop-top wire fence, dangling plump yellow fruit on both sides. Brilliant Scarlet Runner beans coiled up a tropical looking sumac tree. Cabbages and romaine folded into proper heads, while yellow crookneck squash cascaded down a hill of compost. Tomatoes, staked and trained by the book, grew red in the sun. To our delight, the small city yard provided us with almost all the fresh vegetables we needed through the summer and into fall.

To use the yard to the fullest, we laid the garden out in beds (rather than rows) and planted the beds intensively so that every square foot of earth was growing vegetables, herbs or flowers. Even today, with room to spare in a country garden, we continue to grow vegetables and fruit in beds tended with basic hand tools. Chapter 3 details how to design, build and plant intensive beds that make the best use of any space. Throughout the book, photos show small, easily maintained beds of odd shapes and dimensions filled with lettuces, beans, carrots, even corn. Staking tomatoes and sending cucumbers and pea vines upward on strings, wire, netting, or trellises also brings in an abundant harvest from small spaces. For most home gardeners some variation on intensive gardening is the most efficient way to grow — planting a little of this and that in whatever space you have, back

yard or front, along a walkway, up a fence or porch. Food plants take their place beautifully in any landscape.

GOING TO THE COUNTRY

In July, just as our second city garden was overflowing with growth and color, we were given notice that we would have to move out by the end of August. Confirmed city slickers up to this point, it had never occurred to us to search for a place in the country. We had no car. Where would we work? What was outside the city anyway? Still, when a friend told us about land four hours' drive north, we decided to investigate. The land, she said, belonged to a couple, both university professors, who lived in town but had bought property to preserve it. In a spirit of experimentation, they had allowed some of their students to build a geodesic dome there. A succession of students had lived in the dome. Some had tried their hand at gardening, but all had pulled up stakes eventually, usually after the first winter. The dome now stood empty, our friend said, and went on to assure us that the professors, almost second family to her, would not mind if we moved in and established a garden on a half-acre corner of the 300-acre parcel.

And so, one Saturday, rake and shovel in hand, tent and packs on our back, we boarded a northbound bus, got off three hours later, and reboarded an old green school bus that traveled on from there on summer weekends. The driver opened her doors for us at a gravel sideroad; from there, rough map in hand, we hitchhiked and walked the remaining six miles in.

What we saw when we came around the last corner was a flat field waist-high in swaying grass. A towering dead elm tree, gray and barkless, spread its twisted arms against the sky. A leaning barn, sided with weathered wooden shingles, sheltered a flock of swallows. Toppling fence posts, looped with rusty barbed wire, outlined what may once have been a garden. Half-hidden in tall grass, an old iron hand-pump stood beside a shoulder of exposed rock. The flat field was broken here and there by piles of rock, old apple trees and banks of lilac bushes. Later we would come to recognize the signs that tell a story: here a family cleared land; piled stones by hand; joined with neighbors to build shelters; planted shrubs, an orchard, daylilies, daffodils and a vegetable garden; perhaps suffered a fire; rebuilt down the road or moved away.

After pitching our tent by the well, we were eager to find out what lay under the grass. Digging through the thatch of roots, we came up with handfuls of earth so dry it flowed through our fingers like sand in an hourglass. This was not the dark loam we were hoping for, but it was late July of a dry year — and better sand than brick-hard clay. And weren't the magazines filled with tales of unpromising stuff transformed into fertile soil?

Now, to find the dome. A rutted track led us back into the woods where it sat, bug-eyed and silver, like an alien craft landed by accident among the maples. Inside, the dome was cluttered and dirty, but not, at first glance, unlivable. A few overstuffed chairs, braided rugs, an old oak dining table and a hefty wood-burning cookstove were arranged around an open central space. Later, while listening to raindrops pinging musically into pots and pans set under the skylight at the dome's apex; and later still, as we shivered in woolen hats and gloves, our feet propped on the open oven door, we understood that this home-sweet-dome leaked water and heat in opposite directions.

Clearly we had some mulling-over to do. Nothing in our experience had prepared us for being in the country — and especially here. The change from city life to living on the land would be drastic and complete. Winter would present special challenges — firewood to cut, water to haul from the old iron pump two fields away, an outdoor privy. There would be no easy way to run out to a store. We would be totally isolated. But the good news was that here was an opportunity to garden to our heart's content immediately: there was no need to save money and search for land to buy. We could simply start.

It has been my experience that at life's inevitable crossroads — times of difficult decisions — there is a wise voice of guidance, either within or without, if we are still and silent enough to hear it. Was it by coincidence, then, that on the bus going home we happened to sit next to a woman who said exactly what we needed to hear to tip the balance? When we told her what we were contemplating, she asked: "Is there anything keeping you in the city? Why not give yourselves a year, try it out, see how you like living in the country? You're not burning any bridges — you can always go back."

Two weeks later, August 7, 1975, my brother-in-law hauled us (and two cats) back to the land, trucking our few possessions and enough food to last a couple of months at least. After helping us move in, he pulled away with a wave and some parting words: "You'll never make it here." John tells me that at that moment he made up his mind to meet the challenges presented in this new life and see them through. A line from the *I Ching* had stayed with him: "Perseverance brings good fortune."

DIGGING IN

We had come to garden. Taking a clue about where to start from the line of leaning fence posts, we began to clear space. Sputtering with effort, the second-hand rototiller, since retired, chewed into the wiry grass roots. This was no tame lawn. We soon learned to identify quackgrass and bindweed, no friends to gardeners. Or were they? As we tilled, it occurred to us that this sandy soil would have been gone with the wind long ago without the closely woven roots protecting it from erosion. In a few days we had opened up a long narrow strip of earth.

Curious to test the soil's potential, we decided to sow a row of Purple-Top White Globe turnips. Over the next weeks, until the first snowfall called time-out, we continued to dig and rake and shape beds for spring. Despite the improbable mid-August planting date, our turnips grew fast, fat, and round in the cool, wet fall weeks. By late October we had a first harvest: two bushels of roots — an encouraging start. We ate a lot of turnips with our rice and beans that winter —

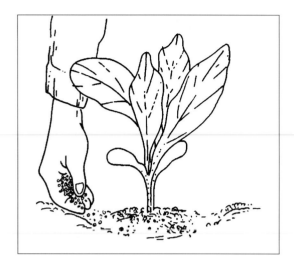

At mid-growth, many vegetable plants benefit from a palmful of blood meal or balanced natural fertilizer sprinkled in a circular band around them and worked gently into the ground with shallow cultivation.

curried turnip, stir-fried and mashed turnip, shredded turnip salad — and we haven't planted them since.

WINTER WONDER

How to describe that first winter? The landscape painted in swaths of subdued color: black-and-white birch trunks and shadowy cedars against the purple-gray haze of the leafless forest; the pale gold stalks and seedheads of last summer's wildflowers crackling above the encrusted snow. The sky a brilliant blue for a spell, then drained of all color for days on end — even the sun was cold and ghostly.

Indigo night skies glittered with more stars than we'd ever seen; moonlit shadows lay across the blue-white snow. The silence was enchanting: Some nights were so still that at first the nosound made us as uneasy as the creak of branches and the howling wolves. Gradually we began to feel safe. During the first howling blizzard we realized how much shelter the trees gave. Moving from open field to woods, our buckets of water

bouncing on a toboggan, was like closing a door on the gale; it was always warmer and calmer in the forest. Chickadees, swooping down to take sunflower seeds from our hand, welcomed us.

It was a winter of new experiences. Priorities were pared to life's basics, first among them keeping warm. Lacking cut and dried wood, we burned what a neighbor called "gopher wood — you need 'er, you go fur 'er." Cutting dead elm trees with ax and Swede saw, we discovered that wood does warm you twice.

HOMEWORK

At one o'clock, every day but Sunday, John or I would trudge down to the road, park ourselves in a seat cut in the snowbank, and wait for the mailman's station wagon, often the only car to pass all day. The mail brought gardening books from the library and seed catalogs from all over. In these weeks we took a crash course in food-growing. Seed and nursery orders reflected not only a curiosity that now had room to grow, but also a wish to raise enough vegetables (and eventually fruit) to feed ourselves all summer and fall with plenty left over to store for winter.

By early March, as the days grew mercifully longer, seedlings began to sprout in pots and flats by the windows. Salvaged lumber and old storm windows became two cold frames to be set outside the moment the snow subsided. More scrap lumber and a pair of old bicycle wheels were transformed into a wobbly version of those expensive two-wheeled garden carts pictured in gardening magazines. We'd be making many trips with tools and plants from dome to garden.

Never was spring more welcome, a stirring reveille after the long spell of sleep. Wet moss shone with the vibrancy of emeralds against the glistening snow; spreading junipers shook off winter's weight and sprang back to growth. Ravens heralded the change. The snow curtain receding from our patch of cleared earth brought to light moist dark beds full of potential. In the woods, white patches still lay in hollows and in the shadow of rocks, but the warming sun roused us to action. It was time to put away the books, roll out the wobbly cart and load it with rake and shovel, stakes and string, a basket rattling with packets of peas, spinach, onion set — the first seeds of our first full season on the land. A new garden beckoned.

FOR INSPIRATION

Times change. One trial year on the land has become many seasons of making and caring for a garden, putting down roots in a place that is now home. The old dome collapsed one winter under a weighty burden of snow. Luckily we were not in it. Suddenly our small tool shed by the garden had to be enlarged, insulated, and turned into proper living quarters — while we were living in it. The old iron hand-pump, powered with a solar motor in summer, continues to supply all the water for home and garden. Gradually our horticultural horizons expanded to include herbs, fruit trees, and the lovely realm of perennial flowers. Our garden acquired a name — Larkwhistle.

Our purpose in this book is not to provide hard-and-fast rules, but rather to share with other gardeners how we meet the challenges of our site, soil, and climate. Local variations, as specific as the microclimate in your own back yard, need local solutions. For example, although we have plenty of water, we water by hand — see Chapter 5 — because we do not have a conventional pressure system, hoses and the like. Once a week we give each bed a deep soaking. In arid areas this may not be possible, so desert gardeners have come up with ingenious ways to conserve every precious drop: to wit, sculpted sunken beds surrounded by a lip of earth. Such beds can be flooded when water is available and stay moist far longer than the raised beds we use. If we have a few more seasons as dry as the last few, we might be looking to Arizona for gardening lessons.

Planting times also vary widely from north to south. The tomato plants which we put into our garden in late May might go into the ground in April or even March in Georgia. In the far south, the season may never be stopped dead by freezing weather. The chapters which follow are organized according to the sequence of the food gardener's year. The specific timing of seeding and transplanting changes from one part of the country to another, but the sequence remains the same: plant lettuce, whether early or late, in the cool of the year, and set out your peppers when there is no danger of frost. The calendar and charts in Chapter 4 can be customized to suit your area once you know the approximate date of the last frost in spring, and the first frost in fall.

Measuring less than one-sixth of an acre, our kitchen garden yields something good to eat from May until the following March, if you count what is stored, and the hardy roots that stay in the ground all winter. The entire one-acre garden, including all the flower beds, is nearly full-time work for the two of us and helpers. But remember, all the work is done by hand. Larkwhistle is a big country garden, but the food beds are small, almost intimate, and the techniques we use can be translated to any yard. Whether you wish to grow a summer's supply of salad greens, a few tomatoes and peppers, or a full season harvest of all your family's favorite vegetables and fruits, we hope you'll find both inspiration and information aplenty in these pages. On any scale, an organically tended kitchen garden provides the best-tasting and healthiest food you can find — live food. The natural gardener leaves the soil in good condition, a valuable legacy for the future.

2

EARTH CARE
Creating and Sustaining Lively Soil

The roots of the words *garden*, *yard*, and *orchard* all spring from the same source, an old word meaning an enclosed or protected place. As gardeners we are reminded of our responsibility to do our best by the piece of land we tend. It is our duty to protect — and restore if necessary — the fragment of Earth in our care.

Some people treat earth like dead old dirt, but it is actually vibrant with life. How else could it give rise to the constant wonder of growth and beauty? That layer of soil, anywhere from a fraction of an inch to several feet deep, mantles the planet's surface and gives birth and sustenance to all that lives on it and then, in a miracle of recycling, takes back what has died and transforms it into nourishment for new life. The natural gardener looks to the earth itself for soil-building lessons.

LIVELY EARTH

Soil scientists confirm that earth teems with living creatures. In a single teaspoon of fertile soil, they say, live 4 billion bacteria, up to 325 feet (100 m) of mold or fungus filaments, 144 million actino-mycetes (one of the infinitely small — and unpronounceable — organisms responsible for changing organic matter into nutrients for plants), as well as countless other microorganisms such as

To improve the texture and fertility of any soil, spread a generous layer of fine-textured organic matter and turn it under.

algae and yeasts. That's a lot of life in a teaspoon.

The goal of organic gardening is to nourish and maintain life in the soil. Lively earth gives rise to vigorous, healthy plants that are less susceptible to diseases and, curiously, less appealing to insects. I find the notion of 4 billion bacteria as hard to grasp as that of the infinity of stars in space, but I know that gardening organically helps me to feel actively connected to Earth's eternal cycles — the turning seasons, the process of growth, decay, and new growth. I like the sense of cooperating with rather than opposing nature. By now we know the devastating consequences of forgetting our vital links with the Earth. Organic gardening is good medicine, a positive step toward mending our relationship with the world around us.

SOIL SCIENCE

Over the years we have seen our garden Larkwhistle's original soil — pale, dry, and sandy in the extreme — grow darker, richer, and more productive with each application of compost, leaf mold, manure, and other organic matter. Nurturing the soil first means much less time spent later on solving problems that could have been prevented — and much more time enjoying the garden.

The first step toward a flourishing vegetable and fruit garden is to find out what type of soil you have. Gardeners are often advised to have a soil test done. The process involves digging trowelfuls of earth from various parts of the garden, mixing them up, and sending a sample to your local department of agriculture for testing. You can also buy soil-testing kits, some more sophisticated than others, that let you play chemist in your own backyard.

In large cities, or if you are planning a food garden close to an older house that has been shedding paint flakes for years, it is wise to have the soil tested for lead, arsenic, and other toxins. In contaminated soils, many food plants can accumulate toxins at unhealthy levels. The solution is to dig out the poisoned soil and replace it with good, clean earth.

When John and I first moved to the country, we sent off a vial of sandy soil to the nearest agricultural college. In a few weeks the results were back, and we were left scratching our heads, wondering what to do next. Soil-test results can be a perplexing mix of chemistry and mathematics. For someone who has trouble deciphering instructions for mixing liquid fertilizer, some of the recommendations might as well have been hieroglyphics.

As we were mulling over the numbers, a neighbor stopped by to see what we were up to. He was as baffled as we were about the test results, but he knew the land. Finally, leaning on a fence post, he looked out over the garden-to-be and gave us a piece of advice that we've been following ever since. "It's good land," he said. "Sock the shit to it and it'll grow anything." Now here was advice we could understand.

I can't say that we completely ignored the information on the soil test. Results showed that the pH hovered around neutral, but the earth was deficient in phosphorus, a nutrient essential for strong roots, fruit development, and improved disease resistance. With that in mind, we have made a habit of digging in crushed phosphate rock and bone meal over the past fifteen years. And, of course, we keep socking not only the manure to the land, but also compost, decayed leaves, soggy old hay, and such — a well balanced soil-food diet. Soil tests have changed over the years. Now several government labs specialize in tests for organic gardeners. Test results suggest corrective doses of natural fertilizers and even

tell you how much manure to use.

Generous and consistent applications of organic matter are the surest way to enhance the life of any soil. That may be all you need to know to grow a perfectly wonderful garden. It makes sense: you can't expect a splendid harvest year after year without giving something back to the earth in return.

SWEET AND SOUR SOIL

When it comes to earth care, an organic gardener sets out to accomplish several things: improve soil texture, boost and balance fertility, and sometimes alter pH, which measures the soil's degree of acidity or alkalinity on a scale of 0 to 14. The lower the number, the more acidic the soil, with 0 being the most sour and 14 the most alkaline. Typically, soils range from 4.5 — quite acidic ground suitable for blueberries and cranberries and found mainly in cold, damp areas — to a slightly alkaline 7.5. Once again, the middle ground is best, with most food plants thriving in a pH hovering around neutral (6 to 6.8). In the old days, farmers would taste their soil to see if it was sour (low pH), bitter (too alkaline), or nice and middling sweet, but if you're averse to eating dirt, a soil test will tell you.

Given the typical pH range, you are more likely to have to raise rather than lower the pH. Ground limestone, otherwise known as horticultural lime, is like a sugar for the soil and, like sugar, it is better to add too little than too much. You can always spread more, but you'll never remove it. To raise the pH of sandy loam by one point, use 3 pounds (1.4 kg) of lime spread evenly over 100 square feet (9 m²) and dig in, either in fall or in early spring. On clay loam use 5 pounds (2.25 kg) per 100 square feet. One application should be sufficient for three to five years, but do a test again before adding more lime. Hold the lime in an area planned for berries or potatoes.

However, if the soil test indicated that the earth has too much lime, then powdered sulfur moves the pH toward neutral. Typical applications: 3 pounds (1.4 kg) of sulfur per 100 square feet

An array of natural soil amendments (from left to right): homemade compost, peat moss, bone meal, a balanced natural fertilizer, and kelp meal.

(9 m²) to change the pH from 8.0 to 6.5; 2 pounds (0.9 kg) per 100 square feet moves the needle from 7.5 to 6.5, or 7.0 to 6.0. To dramatically alter the pH from 7.0 to 5.5, apply 3½ pounds (1.6 kg) of sulfur per 100 square feet.

Lime and sulfur help balance extremes, but if the soil holds a generous measure of organic matter, many plants will grow well despite a less-than-perfect pH. Our garden grows most of the common vegetables and some exotics; a raft of herbs, berries, and tree fruit; well over 300 different flowering perennials; and numerous shrubs and ornamental trees. Except for that first soil test, we couldn't tell you what the pH is. We have never applied lime, and the only plant that gets an annual dose of sulfur is a clump of acid-loving Japanese iris — and even it seems to care more about water than the acidity or alkalinity of the soil.

HANDS IN

Garden soil is composed of sand, silt (microscopic rock pieces), and clay in various proportions,

with an admixture of small or large stones. Bringing these inert particles to life is that magical ingredient — organic matter, with all its attendant creatures.

"Feed the soil, not the plants" is another tenet of organic gardening. But before we look at food for the soil, we had better get our hands into the soil itself — literally. One of the best ways to find out if you have sandy or clay soil is to feel it. Both extremes make for difficult growing.

Rub some fairly dry soil between thumb and fingers. Sand particles feel coarse and gritty; very silty soil has the floury texture of talcum powder; dry clay is hard and chunky. If the soil is moist, squeeze a handful into a ball. Clay-based soil feels sticky and may ooze water when squeezed; open your hand and a ball of clay soil will hold together and probably show your fingerprints. Sandy soil, in contrast, tends to fall apart as you open your hand, whereas loam may adhere into a ball, but will crumble when prodded. Loam, lovely loam, is a nicely balanced blend of sand, silt, and clay, with a good amount of organic matter. Depending on what particles predominate, you may have coarse sandy loam, fine sandy loam, clay loam of various densities, and so on. Sandy ground warms up quickly in spring and is a pleasure to dig and weed. Clay ground is slower to warm in spring and harder to dig into in any season.

The garden's state after a downpour also tells you something about its soil. If water sits in puddles for some time and the soil sticks to shoes and shovel, you have clay or clay loam. If rain drains away and you can tread the paths afterward without getting bogged down, you are walking on sandy loam.

What happens in a dry spell? Clay-based soil holds moisture longer than sandy ground, but if it is unmulched or uncultivated it dries to a hard surface often criss-crossed with cracks. Sandy ground retains less water at first and dries more quickly, turning to coarse dust that may whip away in the wind. As water drains through sandy land, it takes soluble nutrients out of the reach of roots. Loam, that happy medium, holds moisture well but lets superfluous water drain through; as it dries, it tends to crumble, turning fluffy rather than baking hard or going dusty.

Fortunately for gardeners, most soils are in the loam category — although you may not think so as you shovel lumps of unyielding clay, or struggle to keep sandy soil even vaguely damp in July. Most hover within a few degrees of neutral on the pH scale. The rest of the good news is that, sweet or sour, clay or sand or anything in-between, all soils respond favorably to similar care and feeding.

SOIL FOOD

A good way to find out how to enhance texture and fertility of soil is to take a hike. See what is happening in the woods or in a meadow at ground level. Leaves slowly moldering on the forest floor are composting; dead meadow grasses seared by winter's frost are being broken down by the damp earth beneath. Turn over a mat of leaves under a lilac bush — that is if you haven't swept them all away — and chances are you'll see earthworms beating a fast retreat into the ground and

sow bugs scurrying away. These are but two of the creatures that work incessantly to turn fallen leaves, dead trees, frosted tomato vines, corn stalks — all spent vegetation — into soil food and, eventually, nutrients for plant growth.

The perfect food for soil and its inhabitants is organic matter, such as plant residues; old hay; grass clippings; leaves; manure; eggshells; banana peels; coffee grounds; ground-up bones; even sawdust, woodchips, and newsprint. Over time, soil life literally digests organic matter, transforming it into smaller and smaller bits that hold together as humus, a dark, porous, sticky substance that wonderfully improves both the texture and the fertility of any soil.

COMPOST

Piles and Pits

The terms "humus" and "organic matter" are often used interchangeably, but organic matter is the raw material you put into the compost heap, and humus is the rich, dark, crumbly finished product; if you can identify it, it's still organic matter. Humus is what organic matter becomes when it is completely broken down.

It is a mark of nature's efficiency that returning lots of organic matter to the earth works, over time, to bring both sandy and clay soil toward a loamy middle ground. Because humus is bulky and fibrous, it breaks up dense, fine-grained clay, allowing air (an important free fertilizer) to enter and water to drain better. Since it is also somewhat spongy, humus helps to bind sandy soil's coarse, loose particles and to hold moisture that might otherwise run through. Organic matter also tends to correct the soil pH, bringing both extremes toward a favorable neutral range.

On the subject of compost, garden writers wax eloquent: "brown gold," "recycled sunlight," "the key to soil fertility," "a great healer and buffer, and the gentle way to restore soil health," "in the dank and mouldy pile the wheel of life is turning." And it's true. Compost is the heart of an organic garden, a symbol of nature's eternal effort to re-create healthy soil and the gardener's willingness to cooperate. Nature has all the time in the world to

When we clean up in the fall, we build a large compost heap, a "layer cake" composed of manure and garden refuse chopped into smaller pieces with a machete. Topped with soil and left unturned, the heap cooks for fourteen months.

turn forest leaves into fertilizer, but a well-built compost accelerates the process, allowing a gardener to significantly improve the soil each season.

Garden books are filled with recipes for turning out perfect compost in fourteen days, a task that involves shredding ingredients, building precise layers of green stuff and manure, and turning the works over and over. The result is rich chocolate-cakey compost that plants all but thank you for.

I don't think we've ever succeeded in achieving that result. What we usually settle for is less-than-perfect compost in about fourteen months. All through the season, our one-acre garden generates compostable material, but literally tons of stuff becomes available in September and October during the fall cleanup when we build "the big pile."

Our fall composting process goes something like this:

1. Haul wheelbarrow-loads of green stuff to the growing heap, which is usually about 8 feet (2.4 m) long and 4 feet (1.2 m) wide, and dump enough plant residues to make a fluffy layer about 1 foot (30 cm) deep.
2. Jump onto the pile, machete in hand, and whack away at the leaves and stalks to chop them into smaller pieces, trampling the heap to about half the original size in the process.
3. Spread a 2- to 3-inch (5- to 8-cm) layer of the freshest possible cow manure over the green layer.
4. Keep building the heap in layers over the next days and weeks until it grows to about 4 feet (1.2 m) high.

In the compost pile, raw ingredients (foreground) are transformed into the best all-round fertilizer and texturizer you can find. Sifting reduces the compost into rich, dark crumbs that are a pleasure to work into the soil or spread as mulch.

are prepared to do; patience saves the back. By fall, the compost should be ready for use. Because fine-textured compost is easier to turn into the garden, we sometimes sift out lumps and chunks by shaking the compost into a wheelbarrow through a screen of ¾-inch mesh fastened to a wooden frame.

Over the summer, we make another compost using kitchen scraps, spent pea vines, seedy lettuces, coarse cabbage leaves, dead-head flowers, out-of-favor plants, weeds before they've gone to seed, manure, and the like. We leave grass clippings where they fall to fertilize the lawn.

Such large-scale composting is appropriate in a big country garden where there is a ready supply of manure and few neighbors to object to the growing pile of "debris" and the occasionally whiffy dung heap. Last fall, when pressed for space, we built a big oval compost, enclosed by snow fencing, outside the garden, a few feet from the road, something that would probably raise cries of protest in suburbia. Personally I think composting ought to be encouraged wherever and however it happens, but many gardeners want to find a tidy, odorless way.

CITY COMPOST

Tidy compost means enclosed compost, and there are a number of ways to do it. Easiest of all is a ready-made commercial composter, usually some variation on a perforated black plastic drum or barrel. One model sits on the ground, which is a good feature because it invites earthworms. Another, suspended horizontally in a metal frame, can be spun around (like those drums full of lottery tickets) to tumble and mix the compost. Though not quite the humus factories they claim to be, commercial composters do keep everything out of sight; they also fill up rather quickly unless you have a very small garden.

5. Top the finished pile with a few inches of soil or a thatch of hay.

You might call this the haul-dump-jump-whack-tread-spread-top-and-wait method. Once built, the heap is left to slow-cook through the fall, all winter (very slow indeed), and over the next summer.

But the compost is not merely taking up space over those months. The fact that compost heaps routinely sprout tomato, cucumber, and squash seedlings (not to mention weeds) tells us there is growth potential there. In the spring, we plant winter-squash vines on top of the heap; the vines seem not to mind the rough texture — they surely appreciate the manure — and I like to think that their roots help aerate and break down the pile.

Turning such a pile by hand is more than we

Homemade compost bins also do the trick of hiding and containing. Bins should be at least 3 feet (90 cm) square, and situated on bare earth, in some shade if possible. If they are easily accessible, so much the better. Two compost bins are better than one, and one is better than none.

Triple bins, side by side, allow you to build one compost, let it simmer while you make a second pile, and then turn the first pile into the empty third bin and the second pile into the first bin. Bins may be made of boards (scrap lumber, if you have it) on three sides, with or without removable front slats or a hinged front door.

Alternatively, use some type of metal mesh — fine-mesh chicken wire, hardware cloth, wire fencing — stapled or nailed to two-by-fours; a hinged front door makes for easy loading and holds the compost in place. Wire mesh may deter rodents, especially if it is sunk a few inches into the ground.

A cylinder of snow fence, a yard or more in diameter, makes a movable enclosure; two or three can fit inconspicuously in most yards. Snow fence can also be used to contain your yard's output of tree leaves, which, if added to the "regular" compost, will tend to mat down and slow the process. The leaves will eventually decay into leaf mold, a valuable fertilizer and conditioner. Shredding leaves and/or adding 2 cups (500 mL) of blood meal to each wheelbarrow of leaves will turn them into leaf mold much faster. Indeed, leaves are one of the finest sources of organic matter you can get — free, mineral-rich, abundant.

If I tended a city garden, I would use some variation on pit composting. The first step is to dig a square or rectangular hole about 18 inches (45 cm) deep in an out-of-the-way corner of the garden; the dimensions of the hole will depend on the site, but 2 feet (60 cm) by 3 feet (90 cm) or 4 feet (120 cm), or 3 feet square are useful sizes. Pile the soil to one side. As you collect spent vegetation from the garden, dump it into the pit. Use anything soft and sappy such as grass clippings, frosted annuals, dead flowers, old vegetables, or the leafy tops of perennials; leave out branches and any twigs thicker than a pencil. If you get an armload of woody stalks from cutting back a clump of phlox, for example, or tough stems left over after the broccoli harvest, chop them up or crush them before dumping them into the pit. The point is to break and separate fibers so that the soil's compost organisms can

enter. You can fold long stalks zig-zag fashion like a carpenter's ruler, or whack them with the shovel blade, a machete, or a wooden mallet.

Once you have accumulated a layer of vegetation about 6 inches (15 cm) deep, tread lightly to compact it by half; then shovel in enough of the reserved soil (about a 1-inch [2.5-cm] layer) to cover. You can also dump the contents of the kitchen compost bucket, covering the pile with soil to deter raccoons and absorb odors. Wet down the pile from time to time, and poke it with a rake handle to let in air. Introducing 300 to 500 earthworms into the compost pit after it is half full will speed things remarkably. You will have to buy the first batch of worms but they will propagate themselves after that. Certainly, earthworms from near and not-too-far will flock to the compost pit on their own.

Such an in-ground compost can be built up level with the surrounding soil or mounded slightly. In either case, finish the layering with a few inches of topsoil. You need not turn the compost, although it will cook faster if you stir it up from time to time. Let it sit in the pit, and in a season or so you will have a deep pocket of exceptionally rich soil. For more compost you will have to dig additional holes.

Some refinements on pit composting are possible. For a deeper pile, surround the pit with a wooden box, about 12 to 18 inches (30 to 45 cm) high and fitted with a hinged lid; space the boards or drill them with holes to let air circulate. Keep layering green stuff and earth until the box is full. If the box is fitted with handles, it can be shifted over a second pit. Or leave it in place, open the lid in spring, set in a few cucumber, squash, or tomato plants (all in sun) and watch them go wild.

Pit composting has advantages. Most compost recipes talk about the carbon-to-nitrogen ratio, the need to layer carbonaceous material, such as dry plant residues, leaves, and straw, with something high in nitrogen, which is an effective compost catalyst. Animal manure is the usual recommended ingredient for nitrogen, but manure is scarce or costly in the city. To boost nitrogen you can add a sprinkling of blood meal to each layer.

A pit compost, made with layers of garden refuse, kitchen waste, and earth, is a tidy option where an open heap may not be appropriate. The earth layers absorb odors, add all-important nitrogen, and introduce some of the soil life responsible for the composting process.

But soil, too, supplies some nitrogen, as well as introducing active bacteria into the compost. Soil also does double duty by discouraging creatures and suppressing smells, which are important considerations in a town garden. A pit compost gives you lots of earth for layering conveniently close at hand.

NATURAL FERTILIZERS

Soil contains three major plant foods: nitrogen (N), phosphorus (P), and potassium (K). Lesser amounts of magnesium, calcium, sulfur, and various trace minerals also contribute to healthy growth.

I wouldn't recognize nitrogen if it jumped up and bit me, but I do know that a row of spinach perks up amazingly when watered with fish emulsion, a fertilizer high in nitrogen; and tomato seedlings that are looking a little peaked and purplish — a sign of low phosphorus — turn green again after a dose of bone meal.

Synthetic fertilizers are scientifically (and conveniently) formulated to contain a certain percentage of each major nutrient. The three numbers on the box tell you how much: 5-10-5 simply means that this fertilizer contains 5 percent nitrogen (N), 10 percent phosphorus (P), and 5 percent potassium (K).

CHEMICAL FIX

So, why not pour on the chemicals? First, chemicals contribute not a whit to the earth's store of organic matter. In fact, rather than improving soil texture, harsh chemical fertilizers can dissolve the organic ties that bind particles into nice loamy crumbs. With this soil "glue" weakened, the earth tends to disintegrate. Chemicals used in the absence of humus can spoil a soil's texture or "friability."

Used alone, chemical fertilizers gradually starve and deplete soil life, including our friendly earthworms. Synthetics provide a quick fix of concentrated nutrients — an overdose will burn or kill plants — but their effect is short-lived as the water-soluble chemicals leach out of reach. Curiously, chemically fed plants tend to be more vulnerable to insect damage and diseases, giving rise to yet more chemicals in the form of pesticides, resulting in a dependency. In time, chemically treated soil can indeed become nothing more than dead old dirt.

NATURAL ALTERNATIVES

Organic gardeners must ensure that the soil contains enough nitrogen, phosphorus, and potassium. Your own homemade compost and leaf mold, as well as decayed animal manures of any kind, are the best all-round, slow-release fertilizers and texturizers you can use. But who ever has enough? From time to time you may need to rely on store-bought natural fertilizers to boost and balance nutrients. Garden centers and mail-order sources stock these alternatives to chemicals. Some, such as rock phosphate and sulphate of potash, come directly from the earth; others, such as kelp meal and greensand, are harvested from the sea; and still others, such as bone meal and blood meal, are animal byproducts.

Each of the natural fertilizers contains a concentrated amount of one of the major plant nutrients. Nitrogen promotes lush leaves and greener greens. Phosphorus goes in part into increased fruit set and earlier ripening, brighter flowers, and enhanced disease resistance. Often described as the "root" nutrient, potash also strengthens disease resistance, gives better flavor and color to vegetables and fruit, and may help plants through times of drought.

• NITROGEN

Blood meal contains 10 to14 percent nitrogen in a concentrated, volatile form. To avoid the risk of burning plants, some experts suggest introducing it into the soil by way of the compost heap. Sprinkling blood meal through the layers lets this expensive powder do double duty as both compost catalyst and fertilizer. The recommended soil dose is 2 cups (500 mL) sprinkled over 100 square feet (9 m²) before spring digging. For direct garden application I favor a balanced natural fertilizer that contains blood meal as one of its ingredients. The Nutrite company in Elmira, Ontario, blends blood, bone, and kelp for a complete organic fertilizer (no filler or processing) with a 5-4-1 nutrient analysis.

Fifty-Fifty is a mix of blood and bone meal containing 6 percent each nitrogen and phosphorus (no potassium). The application rate is 4 pounds (2 kg) over 50 square feet (4.5 m²). The same amount of Canagro's Nature's Fertilizer covers 800 square feet at a rate of 1¼ cups (500 mL) per 100 square feet; a mix of blood, bones, feathers, sulfate of potash, magnesium, and various trace elements, this granular fertilizer has 5 percent nitrogen, 4 percent phosphorus, and 7 percent potassium.

• PHOSPHORUS

Bone meal, or ground-up bone, has been the organic gardener's standard source of phosphorus (10 to 15 percent) for decades. Its value was first recognized in England centuries ago. To fertilize 100 square feet (9 m²), dust on 2 cups (500 mL) of bone meal if a soil test shows that the ground is already fairly high in phosphorus; for fair to low levels, double or triple the dose. Symptoms of low phosphorus are a reddish-purple tinge to leaves that ought to be green, and tomatoes and peppers that grow lush and leafy but set relatively few fruit. Spread the fine white powder when there is no wind or you'll be breathing bone or watching it blow away.

Ground phosphate rock contains up to 30 percent phosphorus and some minerals, released slowly into the soil. To correct a moderate deficiency, spread about 4 pounds (2 kg) of rock phosphate over 100 square feet of garden, an application that will do for up to five years. For plants to benefit from this fertilizer, it has to be in their root zone; and since it doesn't move much in the soil, you'll have to dig it in.

• POTASSIUM

Kelp meal, a seaweed green, mineral-rich fertilizer, is fairly high in potassium (4 percent). As an added benefit, the presence of kelp meal helps release nutrients that might otherwise remain locked in the soil. Be sure not to add more than 1 pound (0.5 kg) per 100 square feet (9 m²) because an overdose can adversely affect growth.

Sulfate of potash magnesium is another name for langbeinite, a mineral mined in the American Southwest. Packaged as Sul-Po-Mag, it provides a concentrated (22 percent) but slowly released measure of potassium, as well as decent levels of sulfur and magnesium. Use 2 cups (500 mL) per 100 square feet.

Greensand, like kelp meal, comes from the sea and contains much of the oceans' wealth of trace elements and minerals. An ideal soil builder, it provides a ready source of available potash and helps unlock other nutrients already in the soil. It also absorbs and holds water for plant use. Spread an application of 3 pounds (1.4 kg) per 100 square feet before spring digging or sprinkle greensand around growing vegetables; there is no danger of injuring surface roots.

High in potash, stove and fireplace ashes have always been dumped on the garden. But be warned, large amounts of caustic ash can injure and kill germinating seeds and small plants. The best plan is to spread ashes thinly — no more than 5 pounds (2.25 kg) per 100 square feet — in conjunction with compost or manure late in fall or very early in spring so that the ash has time to mellow before seeds go in. Granted, you will lose some nutrients to leaching, but better that than burned roots. Always store ashes under cover or their potash will be gone with the rain. Like limestone, wood ash tends to sweeten soil; it has no place in the berry patch or around acid-loving azaleas, Japanese irises, heathers, and the like. Also hold the ashes, or add them in thin layers to the compost, if your garden pH is higher than 6.8.

• For an all-purpose fertilizer, mix 1 part blood meal, 2 parts bone meal, 3 parts wood ash, and 4 parts compost — an excellent blend for side-dressing or spot enrichment.

SCHEDULE OF FERTILIZING

For organized gardeners, here is a three-step fertilizing program — starter, booster, finisher — that supplies a balance of nutrients for individual heavy-feeding plants, such as cucumbers, potatoes, cabbages, tomatoes, or along closely spaced rows of beans, carrots, beets, or corn. You may not need to apply extra commercial fertilizers if you conscientiously make and apply sufficient compost.

• STARTER: Stir bone meal into the transplanting hole; the specific amount (given in later chapters) depends on the crop in question but, in general, the more you apply, the bulkier the final growth.

• BOOSTER: Side-dress with blood meal by sprinkling a band of the powder around the base of plants or along either side of rows. Do this when plants are about half-grown, or about a month after transplanting.

• FINISHER: As flowers and small fruit appear, or several weeks before vegetables reach maturity, side-dress again, this time with Sul-Po-Mag, a source of potash.

There are four principal ways to get the goodness of natural fertilizers into the ground: (1) broadcasting, (2) spot enrichment, (3) side- or top-dressing, and (4) via compost. The method depends on the time of year, the needs of plants, and the state of your soil. At Larkwhistle, we do all of the above, using the fertilizers we have on hand in ways that seem best at the time.

• BROADCASTING: Gardeners who routinely turn over vegetable beds in fall or early spring might opt to broadcast fertilizers before digging and raking. This method works especially well in intensive beds — an area of ground, from 2 to 5 feet (60 to 150 cm) wide, planted fairly thickly with edibles — because nutrients are distributed evenly throughout the space where roots forage. Broadcasting is most appropriate with the less expensive, slow-released fertilizers, such as rock phosphate. You'd go broke spreading blood meal around like grass seed.

• SPOT-ENRICHMENT: If fertilizer is in short supply, and you have a number of transplants to set out, it's wise to concentrate nutrients under each plant. By stirring a handful of bone meal into the transplanting hole for each tomato, for example, you create a zone of fertility that will boost growth all season. If you can mix store-bought powders with old manure or sifted compost, so much the better. This kind of spot-enrichment works wonders in a new plot where the soil is not up to par, but it is appropriate only for bulky vegetables — such as lettuce, cabbages, broccoli, peppers, and eggplant — that go into the ground as individual transplants set at least 8 inches (20 cm) apart.

Clearly you can't spot-enrich radishes or carrots. Instead, sprinkle fertilizer into the furrow before you plant the seeds, or spread it in a band about 3 to 4 inches (8 to 10 cm) wide along the length of the row and then scuffle it in with a hoe.

• SIDE-DRESSING: Plants in active growth take in a lot of food and water. Side-dressing is the practice of spreading fairly fast-acting fertilizer on the ground around each broccoli, or along either side of a row of beans — think of it as a special

To create a localized zone of fertility for leeks over the whole season, we sprinkle kelp meal (or other natural fertilizer) into the bottom of the furrows and stir it in.

treat for hard-working plants. Blood meal gives a quick dose of nitrogen for leafy crops, but a dressing of kelp would be more useful to beans just starting to flower.

It's remarkable how quickly plants respond to side-dressing. We routinely spread a layer of very old manure or compost, several inches thick, around tomatoes, peppers, or cabbages in midgrowth. Clearly, the plants know that it's there, for within days they are sending thin new roots out into the dark humus to draw in nutrients.

• VIA COMPOST: Blood meal stimulates a compost heap, but (as one expert notes) "adding rock powders, such as rock phosphate and greensand, to the compost is a sterling idea." In the composting stewpot, the minerals are changed into a form that is somehow more appetizing to plants.

3

BY DESIGN
A Kitchen Garden Layout

The kitchen garden, which we think of as the heart of Larkwhistle, is a constant source of interest and pleasure. I love to see the peas run up their wire fence, to have a hand in the progress of lettuces from seeds to heads. A ripe melon is cause for a small celebration. Whenever I pick a red pepper or pull a bunch of long fat carrots, I take a moment—it's habit by now—to admire their forms and colors. What can I say: the whole process of growing food is full of wonder and satisfaction. I often linger in the kitchen garden in the early morning (after splashing my face in the chilly water of one of the garden pools) or at twilight, just watching the garden grow. The Chinese have a saying: "The best fertilizer is the gardener's shadow." Shadows are longest at dawn and dusk.

OF ROWS AND BEDS

Vegetables are traditionally grown in an open rectangle of land. The organizing principle is simple: long, straight, single rows. Row planting has one distinct advantage. The arrangement allows a gardener to weed with a machine, running a rototiller, wheeled hoe, or tractor up and down the aisles. In a big country garden, this could well be

Diversity is the hallmark of a healthy natural garden. Sun-loving perennials—blue-flowered anchusa, chives, and peonies—flank beans, lettuces, and peas. Besides attracting bees and butterflies, herbs and flowers add to the bug-baffling mix.

the factor that dictates design. Simply doubling or tripling the rows makes such a garden much more efficient. If beans, for example, are supposed to stand 5 inches (12 cm) apart in a row, there is no reason why you cannot have another parallel row, or two, the same distance away. Why have two skinny rows of carrots separated by an unproductive path when you can get the equivalent of three rows in a single 8-inch-wide (20-cm-wide) band? A wide row of carrots, a triple row of beans: put them together and the arrangement begins to look like a bed of vegetables.

For most gardeners, rows waste far too much space to be practical. Only a fraction of the available ground is growing what you want; the rest is wide open to weeds. Monotonously straight and narrow, long rows offer little to delight the eye. A gardener who has gone to the work and expense of landscaping may wonder if a vegetable garden fits in.

And there are ways. In our experience, the most appealing and workable setup for a kitchen garden is a series of permanent beds harmoniously placed in relation to the rest of the garden.

A bed is an area of soil from 2 to 5 feet (60 to 150 cm) wide, with a path all around it. Length varies, depending on the scope of a garden. If beds are longer than 30 feet (9 m) or so, you might want a bisecting path midway along to save steps. At Larkwhistle, some of the kitchen-garden beds are 4 feet (120 cm) wide and 25 feet (7.5 m) long. Others are odd-sized triangles, curving trapezoids, and half-moon patches arranged

*During a heavy rain, the fluffy raised beds absorb water more quickly than the compacted pathways.
Given an indoor start and protection in a cold frame, tomatoes may be flowering at tulip time;
lettuce is ready to eat.*

around two water-lily pools and four semidwarf apple trees. Paths weave and criss-cross throughout. Some beds are fairly big, others quite small. The odd assortment of shapes and sizes lets us plant just a little Swiss chard here, a long band of carrots there, a little triangle of radicchio or full bed of corn. The design is an attempt to balance practical needs—getting around with wheelbarrow and watering can—with a wish to harmonize the food beds with the flower borders.

If "a long row to hoe" feels like a recipe for backache and boredom, beds sound cozier somehow, more intimate. And they are. You putter around a bed, tending the plants by hand, reaching in to weed or spread mulch. Beds also make a big garden more manageable. Our kitchen garden measures about a fifth of an acre. I would balk at the thought of digging the entire space by hand. But if I take it on one bed at a time, the task doesn't seem so overwhelming. It takes less than a half-hour to turn over the soil in a typical 4 foot by 25 foot bed, and it leaves you with a sense of completion, a job done.

Bed gardening is good for the earth. How so? First, you walk and wheel your barrow around a bed, not over it. The paths become hard, compact, and, mercifully, less hospitable to weeds. But the beds themselves remain light, fluffy, and full of air—a kind of soil soufflé. Beds are a backsaver: because the earth is not compacted by traffic, it may not need an annual digging and, when digging is necessary, the earth turns over easily. The only time we dig into our vegetable beds is when we are turning in compost or manure. At other times, we simply scuffle and loosen the top a few inches with a hefty hoe, often stirring in a dressing of natural fertilizer as we go. A quick rake and we are ready to plant.

Beds allow us to concentrate our soil-building efforts. Since compost is always in short supply, why fritter it away on unproductive pathways? A better plan is to concentrate compost and those expensive commercial fertilizers in permanent beds that will grow richer each season. But before beds can be shaped, there may be some groundbreaking work to do.

First-time food growers may discover, as we did, that their enthusiasm is not matched by muscle, that their interest exceeds their time. The first rules for new gardeners should be: (1) Start small; (2) Concentrate your efforts; (3) Open up only the amount of garden space you feel you can tend; (4) Branch out as you become more experienced. Small can, indeed, be beautiful. A few scaled-down vegetable beds, nicely placed in the landscape and carefully tended, may be every bit as productive as a neglected larger plot—and a lot more satisfying. I have an impression that a lot of people don't grow vegetables because they remember the hot hours spent hacking away at weeds or picking a never-ending line of beans in their parents' big row garden.

SOD OFF

Lawns are shrinking all over as people realize that the effort they put into watering, weed-and-feeding, and cutting the grass could yield a much more interesting return of colorful flowers, aromatic herbs, and organic food. Our garden evolved from a field of quack grass, not tame lawn. Compared to an overgrown field, sod-breaking in a town lot may be less strenuous, but the approach is the same.

"Skim off the turf," one book blithely instructs —as if turf were akin to cream floating on milk. I wish. Converting a stretch of lawn or field into new kitchen garden beds may make you feel as if everything that comes after qualifies as "jes potterin." Here are the steps:

1. With stakes and string, mark out the perimeter of the new site.
2. Using a sharp, square-bladed spade, first slice a line through the sod around the edges, then slice the enclosed turf into a grid of chunks no bigger than you can lift. Push the spade all the way through roots and as deeply into the ground as it will go.
3. Using a spading fork, pry loose a flap of sod, flip it earth-side up, and whack away at the roots to loosen the precious topsoil. Then spear the chunk, lift it, shake it, knock it around, drop

At Larkwhistle, peppers are protected in a simple glass frame. Hay mulch keeps the ground cool and moist for onions and cabbage and, in a triangular bed, snap beans grow close enough to crowd out weeds.

it hard on the ground a few times—all in an effort to release as much soil as possible. If the earth is soggy, invert all the pieces, exposing them to the elements to dry for a few hours, but not so long that the ground bakes to an unyielding crust.
4. Once the grass is gone, dig the patch over with spade or fork, removing more roots, missed bits of sod, and any rocks bigger than your fist. Small stones actually benefit plants and soil by improving the flow of water and air, an important consideration in clay ground. Stones gradually release minerals and, in a dry spell, each one harbors a little reservoir of moisture underneath.

This 4-foot-wide (120-cm-wide) bed is intensively planted with a double row of peas, two rows of lettuce at different stages of maturity, and a row of radishes. Leaves eventually touch to make a living mulch that keeps the soil cool and moist and crowds out weeds.

5. Finally, rake the earth to break up clods of soil and catch stray roots, rocks, and rubbish.

Good-quality sods can be used, if need be, to patch bald spots in the lawn. Otherwise, pile them by themselves grass-side down, in an out-of-the-way place to compost; a tarpaulin over the pile excludes light and discourages sprouting. Never add wiry quack grass runners to the regular compost. Instead, spread them out in the sun to dry thoroughly. Or as an old neighbor jokes, "Burn them and be careful when you spread the ashes."

Fall is an excellent time to clear ground. Winter freezing works wonders on soil texture, especially heavy clay, mellowing and pulverizing it. As weed seeds and roots sprout in early spring, you have another chance to round up potential trouble-makers. I like to start new beds with a clean slate.

MAKING BEDS

With the land cleared and level, we use stakes and string to mark out the growing beds. Because beds are tended by hand from paths on either side, their width is determined by your reach. You'll need to reach at least to the middle while standing or kneeling on one side or the other.

Most of our beds are 3 to 4 feet (90 to 120 cm) wide, and all of them are raised a few inches higher than the paths. In spring, a raised bed warms up sooner than the surrounding ground. It drains water better in all seasons. Both states are desirable where cool, damp clay is the medium. Larkwhistle's sandy earth drains only too well.

Why do we raise our beds then? Primarily, it is to provide the plants with a greater depth of top-soil—not imported soil but earth from the paths. As we stake out the beds, we also run strings to delineate the paths between them. Then with rake and shovel we scrape up a few inches of path soil and scatter this over the bed. The strings are essential guidelines at this point. The uneven earth on the beds is raked smartly up to the string as the bed is leveled. I find the back of a rake useful for tamping and firming the gently sloping sides of the raised bed to prevent mini-landslides later on. A few more passes with the rake over the path gives a smooth walking surface and a neat line between path and bed.

Over the course of a season the edges of beds may get blurred. Often the growing space widens and the walking space shrinks as we seed, transplant, or cultivate. Leaving a stake in the ground permanently at each corner of a bed saves a lot of remeasuring next spring. If you cannot redefine the edges of a bed by sight, raking from stake to stake, it is a simple matter to run a line of string again.

ON THE PATH

We have a neighbor who gardens on stony clay soil. As she dug, shaped, and raked her raised beds, she tossed stones into the pathways and left them there. Later she leveled the stones as best she could and filled around and over them with gravelly sand. The result: fairly stone-free beds and dry serviceable paths that would otherwise be clogged with sticky clay after every rain.

Our kitchen garden paths are nothing fancier

than the naturally sandy earth. Years of foot traffic have made them hard and smooth. The few weeds that do sprout are easily sliced off at ground level without churning up the soil. Sandy paths drain quickly and are never muddy.

We often spread newspapers over pathways and top the paper with old hay or straw. Nothing sprouts through that. The simplest way to handle newspapers for mulch is to open up a whole section and lay it lengthwise for a narrower path, crosswise for a wider one, overlapping the sections. Since almost all newpapers are printed with a carbon-based ink, they present no toxic danger —just ask the earthworms that chew their way through the soggy pulp.

The width of a path, like a road, depends on the amount and type of traffic. Two main streets bisect our kitchen garden. These 2½-foot wide (75-cm-wide) paths make it easy to wheel a barrow full of jostling corn stalks on their way to the compost. From the big paths run 18-inch (45-cm) side streets—for pedestrians only— between beds. A path narrower than one foot is sure to disappear as foliage closes in from either side. A two-wheel garden cart probably needs a 4-foot-wide (120-cm-wide) highway.

ENCLOSED BEDS

For greater tidiness and permanence, raised beds can by surrounded with bricks, rocks, cement blocks, railroad ties, or boards. Perhaps the best material is rough-cut (unplaned), untreated cedar boards, measuring 1 to 2 inches (2.5 to 5 cm) thick and 6 to 12 inches (15 to 30 cm) wide. On average, one-by-eights do nicely. There is no trick to setting up the enclosure. You may have to dig a little trench around the bed, the better to jiggle the boards around until they are level. Shim with stones if necessary. Use a spirit-level, set on a straight board spanning the bed, to bring both sides to the same height. At all corners, sledge a chunk of two-by-four securely into the soil, on the inside of the soil corral, and nail boards to it. If boards bow, align them with additional pieces of wood pounded into the ground.

Enclosed raised beds may be the only way to get around or over the problem of shallow soil, impenetrable hardpan (subsoil you can barely pierce with a pick), or bedrock close to the surface. I know several gardeners who have built such board enclosures, dug out all the topsoil within them, broken up the subsoil as best they could, and then returned the topsoil mixed with an equal amount of compost and peat moss. Add a measured dose of natural fertilizer to the mix and watch your vegetables grow. Such raised beds are a root vegetable's idea of Nirvana. Years ago, before our soil was built up, we made a small (2 foot by 5 foot; 60 cm by 150 cm) but tall (18 inches; 45 cm) wood-enclosed bed that yielded baskets of long, perfect carrots.

PLANTING IN BEDS

In the 1800s, market gardeners on the outskirts of Paris took to growing their crops in beds for the maximum yield in the minimum space. The technique they devised is called "the French Intensive Method." If lettuces ordinarily stand a foot apart in a row, they reasoned, why not plant several rows side by side, the same distance apart. As the plants in such a bed approach maturity, their leaves touch and the space becomes a sheet of green, with very little if any earth visible. This is a good thing. The canopy of foliage shading the ground creates a cool, moist microclimate beneath. At the same time, weeds have a hard time sprouting.

The principle of spacing plants in an intensive raised bed can be summed up like this: the usual distance between rows is roughly the same as the recommended distance between plants in a row. Thus, if we normally set our broccoli transplants 18 inches (45 cm) apart in a row, we can line up a second row 18 inches from the first. But who wants that much broccoli? Instead, we might choose cabbages or Brussels sprouts for the same bed. Most of our beds grow an eclectic mix of vegetables—peas, lettuce, carrots, and onions in one; beets, parsnips, and carrots in another.

The accompanying chart and diagrams give typical spacing and some workable companion vegetables for an intensive bed.

SPACING PLANTS IN AN INTENSIVE BED

	Distance between plants within a row	Distance between rows
Asparagus	18 inches (45 cm)	18–24 inches (45–60 cm)
Beans, bush	4–6 inches (10–15 cm)	8 inches (20 cm)
Beans, pole	8 inches (20 cm) along trellis	poles 2 feet (60 cm) apart with 3–5 plants per pole
Beets	3–5 inches (8–12 cm)	8 inches (20 cm)
Broccoli	18 inches (45 cm)	18 inches (45 cm)
Brussels sprout	18–24 inches (45–60 cm)	18–24 inches (45–60 cm)
Cabbage	18 inches (45 inches)	18 inches (45 cm)
Carrots	2–3 inches (5–8 cm)	8 inches (20 cm) (or in 8–inch/20–cm wide bands)
Cauliflower	18 inches (45 cm)	18 inches (45 cm)
Celery	8 inches (20 cm)	8 inches (20 cm)
Chard	12 inches (30 cm)	12 inches (30 cm)
Chicory	8 inches (20 cm)	8 inches (20 cm)
Chinese Cabbage	8–24 inches (20–60 cm)	18–24 inches (45–60 cm)
Corn	12–18 inches (30–45 cm)	18 inches (45 cm)
Cucumbers	12–18 inches (30–45 cm)	24 inches (60 cm) trained up trellis
Eggplant	18 inches (45 cm)	18 inches (45 cm)
Kale	12 inches (30 cm)	12 inches (30 cm)
Kohlrabi	6 inches (15 cm)	8 inches (20 cm)
Leeks	6 inches (15 cm)	12 inches (30 cm)
Lettuce, heading	12 inches (30 cm)	12 inches (30 cm)
Lettuce, leaf	8–10 inches (20–25 cm)	8–10 inches (20–25 cm)
Melons	24 inches (60 cm)	one row per bed
Onions/Garlic	4 inches (10 cm)	8 inches (20 cm)
Parsnips	3 inches (8 cm)	8 inches (20 cm)
Peas	1–3 inches (2.5–8 cm)	8 inches (20 cm)
Peppers	15 inches (38 cm)	15 inches (38 cm)
Potatoes	10–15 inches (25–38 cm)	18 inches (45 cm) if mulched 30 inches (75 cm) if hilled
Radishes	2 inches (5 cm)	4 inches (10 cm)
Rutabaga	6 inches (15 cm)	8 inches (20 cm)
Spinach	6 inches (15 cm)	8 inches (20 cm)
Squash, summer	18 inches (45 cm)	24 inches (60 cm)
Squash, winter	24 inches (60 cm)	one row per wide bed
Tomatoes	24 inches (60 cm)	36 inches (90 cm)

ORNAMENTAL EDIBLES

Enclosed vegetable beds intersected by mulched or stone-paved paths are refinements that get a kitchen garden off to a beautiful start, but boards and stones are only the bare bones. Whatever the design, plants add a livelier beauty of color, form, and texture.

Virtually all food plants have some charm of leaf, flower, or fruit. Who can deny the beauty of a pepper bush burning with thin, scarlet chilies; or the eggplant's starry mauve flowers and polished purple fruit. Red lettuces and ferny carrot tops are pretty enough to edge flowerbeds. Other vegetables, too, stand out for their special decorative value. Here are some vegetables you might plant even if they weren't edible.

Top marks go to Swiss chard for its glossy, crumpled dark-green leaves and broad contrasting stems. Red-stemmed chard is lovely enough for a prominent spot in any flowerbed. The same is true for kale; its wonderfully textured, blue-green leaves fan open like a great frilly flower.

Scarlet runner beans wind their way decoratively up poles, trellises, or porch pillars in the sun. By midsummer the spot is alight with stems of brilliant blossoms that are very enticing to hummingbirds. The clusters of green beans are a welcome bonus. Closer to the ground, purple-podded "green" beans grow among heart-shaped leaves tinted with some of the bean's dark ink.

Radicchio lovers should know about the variety "Giulio"; the lovely wine-red heads, like leafy roses, mature slowly and not all at once. If some go to seed, you'll enjoy the flowers on the way. The alpine strawberry is a jaunty small perennial for edging; its fruit, either red or white, is the size of the nail on your baby finger. Grow this ornamental edible from seed or start with plants for quicker pickings.

When my friend and I started our first garden

Easy to grow from cloves planted the previous fall, garlic helps to ward off some of the insects that might bother beans growing nearby.

in the city, two things never occurred to us. The first was to spray the vegetables with chemicals—that would defeat the purpose. The other was to lay out the garden in rows with unproductive paths between—we didn't have room to waste. By July we could barely find an island of bare ground to stand on in the sea of green. When we came to the country, we had all the space we could want, and more. But we laid out the garden in a series of beds from the beginning. The beds suit us. They are as productive as we could ever hope for, as lovely as we could wish. In the kitchen garden, use and beauty meet.

4

SPRING STEPS

Sometime after New Year's, a gardener's fancy turns to thoughts of seeds and soil. By May, some of us are once again under the spell of a "springtime passion for the earth." Between those first green thoughts and the appearance of green seedlings, a new season bows in. What a pleasure, after a long stuffy winter, to be out, spade and seeds in hand. We drink in the fresh spring air; our bodies are more relaxed, freed from the winter huddle and heavy clothes. The rhythmic work of raking a bed becomes a kind of active meditation: we feel the lively potential of the dark soil.

For gardeners, April is far from being "the cruelest month," but the tentative weeks between winter and spring — April here, March or even May in other areas — are surely the most tantalizing. One glorious morning entices us out to the garden with warm promises; the next drives us indoors with cold winds, scowling skies and the sting of freezing rain. Who can sit idly by warming their heels while Primavera dances two steps forward, one step back? Besides, if you do, you lose precious weeks of growth. While the weather dithers, gardeners can get the season under way inside. Seedlings started indoors will be garden-ready by the time spring decides to stay.

In May seedlings of squash, cucumbers, and melons take windowsill space as cool weather seedlings—broccoli, lettuce, onions, cabbage, and leeks—are transplanted to the garden.

AN INDOOR START

Not all vegetables are created with an equal tolerance to cold, and not all ripen on the same schedule. Lettuce and broccoli grow better and faster in somewhat cooler weather and are table-ready six to eight weeks after transplanting. For them an indoor start means improved growth before summer begins to swelter, and a welcome early harvest. Leeks and Brussels sprouts are two of the kitchen garden's most frost-proof residents, but both take their sweet time maturing. A few extra weeks indoors results in a more abundant harvest. Peppers, tomatoes, melons, and eggplant — long-season, heat-loving tropicals all — don't get moving until the weather warms up, and then come to an abrupt end on the first frosty night in fall. A spell on the windowsill may make the difference between a fruitful summer and no pickings at all.

In many cases a cossetted period indoors brings plants through their infancy away from drought and deluge, frost or frying heat, not to mention voracious slugs and earwigs. Swiss chard, for example — one of the most decorative of vegetables — is normally sown directly outdoors, but in our garden its first leaves are often decimated by earwigs. Since five or six Swiss chard plants are all we need, we seed a few 4-inch (10-cm) pots in April for May transplanting. Earwigs are a lot less interested in the slightly older specimens.

The snow may still be flying outside when we start seeds indoors in a sunny window.

Seeding Schedule

The indoor seed-sowing season may extend over a number of weeks, from late February to mid-May in most regions. It's a mistake to think that the sooner you start, the quicker you'll pick. Unless conditions in the house are close to perfect — lots of sunlight and night temperatures hovering around 60°F (15°C) — there is nothing to be gained by rushing things. Better results come from setting out stocky month-old seedlings rather than older ones that have grown weak and lanky. For example, we used to sow broccoli the third week in March, when days are often cloudy and the house is fairly warm. Leaning toward the light, the seedlings were also forced by the heat. Low light and high heat make

for weak, wobbly seedlings. We now wait until mid-April when more sun pours through the glass doors. The stripling broccolis that go out in mid-May are less spindly than before and settle into the garden without much ado.

Home Grown

Gardeners who tend to be seed-shy, take heart. Vegetable seeds are among the easiest to sprout, most making an appearance within a week or ten days. Lettuce may show through in as few as three days. But why bother to start your own vegetable seedlings when you can buy them ready-grown at any nursery in May? Starting your own seeds gives the advantage of variety. The garden store may stock a lettuce or two, but seeds open the door to red Bostons, mini-romaines, European exotics like "Merveille de Quatre Saisons," old-fashioned (but succulent) "Oakleaf," and many more. You will always find "Beefsteak" tomatoes at a nursery, a variety that ripens much later than the "Ultra Girls" you can raise yourself.

As well, many commercial seedlings are cramped, tangled, and root-bound by the time you get them. You're forced to wrench roots apart, a traumatic start for a plant that also has to face the rigors of sun and wind for the first time. At home you can schedule seeding and use fair-sized containers. The result is superior plants that suffer very little at transplanting time.

Setting Up: Pots, Flats, and Soil for Seedlings

Seedlings are started in all manner of quirky containers, from half-eggshells and egg cartons (rather small for the purpose) to toilet paper rolls snugged together in a watertight tray (quite good). I'm no fan of the various Styrofoam seed-starting trays. The tray may last for a year or two and then becomes one more piece of toxic junk.

There is little need to buy seedling containers, although peat pots are handy for plants with roots strong enough to push through them. All manner of erstwhile trash can be reused: yogurt and cottage-cheese containers with drainage holes; the bottom half of waxed cardboard milk or juice containers; paper drinking cups. The plastic six-packs that held your petunias from the nursery last spring can grow your lettuce seedlings this time around. One nursery sells a wooden cylinder for rolling your own seedling pots from newspaper. For those who like to muck around, there is a gizmo that presses wet earth into soil blocks. More traditionally, flats — simple, portable wooden boxes — are the first quarters for many vegetable plants.

For years we have made a good start with many vegetables using homemade flats. The exceptions are tomatoes, peppers, eggplant, cucumbers, and melons, which begin their pre-garden life in 4-inch (10-cm) pots. Flats are knocked together with scraps of lumber or plywood and small spiral nails or wood screws. Boxes vary in size: 16 by 18 by 3 inches (40 by 45 by 8 cm) deep is the largest we want to lift when it is full of damp dirt; 12 by 15 by 2 (30 by 38 by 5 cm) deep is the smallest that is useful.

Containers at hand, we turn our attention to the growing medium. At Larkwhistle we stir together our own seed-starting mix, using two parts sandy topsoil from the garden and one part each damp peat moss and sifted compost. To each wheelbarrow full of the blended ingredients we add a spadeful of bone meal. Even though we do not sterilize the mix, as is often recommended — baking soil in the oven at 300°F (150°C) for ninety minutes is a messy, smelly business, and an impossible task in any volume — disease or fungus problems have been negligible. We make the mix for spring seedlings the previous fall and then store it under cover, often right in the flats and pots we will seed in spring.

You may lack the inclination to blend and bake a batch of soil (or forget to do it in fall). You may not have access to the sandy earth that makes such a good base; clay ground quickly puts a stranglehold on tender sprouts. Commercial seeding mixes, usually a blend of peat moss, vermiculite, and small amounts of nutrients, are a good alternative, as is a homemade blend of equal parts potting soil and perlite. Store-bought ingredients have several advantages over garden soil. They are available at a time when the garden may be muddy or crusty with frost. They are weed-free, so you are not left scratching your head,

wondering which bits of green are peppers and which are plantain. Commercial mixes are formulated to be lightweight and porous to both air and water while holding moisture that seedlings need. Most significantly, the blends you buy are sterile, free of the fungus spores that often menace seedlings in unsterilized ground. You avoid the discouraging prospect of watching your nice young tomatoes suddenly keel over from "damping off."

Damping-off spores breed and attack at soil level, causing stems to wither. As a preventive step, we sometime top pots or flats with a half-inch layer of vermiculite ("puffed" mica), or milled sphagnum moss (not peat moss). Seeds are planted right in the vermiculite. The resulting seedlings will have a sterile "collar" around their vulnerable necks. You can also foil spore growth by cultivating around seedlings — an ordinary kitchen fork is a handy scratcher — leaving a layer of fine dry soil on top. A spray of cool chamomile tea seems to stop the fungus, as does a dusting of crushed chamomile flowers (those sold for tea). Grow seedlings a little on the dry side with good ventilation — it's good for them, damping-off or not.

Seeding Steps

Start seedlings as follows:

1. Fill flats almost to the top with moistened growing medium and tamp by hand, or with a flat board, to level soil and squeeze out air pockets. Top up with more soil mix or vermiculite.

2. Using a ruler for accurate spacing, make shallow thumbprint depressions 2 inches (5 cm) apart in the surface; such spacing is ideal for lettuce, broccoli, cabbage, Brussels sprouts, cauliflower, and endive. For seedlings of leeks, onions, and parsley, which can stand a little more crowding, draw short, shallow furrows, about 1½ inches (4 cm) apart, across the soil.

3. Drop three or four seeds into each thumbprint. Scatter seeds thinly along the little rows. Cover seeds lightly with a quarter-inch of soil and pat to firm.

4. As seedlings grow, thin to the sturdiest one in each little hollow. Thin those in rows until they are a scant inch apart. Scissors are handy to snip

CALENDAR OF INDOOR SEEDING AND
OUTDOOR TRANSPLANTING

At Larkwhistle, where the last spring frost occurs in late May (circled), this is the spring schedule of seeding indoors and transplanting outdoors. To make a customized calendar for your garden, determine your spring frost-free date and circle the appropriate period. Using check marks, shift the schedule backward or forward the corresponding number of boxes. For example, where frost is finished in early May, leeks and onions are seeded indoors in mid-February, hardened off in early April, and transplanted outdoors in mid-April.

	Mid-Feb. 10-20	Late Feb. 20-28	Early March 1-10	Mid-March 10-20	Late March 20-31	Early April 1-10	Mid-April 10-20	Late April 20-30	Early May 1-10	Mid-May 10-20	**FROST-FREE** Late May 20-31 **FROST-FREE**	Early June 1-10	Mid-June 10-20
Leeks Onions			seed indoors						harden	transplant			
Parsley				seed indoors					harden	transplant			
Peppers Eggplant						seed indoors				harden	transplant*		
Tomatoes						seed indoors			harden	transplant*			
Lettuce						seed (1) indoors		seed (2) indoors	harden (1)	transplant (1)	transplant (2)		
Cabbage Broccoli (early) Kale Swiss chard						seed indoors			harden	transplant			
Melons Winter squash Zucchini Cucumber Basil									seed indoors		harden		transplant
Cabbage Broccoli (late)											seed indoors		transplant

*Protect from frost if necessary

SPRING SCHEDULE OF OUTDOOR SEED SOWING

Sowing seeds in the garden need not be a frantic, one-day task. Better to relax and do a little seeding now and again from early spring until mid-summer. Hardy vegetables withstand frost and grow better in the cooler weeks of spring. Others, such as tropical tomatoes and melons, thrive in warm weather. The charts below show you when to seed (and, in some cases, transplant) into the garden, using spring's last frost and fall's first frost as benchmarks.

APPROXIMATE DATE OF LAST SPRING FROST: _____

VERY HARDY	HARDY	SEMI-HARDY	TENDER	HEAT-LOVING
Sow 5-7 weeks before last frost	Sow 2-3 weeks before last frost	Sow 1-2 weeks before last frost	Sow on or just after last frost	Sow 1-2 weeks after last frost
leeks	lettuce	beets	beans	cucumber
onions	mustard	carrots	corn	lima beans
(seeds/sets)	turnip greens	parsnips	pumpkin	eggplants*
peas	chervil	radish	summer squash	tomatoes*
spinach	coriander	broccoli*	winter squash	peppers*
dill	parsley	brussels	zucchini	canteloupe*
garlic		sprouts*		watermelon
shallots		cabbage*		peanuts
		cauliflower*		sweet potatoes
		kale		
		kohlrabi		
		Swiss chard		
		potatoes		

* Best as transplants

SUMMER SCHEDULE OF OUTDOOR SEED SOWING

APPROXIMATE DATE OF FIRST FALL FROST: _____

Sow 10-12 weeks before fall frost	Sow 8 weeks before fall frost
beets	bok choy
carrots	lettuce
Chinese cabbage	kohlrabi
endive	Oriental radish
radicchio	snow peas
rutabaga	spinach
	turnips

away the surplus without disturbing roots of seedlings you wish to keep.

5. About a week before transplanting, slice through the soil between plants — just as if you were cutting a tray of brownies into squares — leaving each seedling at the center of its own block of earth. An old spatula is a useful tool for lifting the blocks.

In the past few years we have taken to filling our flats with small containers, round or (preferably) square pots, either of recycled plastic or pressed peat. It is the better part of wisdom to sterilize second-hand pots in a solution of one part bleach to six parts hot water, but I have to say we've never done so. Pots 2 to 3 inches (5 to 8 cm) across are suitable for most vegetable seedlings. In each pot we sow three to five seeds, with a view to thinning eventually to the strongest single one. Containers eliminate the stress of damaged roots that may result from transplanting directly out of flats. However, flat-grown seedlings (without containers) have done well for us for years. The secret seems to be adequate spacing and careful lifting at transplanting time.

Seeded flats or pots are watered from below by sitting them in a tray of lukewarm water. You can also rain on them gently from above with a hand sprayer tuned to a fine mist. To water from the bottom later on, set pots in a watertight tray, such as an old cake pan or metal cookie tin.

Soil must be kept moist but never soggy until seeds sprout, something better done by misting than by draping a suffocating sheet of plastic over the containers. Tepid water is better than a shocking cold shower. We seldom feed seedlings — the compost and bone meal are nourishment enough — but if they show hunger signs, such as pale or purpling leaves or lackadaisical growth, a reviving drink of liquid organic fertilizer, mixed half-strength, makes a visible difference.

Bottom Heat

Once pots and flats are seeded, they need a warm spot for germination. Gentle bottom heat rouses

Planning is the key to making the fullest use of garden space. The diagrams below and opposite illustrate two examples of how beds can change over the course of the season. Planted in spring, the first crop of vegetables gives way to a second, as new plants are either seeded or transplanted in midsummer for fresh eating in fall. Careful spacing puts plants quite close together without overcrowding them. The distances between rows add up to a total width of four feet (1.2 m), a handy size for tending from paths on either side. The length of the bed depends on the space you have available.

FIRST PLANTING

SECOND PLANTING

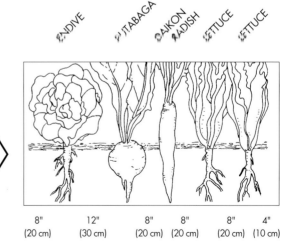

PEAS	PEAS	ROMAINE LETTUCE	CARROTS	ONIONS
6" (15 cm)	6" (15 cm)	12" (30 cm)	8" (20 cm) 6" (15 cm) 6" (15 cm)	4" (10 cm)

ENDIVE	RUTABAGA	DAIKON RADISH	LETTUCE	LETTUCE
8" (20 cm)	12" (30 cm)	8" (20 cm) 8" (20 cm)	8" (20 cm)	4" (10 cm)

dormant seeds. We balance flats on a base of inverted clay pots set directly on top of the wood stove. When the soil in the flats feels warm to the touch, we swaddle them in old blankets to retain the heat. Often, one warming is enough to persuade seeds to sprout.

An electric heating pad or radiator also warms pots and flats. And there is another "technological breakthrough" — special heating cables to run under your flats. Actually, a "grow-mat," a rubber square embedded with heating cables, sounds useful for large batches of seedlings. Or you could simply put seeded trays on a nearby kitchen counter when the oven is in use.

Let There Be Light

As soon as the little green backs show through, seedlings need sunlight and lots of it — at least five hours for lettuce and parsley, more for broccoli and Spanish onions, and a minimum of eight hours for the tomatoes, peppers, and eggplant. An unshaded bay window facing southeast to southwest is perfect. East and west windows are fine, too, if you are home to shift your seedlings. Supplementing the sun with fluorescent lights helps. A cool room temperature is better than too much heat, which forces weak stretchy growth.

In the absence of sunlight, seedlings will grow along merrily under fluorescent lights, either the standard cool-white ones or special (and costlier) grow-lights that include more of the infrared spectrum. One 4-foot tube of each, set in a reflector, provides excellent light over a 4 foot by 1 foot (120 cm by 30 cm) space, enough for 54 3-inch (8-cm) pots, or 144 2-inch (5-cm) pots. Because fluorescents radiate very little heat, plants can sit a mere 3 inches away from them. It is handy to be able to raise the lights or lower the plants as necessary. Small plants need about the same amount of rest as you do, so it's lights out for eight or nine hours every night.

Cold Frames

Nothing is more useful for the days between indoor safety and the open air than a simple cold frame, a bottomless sloping wooden box topped with a transparent cover. There are several choices for glazing. Clear plastic is cheap; a sheet of clear corrugated acrylic is much more lasting. Both are lighter and easier to work with than the old storm windows that cover all our cold frames.

We build cold frames to fit the windows, using leftover lumber — 1- or 2-inch (2.5- or 5-cm) stock or even odd pieces of plywood — if we have it. Not surprisingly no two frames are alike. The salient points are that the back of a frame is approximately twice as high as the front, and the front is at least 5 inches (12 cm)

FIRST PLANTING

SECOND PLANTING

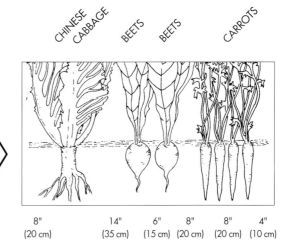

FIRST PLANTING — PEAS · PEAS · EARLY CABBAGE · SPINACH · SPINACH

| 6" (15 cm) | 6" (15 cm) | 12" (30 cm) | 12" (30 cm) | 6" (15 cm) | 6" (15 cm) |

SECOND PLANTING — CHINESE CABBAGE · BEETS · BEETS · CARROTS

| 8" (20 cm) | 14" (35 cm) | 6" (15 cm) | 8" (20 cm) | 8" (20 cm) | 4" (10 cm) |

About a week before transplanting, slice through the soil between flat-grown seedlings. Later, each lettuce or cabbage can be lifted with a block of soil intact and minimal root disturbance.

high but no taller than 8 inches (20 cm) or you'll shade the interior.

One neat and sturdy cold frame is fronted with a piece of two-by-eight cedar (or pressure-treated lumber) with two pieces of the same stock making the back. The sloping sides are fashioned of another length of two-by-eight cut on a diagonal from corner to corner, the halves fastened to two lengths of two-by-eight.

For "high-tech" and well-heeled gardeners there are aluminum and acrylic cold frames fitted with an electronic device that automatically raises and lowers the top to keep the interior temperature steady.

A cold frame should be situated in a sheltered spot, facing the sun and handy to the house if possible. Our frames, oriented vaguely south, sit on the ground in the garden. The first seedlings, barely two weeks old, go into the frames by the third week in April when frosty nights are still

commonplace. These are the cool-weather crops: lettuce, cabbage, broccoli, Swiss chard, leeks, and parsley, and with them such hardy annual flowers as asters, sweet peas, stocks, mignonette, and snapdragons.

Nights may be chilly in April, but a calm sunny day sends temperatures in the frame soaring. By mid morning we check to see if windows need to be propped upon for ventilation, a necessary airing that accustoms seedlings to the winds they will soon be facing in the great outdoors. If you leave home in the morning, and the forecast is for sunny and mild weather, you'd do well to take the sash off completely and soak flats and pots thoroughly. A few hours before sunset, windows go on to retain warmth. If an unseasonably cold night threatens, we cover frames with an assortment of old woolen blankets — the thrift shops are a good source — and feather-spewing sleeping bags.

By mid-May, as we transplant hardy vegetables, vacant frame space is filled with pots of heat-loving tomatoes, peppers, eggplant, perhaps melons. If night temperatures are predicted to dip much below 45°F (7°C), we haul these sensitive sorts back indoors until morning.

A cold frame is used not only to harden plants to outdoor conditions but also to serve as the starting ground for certain hardy vegetables. Hereabouts, a number of older gardeners routinely sow seeds directly in the soil of a cold frame in preparation for later transplanting. If you want to grow some starter plants, but lack suitable window space or don't care for the fuss and expense of fluorescent lights, a frame makes a fine nursery. It is not lack of light in early spring that inhibits growth — the sun is on the rise and days are long enough — but the absence of heat. Buffer the breezes, warm the ground with a frame, and you can sow seeds in a frame weeks before you could plant them alfresco.

To grow seedlings directly in a frame, set it up over bare earth in a sunny corner of the garden, or by the south wall of the house or outbuilding. On cold clay soils, better results accrue from digging out 8 or 10 inches (20 or 25 cm) of topsoil from the frame. Turn and break up the ground beneath for drainage and aeration before replacing the clay with a mellow mix of light topsoil, fine compost, and/or bagged manure and a dusting of bone meal or organic fertilizer. Stir the mixture together, rake to a fine tilth, and you are ready to seed.

Vegetables suitable for direct sowing in a frame include lettuces of all kinds, cabbage and broccoli, kohlrabi, Swiss chard, and kale. About six weeks before spring's average final frost date, sow seeds by dropping them one by one, an inch (2.5 cm) apart, into shallow furrows drawn from back to front. Space furrows 4 inches (10 cm) apart. Cover seeds with a quarter-inch of light soil or sifted compost, water with a very gentle spray, and fit the cover over the frame. After they sprout, thin seedlings before they grow crowded to one plant every 3 inches (8 cm) in the row. Seedlings will grow vigorously in the frame's gentle heat but will never stretch for light as they are

Seedlings grown indoors must be gradually acclimatized to unfiltered sun and drying winds, a process called "hardening off." A cold frame is ideal for the transition.

apt to do under less-than-ideal indoor conditions. Ventilate the frames just as you would if they held pots and flats. Even frame-grown seedlings must learn the facts of outdoor life gradually — fresh breezes one day, the caress of the unfiltered sun for a few hours the next.

TRANSPLANTING

There comes a time in May when a gardener is looking at a frame or windowsill full of seedlings and the forecasts are calling for a mild week, a few overcast days, a chance of showers — transplanting weather. After tending seedlings for a month or more, I always get a bit nervous about

At transplanting time, dig oversized holes and stir in sifted compost to concentrate nutrients around each plant. Set most seedlings slightly deeper than they were growing, firm soil well, and water.

fine-textured manure and damp peat moss. (Compost is also fine on its own.) To each bucket of the blend, add a heaping handful of bone meal and a little less kelp meal, or use a handful of a balanced organic fertilizer.

I have a pint-sized spade that is just right for transplanting. After measuring and marking the distance between plants, I dig an oversized hole for each seedling. Then I ladle a spadeful of transplanting mix into each hole and stir the organic stuff into the soil. Finally I firm the earth with a gloved fist.

Pots and trays should be watered thoroughly before transplanting so the damp soil clings to roots. Most seedlings can go into the ground a little deeper than they were growing in containers; deeper planting helps to anchor and stabilize lanky plants, leaving them less prone to a wind whipping. Set in up to its bottom leaves, a tomato plant quickly sprouts new roots from its buried stem; the same applies to broccoli and cabbage. Lettuce, however, resents a depth change.

Nestle transplants into the soil, making sure there are no air pockets under them. Fill in around roots with fine earth or transplanting mix, then poke around with fingers or the trowel handle to ensure good earth-root contact. Firm the soil by pressing down gently around the transplant. At this point, we sculpt the earth to form a shallow "soupbowl" around each plant; water poured on now and throughout the season will be funneled right to the plant's roots. Seafood soup — a feed of fish emulsion or liquid seaweed mixed to half the usual strength — is often on the menu for new transplants.

Cutoffs

Is there anything more frustrating than going through all these steps only to find gaps in the row next morning. Closer inspection reveals cut-off seedlings wilted on the ground. Dig around the stub with your finger and chances are you'll unearth a fat gray cutworm that spews a stream of green — your digested seedling — when stepped on. All God's creatures have a role, they say — and I don't doubt they do — but this smacks of vandalism. What kind of a meal is a

setting them out. What if frost strikes in the night, a fat cutworm slices stems, earwigs chew them up, the sun fries the small fries? It's not exactly a jungle out there, but threats lurk.

It is strange but true that insects are more apt to bother plants that are enduring some stress — too much fertilizer, lack of water, or faltering growth. Transplanting is potentially very stressful, but there are ways to reduce the trauma. Care taken at this juncture will be repaid abundantly later on.

First, if at all possible, choose a calm overcast day for transplanting; if a drizzly day follows, so much the better. In sunny weather, transplant in the late afternoon or early evening. Before I set out small plants — perennial, herb, or vegetable — I like to stir something nourishing into the soil for each one. An easily prepared transplanting mix consists of equal parts sifted compost or

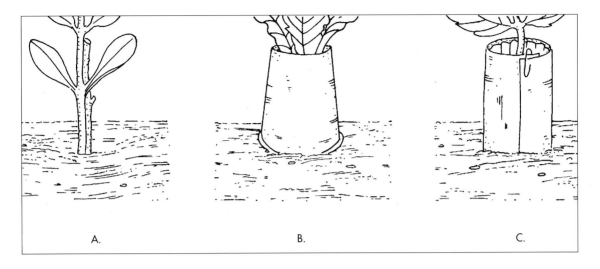

Where cutworms are active, protect new transplants with: A) sticks or nails pushed into the ground next to stems, B) bottomless paper cups or tin cans snugged over seedlings, or C) a collar of corrugated cardboard held in place with a paper clip.

millimeter of stem? There are ways to outwit a cutworm, a common pest that does its dirty work at night, curling around stems near ground level and chewing through. Most effective is a physical barrier: we always stick two thin 3-inch (8-cm) nails an inch into the ground, one on either side of vulnerable stems. Some gardeners wrap stems loosely with a collar of tarpaper, tinfoil, or cardboard, pushed into the ground. Paper cups, toilet-tissue tubes, or tin cans (minus tops and bottoms) also keep cutworms away; and a circle of ashes or crushed eggshells is said to deter ol' cutty, too. As you cultivate around recent transplants or along a row of just-sprouted seedlings, you'll likely turn up a number of the curled culprits for quick dispatch underfoot.

Earwigs love to snack on seedlings — they are as fond of basil as you are. Their trademark damage is a lacy network of holes. A spray of insecticidal soap is a sure control, but you must hit the insects directly, not just coat the leaves. If we notice damage by day, we're out on a flashlit garden tour some time after dark when earwigs are active.

5

TROUBLE
Insects, Weeds, Frost, and Water

FROST PROOFING

All the seedlings are in the ground. Gentle rains fall on schedule; the late spring sun is warm and encouraging. The garden is coming along beautifully. Suddenly winds shift into the north; by evening, under a clear sky, they die down, leaving chill air in their wake. Over the horizon a full moon rises. You can see your breath. All signs point to a frosty night. It's time to take steps to protect the plants.

Our garden lies in a slight hollow on the north side of the woods where cold air settles on a calm night — a classic frost pocket. Although the "official" frost-free date here is June 1, every couple of years the garden feels the silver sting as late as June 10. Passersby must wonder at a garden spread with blankets and at rows of inverted flower pots lined up on the beds.

Even a light covering will deflect frost. In the garden shed we keep a stack of 5-inch (12-cm) fiber pots that we pop over the heads of susceptible seedlings. Since frost usually strikes on a calm night, we don't weight pots down but simply "screw" them a little into the ground. Bigger pots

An array of herbs and flowers weave through the beds of edibles. Silver Artemisia absynthium *and feathery green yarrow lend their pungent, bug-repelling scents to a mix that includes Rugosa roses, dianthus or pinks, and big blue Italian bugloss, a giant forget-me-not relative with edible blue flowers that draw bees and butterflies.*

slip nicely over tender zucchini plants; large paper grocery bags, doubled if you have enough, keep tomatoes safe if not particularly warm. Layers of newspaper must be held down with soil or rocks or they'll be everywhere.

Threadbare blankets, propped up on short sticks, are useful for covering beds of small bean plants or blooming strawberries. As a last resort we carry a few armloads of bedsheets and bath towels into the garden. We may wake up the next morning to a south wind returning and no frost, but why risk it? Who wants to see two months of work ruined in a night?

As a season stretcher and frost deflector, plastic sheeting has its advantages. Clear plastic tunnels held up by wire hoops protect plants beneath. Designed especially for garden use, slitted plastic row covers exhale the buildup of hot air. Then there are water-filled plastic teepees (Wall-O'-Water) that sit over individual plants; the water absorbs heat during the day, releases it at night, warding off a fairly sharp frost in the process. One catalog shows a plastic "cloche" meant to give seedlings, a head start and shed frost, but the translucent cylinders strike me as too small and too expensive. In any event, you can reuse any big clear plastic jug for the purpose: slice off the bottom and unscrew the cap to vent hot air.

Am I wrong to think that all this plastic has little place in an organic garden? After a season or two you end up with a bundle of nondegradable garbage that took its share of petroleum and chemicals to make. Even so-called photodegradable plastic does not truly return to the soil in any usable form; it just breaks up into tiny bits that look "gone." If we are choosing natural over chemical fertilizers for the Earth's sake, isn't some consistency called for? The refuse we don't want around our gardens ends up littering some other part of the larger earth-garden.

That said, I do like the new lightweight fabric covers sold under several trade names. Made of "spun and bonded" polyester fibers, the cloth lets in about 85 percent of available light and all the rain. It also buffers the winds to create a cozy microclimate underneath. Because they weigh next to nothing, cloth covers "float" ever so lightly, right on top of plants; as your cauliflowers grow, the fabric billows up like rising bread dough. We secure the sides with stones or, more conveniently, long sticks or lengths of lumber. On the down side, the stuff tears too easily; if you get three seasons out of it you're doing well. We often reuse badly torn Reemay (one of the brand names) by closing a rip and keeping it together with stones. Even fairly small remnants are useful to cover small sections of garden. Garden fabric gives some frost protection as well.

INSECTS

There may never be complete peace between gardeners and insects, but it is a mistake to cast all bugs in a bad light because of a handful of troublemakers.

Natural Balance

A healthy garden is literally — and quite naturally — swarming with flying insects and crawling with earthbound creatures. Bug counters estimate that every square yard in an average garden is home to more than 1,000 insects of many kinds. Obviously, only a fraction pose any threat to plants; otherwise the garden would be eaten to shreds in no time. The rest do the beneficial work of returning organic matter to the soil, opening up underground air channels, pollinating your cucumbers, and keeping the birds well fed. Some bugs — bless 'em — eat other bugs: spiders, ladybugs, praying mantises, assassin bugs, rove beetles, and parasitic wasps are among a gardener's best allies.

All this is easy to forget when earwigs are mowing down carrot sprouts or turning basil into lace; when cutworms are toppling tomato seedlings and flea beetles are riddling the radish leaves. The temptation may be to reach for the "big guns" — a sprayer full of chemicals — and show the bugs who's boss. The problem is that many chemicals kill friend and foe alike. You may win the battle, but you'll never win the war. When the next generation of aphids appears, where are the ladybugs that devour them? If insect-eating birds haven't been harmed outright by the spray, they may leave when their food supply suddenly dwindles. The lull in plant damage by insects is sure to prove a short-lived illusion.

It is no coincidence that talk of pesticides often takes on a military tone. Much of the arsenal of garden chemicals was originally developed and stockpiled as weaponry — nerve gases, defoliants, and the like — during the last two wars. In peacetime, the chemical companies targeted farmers and gardeners as a ready market for the toxic leftover inventory.

A garden is a place of peaceful cooperation, not a battlefield. Insects are part of the natural balance. Our approach to bugs can be summed up as: innocent until proven guilty. When we need to protect our plants, we do. But if we're not sure about the eating habits of a mysterious iridescent beetle that comes to light as we dig, we let it be. (Sometimes, as a precaution, we'll throw the creature over the garden fence, a tactic that works only if you have no neighbors within bug tossing distance.) After a while, you come to recognize the garden's principal pests; you learn the difference between leaf-eating Mexican bean beetles and their near look-alikes, the aphid-eating ladybugs. You can spot the calling cards of creatures that dine by night: a silver slug trail, the telltale toothmarks of earwigs. You can take specific steps to correct the balance only when you know what you're up against.

Prevention

When it comes to trouble (with a capital T and that rhymes with P, and that stands for pests) prevention is better than cure. Tests have shown that insects are drawn to plants that are weak, ailing, pumped up with chemical fertilizers, or otherwise stressed. A healthy garden, built on a foundation of lively organic soil, is less apt to be bothered by bugs. If insects are giving you a rough time, look to the soil first.

Diversity is another key to a balanced environment. Snakes and toads should always be welcome in a natural garden. A big old clay pot, inverted and propped up on one side with a stone, may persuade a toad to set up house in a shady corner. Enticing birdhouses and shrubbery offer shelter to swallows, flycatchers, and finches. Last season a pair of perky redstarts took up residence in our garden. From dawn till dusk they flashed from fence to branch, to cabbage patch, to rosebush in a tireless search for insects — regular little bug-catching vacuum cleaners. Robins, cliff swallows, phoebes, and catbirds joined the hunt.

Companion planting has its adherents. Some books provide detailed lists of good companions and bad: plant beans next to potatoes to repel the Mexican bean beetle; chives near tomatoes, strawberries, and broccoli will ward off aphids. Although I'm intrigued by the possibilities, our approach to companion planting is rather more chaotic — but companionable nonetheless. Woven throughout our kitchen garden are an array of aromatic herbs that add randomly to the bug-baffling mix. At the ends of kitchen-garden beds, clumps of sage, winter savory, chives, tarragon, and Greek oregano are within easy reach as we gather ingredients for a salad or stir-fry. Seldom picked for use, rue and wormwood lend their pungent presence to the jumble. Catnip, chamomile, and horehound pop up as volunteers.

One of the simplest things you can do to prevent a pests population explosion is to clean up the garden thoroughly in fall, a time when insects are searching for a place to lay eggs or hibernate. There is no point working against yourself by leaving a litter of spent vines and stalks, old fruit and foliage lying around the garden. If you can bury all debris in a hot compost heap, so much the better. Turning the soil in fall also exposes various eggs and grubs to the birds or freezing temperatures.

Getting the Bugs Out

As sure as plants grow, some insects eventually show up to feed on them. The first step is to identify the culprits. A comprehensive illustrated insect guide is a valuable tool. *The Healthy Garden Handbook* from the editors of *Mother Earth News* gives clear mugshots of the garden's "most wanted" and suggests a choice of controls.

Plants can cope with a certain amount of grazing and may even rebound with increased vigor after the pest's cycle is over. Let's face it: often a gardener's pride suffers more damage than do the plants themselves. If the problem escalates, handpicking is a benign and effective way to control many insects. If potato beetles are getting the best of the patch, knock them off into a pail of water with a dash of dish soap in it. Better yet, search the undersides of leaves early in the season and crush the egg clusters by hand. Provided that the garden is not vast, handpicking is an excellent way to control larger, slow-moving pests that eat by day. Many a slug, earwig, and caterpillar has felt the full force of the sole of a wooden clog in our garden. Sometimes, as I grind, I'll say something like "May your dead body enrich the earth" to ease my conscience and remind me that nothing is wasted in nature.

Slugs and Earwigs

I've tried handpicking slugs by night, but the slimy things slip through my fingers. A few shakes of salt reduce a slug to bubbling gel in no time, but too much salt can injure foliage. A neighbor stalks slugs with a flashlight in one hand and scissors in the other. I'll spare you the gory details except to say that I've heard her referred to as the "slug slasher."

Here is an improvement on beer-baited slug traps: sink yogurt or cottage-cheese containers into the ground up to their rim; fill them almost to the top with a 50/50 mix of molasses and water into which is stirred a few teaspoons of brewer's yeast and bran. Empty the drowned slugs into the compost every few days.

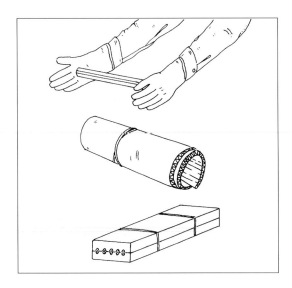

Earwigs like to crawl into dark, close quarters. Trap these nocturnal pests in pieces of old garden hose, a loosely rolled cardboard cylinder, or two pieces of grooved wood, held together with elastic bands. Such simple traps often lure a number of earwigs.

Earwigs have become notorious pests recently in this area. I hate to pinch them because they pinch back. Insecticidal soap kills earwigs on contact but that entails a midnight garden tour. You may prefer to set some traps and get some sleep. Earwigs love to hide in tight dark places. One gardener reports wonderful success trapping earwigs in foot-long lengths of old garden hose laid on the ground in places where the nocturnal raiders have been busy — in the carrot patch, for instance, or near Chinese cabbages. A few drops of cod-liver oil or fish emulsion in the hose sweetens the trap. In the morning she picks up the hose gingerly with gloved hands, being careful to first block the exits at both ends, and shakes the earwigs into a pail of water with a slick of cooking oil on top. Lacking old hose, roll up tight tubes of corrugated cardboard. Earwigs crawl into crevices in wood as well. Chisel or cut some grooves into two small pieces of board; clamp the boards together with rubber bands and lay the trap in the garden. Balls of

crumpled newspapers or cloth, baited with fish oil, draw the pincered nightcrawlers for morning collection.

Barriers and Live Traps

Sometimes a physical barrier is the best way to ward off pests. Crushed eggshells or sharp sand spread in a band around susceptible plants may keep soft-bellied slugs and snails at bay. A dusting of wood ash is said to discourage a range of insects. The new "floating row covers," made of very lightweight translucent fabric, exclude flying pests such as cabbage moths, flea beetles, and root maggot flies.

In many areas, deer and rabbits freeload off a gardener's efforts. Both mammals are forever sniffing the air for threatening scents. Some gardeners sprinkle blood meal around beds, or hang it in cotton bags at waist height from a fence or branches, to signal "danger zone — stay away." Live traps capture nocturnal bandits, like raccoons, that raid garden produce.

Sprays and Dusts

For an organic gardener, insect sprays are a last resort. The choice is between either homemade or commercial. From the kitchen come several recipes that are more repellant than lethal.

• ALL-PURPOSE SPRAY: Blend together a few peeled garlic bulbs, a small onion or a handful of chives, a tablespoon of cayenne pepper in a quart of water. The addition of pungent herbs such as peppermint, cedar leaves, wormwood, or coriander boosts the brew. Let it steep for an hour or more. Strain through cloth and add a tablespoon of pure liquid soap or cooking oil to help the spray stick to leaves. Store in a cool place. Spray full strength to repel aphids, flea beetles, thrips, and others. To make a "solar tea," chop the same ingredients and steep in water in a clear glass jar set in the sun for a few days.

• GARLIC SPRAY: Garlic's antibiotic properties make it a natural for controlling downy mildew on cucumbers and melons; rust, anthracnose, and bacterial blight on beans: and the early blight that hits tomatoes. Remember, though, that it is wiser to plant disease — resistant varieties whenever possible.

To make a pungent bug chaser, press 4 or 5 big garlic cloves into as many tablespoons of mineral oil. Let steep for a day. Add 2 cups of water and a teaspoon of pure liquid soap and whisk together. Strain through a square of cotton and store the concentrate in a glass (not metal) container. Use 2 teaspoons in a quart (or liter) spray bottle aimed at your worst pests.

• CEDAR LEAF SPRAY or CEDAR MULCH: Remember the lovely resinous scent of that big old cedar chest used to store blankets and woolens? In the garden, the repellant properties of cedarwood deters cucumber, bean, and potato beetles, as well as red spiders and squash bugs from susceptible plants. Simmer a couple of double handfuls of cedar chips, bark, or sawdust (from a local lumber mill) in a big pot of water. Strain and store for future use as a foliar spray. A cedar mulch should keep the potato patch beetle-free; cedar chips in the pathways may also help repel various pests. Smells nice, anyway.

Natural Pest Controls
A Buyer's Guide

One shelf in our garden shed holds the few safe but effective natural pesticides that help protect the kitchen garden from hungry predators. As a last resort, when insects threaten to do more than cosmetic damage, we spray or dust only the infested area, trying if possible to hit the culprits directly. All of the following are available from garden centers or mail-order sources.

• INSECTICIDAL SOAP: High in fats and mineral salts, this specially made soap coats and smothers insects. Effective against aphids, whiteflies, earwigs, flea beetles, leafhoppers, and others, soap spray does not harm beneficial insects and quickly biodegrades. The ready-mixed pump-spray bottle — a little soap, a lot of water and plastic — is an overpackaged waste of money compared to the concentrate that you can mix easily yourself. I like to have a spray bottle full and ready to grab — "Quick, get the soap!" — whenever we uncover a nest of earwigs.

• BACILLUS THURINGIENSIS (BT): This biological control for a variety of caterpillars, loopers, and cutworms should be on the shelf of any gardener wanting to grow cabbages and kin. Trade names include Thuricide, Dipel, or simply Liquid Organic (Biological) Insecticide. Used as needed, BT all but guarantees worm-free broccoli. Because it degrades quickly, we respray with BT after rains or whenever we see new caterpillar damage. Mix only what you need and use it up in a day because the active ingredient soon loses its punch.

• DIATOMACEOUS EARTH: Made from the pulverized shells of tiny fossilized ocean plants called diatoms, this natural dust feels like coarse flour to thick-skinned gardeners but more like broken glass to soft-bellied slugs and insects. Kills on contact by piercing ectoskeleton or innards, causing pests to dry up. Controls aphids, thrips, mites, earwigs, slugs, snails, tomato hornworm, and others. For full effect, dust onto dry foliage or soil and reapply after a rain. This can get expensive.

• PYRETHRUM: A heavyweight botanical insecticide derived from the flowers of an innocent-looking white daisy, *Chrysanthemum cinerariafolium*, pyrethrum knocks out a range of bugs, including various beetles, caterpillars, aphids, and thrips. It is also toxic to fish, frogs, snakes, and beneficial insects, including bees. Spray at dusk to spare the bees, and do not use where spray can drift into garden pools or streams. Although it breaks down into harmless compound fairly quickly, you're advised to hold the spray during the week before harvest and to avoid pyrethrum products that also contain piperonyl butoxide, a suspected mutagen.

A hardy perennial, pyrethrum can be grown in the garden as a source of homemade insecticide. Sprinkle the crushed flowers, fresh or dried, around and over bugged plants. To make your own spray, steep a palmful of ground dried flowers in 2 quarts of hot water for a half-hour, strain, and add a teaspoon of pure liquid soap.

• ROTENONE: Another widely available, plant-derived bug killer, rotenone is made from the roots of several tropical plants, including derris. Deritox is one brand name. Again look for the pure product, unadulterated with synthetics.

Harmless to warm-blooded animals, rotenone controls flea beetles, cucumber and potato beetles, squash bugs, leafhoppers, and various caterpillars. Dust or spray carefully on a calm evening to avoid breathing it in or spreading it beyond the infested area. Potent but not long-lasting, rotenone should be purchased fresh at the start of a new season and applied, like pyrethrum, as a last resort.

WEEDS

"One year's seeding makes seven years weeding," runs an old saw. You can save yourself a lot of work by never allowing weeds to go to seed in and around the garden. Nip them in the bud; better yet, catch them long before. Weeds are either annual or perennial. Once you root out an annual, or sever its top, the deed is done. I prefer to rake up annuals and haul them to the compost, rather than leaving a mess of weeds strewn around the garden where they may shelter insects or take root again.

Perennials are another story. Although our kitchen garden grows on land that was once woven through with quack grass and bindweed, two of the most tenacious and "spreadaceous" perennials going, I can honestly say that weeds pose very little problem. As we broke new ground, we were careful to unearth all the roots we could find. Never add perennial weeds to a compost heap.

Bindweed is a pretty perennial morning glory intent on strangulation as it twines up its neighbors in a bid to see the sun. Its roots, like rubbery spaghetti, go down too deep to dig out entirely. Like most perennials, bindweed feeds its roots through its leaves. Whenever we turn over a bed, we yank out as much root as possible. Later, during cultivation, we slice off the top growth. Over the years, bindweed has scaled down its ambitious takeover plans — and has even given up altogether in some places.

Smothering weeds with mulch is a good plan, especially in pathways where a thick layer of newspaper or overlapped cardboard under hay, leaves, or straw will keep even the most determined interloper in the dark. A closely planted vegetable bed leaves little room for weeds.

Weeding conscientiously at least once a week in the early part of the season will make your work easier later when it's hot. And it's best to turf out small weeds before they have a chance to steal food, water, and light from garden plants. A small sharp hoe is useful for close work in intensive beds; a pronged weeder snaps off taprooted weeds, such as dandelion and burdock, underground.

WATER
Doing More with Less

Larkwhistle Garden is watered entirely by hand. Throughout the garden there are a number of strategically placed concrete pools — two in the kitchen garden — all linked by underground pipes to a holding tank under the farm's original old hand-pump (that is solar-powered during the summer). Water from the slightly elevated wellhead flows by gravity into the pools where it sits, warming in the sun. To water, we dip cans and buckets into the pools and go from there. I get a great kick out of paddling around barefoot, plunging the pails into the water, splashing around, getting soaked with the garden. When children visit, watering is their favorite activity.

Because we water by hand, we've found ways to do more with less. Whether you use cans, hose, or sprinkler, the following conservation techniques are appropriate to any garden.

• Start with the soil: add an abundance of spongy organic matter every season; humus (paradoxically) soaks up and holds moisture while opening the soil for improved drainage.
• Plant garden beds so that the leaves of maturing plants touch to create a cooling and water-conserving "living mulch."
• Sculpt the earth to hold water where you want it. With your hand, make a shallow "soup bowl" around individual tomato, lettuce, and broccoli plants. Form a water-holding trough between double rows of peas, carrots, onions, and spinach. Rake a raised rim of soil around the perimeter of a bed to prevent runoff. Such earth sculpting helps funnel water to roots.

• Localize water on beds and around individual plants and apply it to the soil rather than to foliage, if possible.

• Water deeply about once a week — think soak, drench, saturate. The soil should be moist down about one foot (30 cm). If in doubt, check with a long trowel or small spade. Water seedlings and small plants more often if you can.

• Water early in the morning to send plants into the heat of the day with a reviving drink. Alternatively, water in the late afternoon until dusk; cold water will be moderated somewhat as it filters through sun-warmed soil. Remember to water early enough so that foliage dries by nightfall; damp leaves are a breeding ground for mildew and fungus. Working in a wet garden may also spread diseases.

• Once the soil has warmed up somewhat in June, wait for a real soaker, then lay an organic mulch around the thirstiest plants to conserve moisture.

• Pay attention to signs of wilting leaves in the morning or evening — time to water. A certain amount of wilting is natural under a hot mid-day sun. Avoid watering at mid-day because it tricks plants into opening their "pores" then when you turn off the tap, the tomatoes may actually lose more water through their leaves than they take up through their roots. Also, much of the water applied at mid-day evaporates.

• Sink large, perforated, topless tin cans or plastic jugs into the ground next to tomatoes, peppers, and such; filled with water, the container will gradually leak moisture to roots.

• Pay particular attention to watering when fruits such as cucumbers and tomatoes are swelling, when broccoli heads are expanding, when ears of corn are growing plump — that is when the parts you want for food are moving toward maturity.

• Use a round of hand watering as a good excuse to feed plants a drink of liquid fertilizer in the form of fish or seaweed emulsion or a garden tea made from manure or compost.

• Cultivate often.

At any season, garden fabric protects susceptible plants from flying insects. Permeable to sunlight and rain, the cloth floats lightly over vegetables and irises as they grow.

The Cultivated Garden

Cultivation is the practice of scratching and stirring a shallow surface layer of soil — and it is one of the best things you can do for the garden. The tool for the job is a pronged cultivator — a "scratcher" we call it — with either a long or a short handle. On clay ground, a loose top layer prevents baking, cracking, and crusting over. In a sandy garden, surface cultivation creates a "dust mulch," a crumbly dryish layer that blocks the upward evaporation of moisture from below by breaking the continuous soil "wick." After every rainfall, we try to get around to cultivating all the unmulched kitchen-garden beds. After watering, we fluff up the soil around plants. Stirring the soil conserves water and lets the earth breathe — and a freshly cultivated bed looks so lovely. Weeding and cultivating go hand in hand. I have a lovely little combination hoe/cultivator, a gift from an older gardener. The blade slices weeds; the four-pronged flip side loosens the soil. Think of cultivation as giving the earth a good back-scratch.

6

SOW COOL

Peas, Spinach, Onions, and Leeks

"They're hoeing the snow up there," was the story that circulated among our neighbors (and finally returned to us) our first spring in the country. Eager to dig in, we did indeed chase the last remnants of snow with hoe and rake — and we've done the same thing many an April since. Larkwhistle's light sandy soil is by nature "early" soil; that is, it warms and dries sooner than heavier ground, which is just as well since we are by nature impatient gardeners, especially in April. Sand also drains better than clay soil, so that melting snow leaves it moist but not sodden. Most years, the very day after snow recedes, we are able to open shallow furrows in the cool earth for onion sets, peas, and spinach seed. In April we're grateful for early soil that brings snow peas and scallions for the wok by late June, lettuce and radishes for the salad bowl by the end of May, a time when many gardeners are just getting around to sowing their first seeds outdoors.

NEW TRADITIONS

"Sow as soon as the ground is workable," say the instructions on the back of a packet of spinach seeds. "Better safe than sorry: The 24th of May is

Trained to climb up chicken-wire fencing, pea vines occupy much less space and are easier to pick than unsupported plants. Across the hay-mulched path, lettuces and leeks share a bed bordered by self-sown calendulas and sweet alyssum.

the time to put in the garden," says traditional wisdom. Trust the seed packet.

A May harvest depends on an April planting. "But it's still so cold," I hear you protest. And yet, look around: all kinds of wild plants and weeds are putting on a burst of growth in April. Certain vegetables, too, some of them related to the dandelions and lamb's quarters sprouting in lawn and garden, are built to survive frost, thaw out, and keep growing. Not only do the hardy ones endure cool weather, most actually need it for best growth.

PEAS

Snap, Shelling, and Sugar

Cool weather crops include one of the best-tasting vegetables — fresh green peas. My first mouthful of peas right from the pod came as a sweet surprise. The peas I knew to date, straight from the tin, were more gray then green, more starch than sugar — a miserable fate for such a good vegetable.

Many vegetables can be grown from nursery transplants, but not peas: the first step is to look for seeds. There are three kinds of peas — shelling peas, snow peas, and snap peas — and for each a range of heights. Shelling peas — the kind you remove from the pods — take up the most space for what you get, but are probably the most delicious. Flat, edible-podded snow peas — the French *mangetout* — are very productive of flat pods for stir-frys and crudités, but lack sweetness and tend to toughen as the peas fill out.

A few years ago snap peas — the now famous "Sugar Snap" started it all — made a splash in seed catalogs. Here, after years of work, was a brand-new vegetable combining the fiberless pods of snow peas with plump sweet seeds inside. A great treat right off the vine, "Sugar Snaps" are as close to candy as you can grow. Those vines, however, stretch to an unwieldy 6 feet (1.8 m) or more, a drawback for many gardeners. At 2 feet (60 cm), "Sugar Ann" snap peas have lost not only stature but also a measure of sweetness.

Peas Ease

Virtually free of pests and diseases, peas are one of the easiest of vegetables to grow, provided their few needs are met. These are: early planting, cool moist soil, and support for the taller types.

All three kinds of peas are among the earliest seed we plant, with the first batch usually going in at the beginning of April, a day or two after the snow has faded. Early planting brings the vines to fruitful maturity by July, so that most of their growth takes place in the cooler days of May and June. Hot dry weather is a pea plant's idea of stress, and stressed plants, like stressed people, are more susceptible to sickness. To extend the harvest of shelling peas, we sow a second time, three weeks to a month later.

Peas do well in a range of soils, with a preference for rich sandy loam. Fertilizers high in phosphorus and potash — phosphate rock and kelp meal are two choices — help produce sturdy vines full of fruit. Too much nitrogen, in contrast, pushes foliage at the expense of pods. Well-aged manure and/or compost are always helpful.

Think Ahead

To get a jump on spring, it's wise to prepare the earth in the pea patch the fall before, spreading the required fertilizers and digging them in. If your soil stays cold and damp for weeks in April, consider raking the space into a raised flat-topped mound in October; a rise of even a few inches means better drainage and faster

warming. Where the soil tends to be hot and dry, sculpt a shallow, rain-catching trough for pea seeds instead.

A band about 16 inches (40 cm) wide will accommodate a double row of peas down the center with space for cultivating or mulching on either side. A wider raised area, however, makes room for other vegetables and cuts down on unproductive paths. In our garden, peas typically grow along the north side of a 4-foot-wide (120-cm-wide) intensive bed; for company they may have lettuce, onions, carrots, and spinach in front, an arrangement that gives way to a second planting of endive, Chinese cabbage, and late lettuce in midsummer. I can't say that the peas are the easiest to pick in this wide-bed setup — it would be much handier with a path on both sides — but the inconvenience is balanced by the full use of space. And it makes a rather lovely planting, too, with red and green lettuces snugged up to the pea vines and a feathery edge of carrot tops.

Peas are gregarious; there is no point planting a skimpy single row when you can get double the pods in a little extra space. To plant, hoe open two side-by-side furrows, about 3 inches (8 cm) deep and a hand-span (7 to 9 inches; 18 to 23 cm) apart. Drop seeds in one by one, leaving an inch or so between them. Use a rake to knock in the sides of the furrows, covering seeds with about 1½ inches (4 cm) of earth; thump the back of the rake along the row to firm. If you want to get fancy and conserve water later on, sculpt the earth over the rows to leave a ridge on each side; then, if vines are laden with pods in a hot dry July you can flood the little trench and water will be funneled to thirsty roots.

I have to confess that the first pea seeds we plant are usually pink, coated with fungicide that sterilizes soil around each seed so they will not rot in the cool ground. I know that this is heresy coming from an organic gardener, but pink peas are our one concession to chemical help toward an earlier harvest.

Pea Props

All but the shortest pea vines need some support; left to topple they take up more than their share of space, and pods are hard to find in the leafy tangle. Ideally the time to put in props is just before the rows are seeded. We seldom do, but always wish we had when, wincing at possible root damage later on, we are hammering in posts between young plants already entwined.

Pea tendrils will curl around anything fine. For the hip-high "Green Arrow" vines we use a 25-foot (7.5-m) length of wide-mesh chicken wire nailed to slim cedar posts spaced 5 feet (1.5 m) apart. Usable year after year, the fence is unrolled, stretched tight, and sledged into place each spring — this is a job for four hands. Fencing means we can grow a neat double row along the back of an intensive bed without smothering shorter things in front; if left unsupported, the vines would easily take up the whole space, and the path to boot.

If available, twiggy branches pushed into the ground between a double row provide a network of support and make for easy picking. Once, when a neighbor thinned out a stand of birch trees, we hauled home bundles of 6-foot-long (1.8-m-long) tree tops for a double row of "Sugar Snaps"; laced together with binder twine, the branches looked first like a leafless hedge and then like trees full of peas. Other options are various arrangements of lumber and twine or special nylon pea netting.

Usually spring rains keep peas watered, but if a dry spell hits as vines are flowering and fruiting, be sure to soak the patch deeply twice a week, if possible flooding the soil — here's where that trough comes in — rather than wetting the leaves. A ground-covering mulch of grass clippings, straw, or last fall's leaves, snugged up to the base of the vines, goes a long way toward keeping the earth moist and cool, conditions very much to their liking.

Harvest Time

Quick to pick, snow peas are ready when they are still flat and tender, before they grow puffy, curled, and fibrous; once flowers appear, pods are close at hand. Pick "Sugar Snaps" (or equivalent) when they are plump, bright green, and tender; if you pierce the pod with a thumbnail, just under

"Sugar Snap" peas climbing up strings or netting quickly transform a teepee of poles into an edible hideaway for children.

the little green cap, you can pull out and down to pick the pod while removing both the cap and string all in one step — a real kitchen time-saver.

It can be tricky to know when shelling peas are ready; pods may look full but be only inflated, the peas mere pebbles inside. If squeezing doesn't tell you, unzip a few pods to see. If you are tempted to leave pods on the vine a few extra days, remember that all peas change quickly from sweet and tender to bland and grainy. For best flavor, pick peas just before you intend to cook them — if you cook them, that is.

In the Kitchen

Shelling and snap peas are the favorite grazing food in the garden; a certain percentage never make it to the kitchen. Of those that do, some never reach the kettle; handfuls are munched raw while shelling, and even the cat pounces on rolling peas and eats them eagerly. Snow peas get the classic stir-fry treatment with garlic, ginger, and soy sauce. If "Sugar Snaps" are at their best raw, brief cooking makes shelling peas even more succulent.

Risi et Pisi is a perfectly simple Italian dish of rice and peas. Cook them separately, then gently stir together; season with a little sweet butter and salt, lots of grated Parmesan or Romano cheese and freshly ground pepper. A few sautéed mushrooms are a nice touch, but simpler may be better.

SPINACH

On that first spring planting day, a packet of spinach seeds always rattles around with the peas and onion sets in the garden basket. Here is a cold-hardy crop that must go into the ground early for decent results. The reason? Spinach thrives in cool weather during spring's shorter days, but responds directly to higher temperature and June's lengthening days by sending up a seed stalk— end of harvest. The sooner it sprouts, the more time spinach has to grow leaves before the bolt. Certain varieties are listed as "longstanding" and "slow bolting," but nothing will postpone the inevitable except an early start.

Gardeners like to say that there is no comparing the taste of store-bought with fresh-picked. Well, yes and no: I doubt that you could tell the difference between acorn squash from the market and from the garden; you may not know store-bought zucchini, peppers, or eggplant from those you grow, except that you know what's on them. But other vegetables, spinach among them, lose a fair bit of sparkle sitting in a truck and on the produce shelf for even a few days.

Seeding and Thinning

The lively crunch of a spinach salad just minutes from the earth is within easy reach of anyone with a bit of space in the sun — even a little shade will do. As a leafy crop, spinach responds with lush, dark green growth to an extra helping of nitrogen in the soil. To that end, we turn in a few inches of decayed cow manure or compost along the row; a dusting of blood meal also boosts the N rating, while a blended organic fertilizer covers the spectrum of nutrients. Lime or wood ashes may be needed in acidic ground to bring the pH up to around 6.5, a level that most vegetables prefer but spinach demands.

A maxim of intensive gardening says that the distance between plants in a row can also be roughly the distance between rows, as long as you leave room to cultivate. Since full-grown spinach plants should stand 5 or 6 inches (12 or 15 cm) apart along a row, we plant spinach seed in either double or triple rows, with a hand-span (7 to 9 inches) between each row. Drop the largish seed one by one, about 1 inch apart, into a shallow furrow, then cover with ½ to ¾ inch of fine-textured earth, before tamping gently with the back of a rake or by hand. If your soil tends to crust over, consider topping the seeds with sifted compost instead.

When seedlings grow to touch each other, it's time to thin. I know several otherwise sensible gardeners who balk at this step; and I can understand why: I'm still surprised that seeds sprout at all — hope I never get over the wonder — and when they do, I feel like an ingrate, somehow, tearing half of them out. But there's nothing gained by crowding plants.

The first thinning leaves small plants about 3 inches (8 cm) apart. Later, when they touch again, you can go over the rows once more, removing every other plant, a thinning that counts as a salad harvest and may last a few days. After that, harvesting means picking larger outside leaves, allowing the rest to fill out for the next time.

A tip: If spinach growth has stalled or slowed, a drink of dilute fish emulsion usually shows dramatic results in a spurt of growth and darker leaves. Spinach is a thirsty vegetable in any case, and if spring rains fail, plan to soak the patch every three or four days; avoid sprinkling in the evening for fear of encouraging fungus. To further ward off blights and blue mold, look for hybrids such as "Melody," "Indian Summer," and "Tyee" with built-in tolerance. We habitually plant the old-fashioned "Longstanding Bloomsdale."

Pests

Although disease is rare in our spinach rows, several bugs routinely show up. Most destructive are some species of cutworm — worldwide there are a frightening 20,000 variations on this grayish-brown caterpillar (the larvae of night-flying moths). The cutworm helps itself to a spinach salad during a night out of the ground. By day the coward hides, but the damage is done. Spraying spinach with *Bacillus thuringiensis* ensures that the cutworms eat their last meal, otherwise you will probably unearth the curled-up creatures as you cultivate alongside the rows. I have to tell you that they pop horribly when stepped on.

Flea beetles can riddle young spinach, but the tiny dark hopping insects are easily foiled by a covering of horticultural cloth, such as Reemay, draped over the rows. Even in the absence of beetles, spinach seems to thrive under Reemay, especially during the first three weeks or so of growth.

Once it grows seed stalks in late June, spinach is fit only for chicken feed or compost. Then garden space opens up for a midsummer planting for fall picking. You can reserve the row for another spinach seeding in August that should yield new greens as the maples turn. Other follow-up vegetables include endive, Chinese cabbage, daikon radish, late lettuce, fall turnips.

Pick of the Crop

Cooked (or, rather, overcooked) is how many people learned to hate spinach. Raw is how many learned to love it. Most of our pickings go directly into the salad bowl, by way of a grit-removing deluge and a quick turn in the salad spinner. Spinach Parmesan is another way to enjoy this vegetable.

LEEKS AND ONIONS

If leeks are the gentry among alliums, onions are the peasant cousins, hard-working, handy, and sometimes taken for granted. But so many dishes start with a skillet full of sautéed onions that I can't imagine cooking without them.

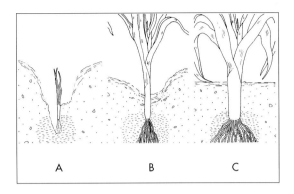

A) In spring, transplant leek seedlings into the bottom of a 3- or 4-inch (7.5- or 10-cm) deep trench. B) As leeks grow, gradually fill the trenches with soil. C) At harvest time, you'll dig long, beautifully blanched leeks with lots of the tender, mild white portion.

To "know your onions" is said to be a mark of wisdom, and it is a wise gardener, indeed, who can sort them out: red, white, and yellow; sets and multipliers; Spanish and Egyptian. I'm not keen on multiplier onions: from a fat spring-planted bulb you get a bunch of skinny green onions that are a nuisance to clean. The simplest way to grow onions is from sets. Plant an onion set in spring, harvest a full-grown bulb in September.

A set is a miniature bulb grown from crowded seeds the year before; you could grow sets yourself, but nobody does — wicker baskets at hardware stores filled with crackling sets are another sign of spring. A tip: If you are picking out sets by hand, go for the smallest of them; bigger ones may already have a flower stalk in embryonic form at their centers and you don't want your row of onions going to seed at the expense of bulbs.

Being quite cold-hardy, sets go into the ground first thing in spring with the peas and spinach. Before planting, turn an inch or two of fine-textured compost and/or a measured amount of a blended organic fertilizer into the soil; manure used at this stage should be old, dark, and crumbly. Lacking a complete fertilizer, bone meal or phosphate rock and a very light dusting of wood ashes and blood meal will help. See that the ingredients

Orange tulips in the background show just how early in spring spinach can be ready to eat.

are well mixed through the top 8 inches (20 cm) of soil before raking the space smooth.

We always plan to harvest both green onions (or scallions) and mature cooking bulbs from the same row. To do this, push onion sets, pointed side up, into the loose soil to the depth of your knuckle, spacing the individual sets about 2 inches (5 cm) apart. This distance is much too close for full-sized bulbs, but later, if you pull every other one as salad onions during May and June, the remaining bulbs will be properly spaced to fill out to maturity.

A second tip: The best part of a green onion is the white below the leaves; plant onion sets down deep — 3, even 4 inches of soil over their heads is not too much — and they will stretch to see the light, blanching all of the underground portion tender and mild. This is best done in a space reserved solely for green onions.

"What are you going to do with all those onions?" my brother once asked, looking around

at five 25-foot (7.5-m) rows. Lots: once they get going, we harvest onions almost every day, not only as spring scallions and mature bulbs for fall/winter use, but at any size all summer long. Onions start off stir-frys and ratatouilles, season coleslaw and tabouli, are sautéed with ginger, lemon thyme, lemon juice, and tamari for a sauce to pour over poached white fish.

Of Mulch, Maggots, and Mold

Although they will put up with a dry spell, onions need a fair bit of moisture to plump up. Plan on a soaking every seven to ten days, if rains fail. For a quick boost of nutrients, we water the rows once or twice a summer with fish emulsion or an equivalent. A mulch of grass clippings, last fall's leaves, or what-have-you, pulled right up to their little necks, keeps onions moist and discourages weedy competitors.

Some gardens are bothered by onion root maggots, the larvae of a fly that lays its eggs on the soil next to onions; mulch applied early is an effective barrier to the maggot's destructive tunneling. Infested roots should be pulled and destroyed to stop the cycle. In wet areas or in damp clay ground, mulch may encourage moldy onions; in this case, it is better to cultivate shallowly around bulbs to suppress weeds and leave a fine dryish surface. Use wood ashes or diatomaceous earth around unmulched onions if maggots are a threat.

Home Stretch

Some gardeners say you must bend onion foliage to the ground in late summer or bulbs will not mature. Others disagree. Foliage begins to ripen naturally, like any daffodil or lily, when the time is right. When most of the tops are half-toppled anyway, we ease them all over in one direction for the sake of a tidy row.

Once leaves have withered to yellow, pull the onions and, with the remnants of foliage covering the bulbs, let them cure in the garden for a summer day or two. In wet weather, bring them in under cover to some place warm, dry, and airy for a week and spread them out in a single layer. When the curing is complete, twist or cut off the shriveled tops and you have onions to store — we use mesh bags from store-bought onions — for months to come.

Leeks from Seed

The *Allium* genus brings lots of flavor to the kitchen garden in the form of onions and leeks. Onions of any color come from either seeds or sets, and leeks are grown only from seeds.

It's a mystery to me why leeks are so expensive, commonly a dollar apiece, when they are only marginally trickier to grow than ordinary cooking onions. Lack of demand may account for the price; but who is willing to pay that much? Perhaps it's the leek's association with stylish French cuisine; and yet this mildest of alliums is a staple of day-to-day home cooking in much of Europe. It is much cheaper to grow your own leeks: a patch of ground 10 feet (3 m) long by 1 foot (30 cm) wide will yield about 50 leeks from an 89-cent packet of seeds.

Leeks must be started from seed very early indoors. We sow leeks around March 1, or ten to twelve weeks before the average date of the last spring frost. The sooner you start them (within reason), the bigger the leeks you'll harvest. Bigger is not always better in the vegetable garden, but in the case of leeks, a big leek is every bit as good as a little one, only more so. Here are the steps from seed:

1. Fill an 8-inch-diameter (20-cm-diameter) bulb pot (shallower than a normal flower pot) or a 3-inch-deep (8-cm-deep) wooden flat with moist seed-starting mix.
2. Mark off shallow furrows across the flat in rows spaced 2 inches (5 cm) apart, or draw a spiral furrow around the flower pot with your finger.
3. Sow seed individually, ½ inch (1 cm) apart and cover with ¼ inch (5 mm) of soil.
4. Keep container warm until seed sprouts, usually within a week.
5. As soon as the small green backs show through, shift container to the sunniest window or a few inches below fluorescent lights.
6. Water seedlings as necessary, and feed once or twice with fish emulsion mixed half-strength.
7. If leeks grow too tall, trim tops back to 4 inches (10 cm) with scissors.
8. Shift containers to a cold frame (if you have one) when the daffodils are in bloom; being quite hardy, leeks can then live full-time in a frame, where they will need routine watering, ventilating, and bundling up with old blankets on really cold nights.

In the Trenches

So far the process for seed-grown leeks is the same as that for onions. At transplanting time, however, leeks need special treatment. Like scallions, the prized part of a leek is the white section below the leaves; planting in trenches ensures that a good chunk of leek will be blanched white and tender underground.

We transplant leeks into the open garden when the tulips start to flower (about mid-May here), keeping an ear to the long-range forecast to avoid exposing seedlings to the trauma of a cold snap — they'll survive frost, but it's a rude and unnecessary shock.

I find a hefty round-bladed hoe, the kind used for hilling up potatoes, ideal for opening a trench about 5 inches (12 cm) deep and wide; otherwise a small shovel or border spade (half normal size) will do. Stir a 1-inch (2.5-cm) dressing of compost and/or some organic fertilizer into the trench bottom, and you are ready to plant. Ease the young leeks out of the containers and lay them near at hand, with roots covered. With a trowel open a wedge-shaped slit in the bottom of the trench; holding the seedlings by their leaves, plant each leek so that at least half of it is buried when you fill in with soil. Space seedlings 4 inches (10 cm) apart. The row complete, water gently; you don't want a mud-slide in the trench.

As the leeks grow, gradually fill the trench with soil from the sides. If times are dry, we soak the row, watering with fish emulsion twice over a summer, before adding the next level of soil. Once trenches are topped up, a mulch helps suppress weeds and maintain moisture. Leeks are wonderfully free of pests and diseases; indeed,

Two steps in one: as we draw earth into the trenches to cover the tender white bases of leeks, we are also getting rid of weeds.

like onions, they may help keep bugs at bay.

A leek is ready to eat when it is as fat as your thumb, usually sometime in August, but with the summer garden full of food, we let them grow on into October. When you dig or pull a leek, half of its roots come up with a clinging ball of dirt. I like to clean leeks next to the compost heap; pull back two or three of the tough outer leaves right to the roots, and then slice off roots and leaves with a knife. Trim away most of the foliage and you are ready to swish the leeks in a sink full of water to dislodge grit in their crowns.

SPINACH PARMESAN

2 or 3 handfuls	spinach leaves	2 or 3 handfuls
2 tbsp	olive oil	25 mL
2	garlic cloves, minced	2
½ cup	grated Parmesan cheese	125 mL
½ cup	dry bread crumbs	125 mL
pinch	nutmeg	pinch
2 tsp	fresh tarragon, minced	10 mL
½ cup	milk or cream	125 mL

Carefully wash spinach and shake dry. Steam spinach gently until wilted and cooked through. Drain it in a colander, pressing out excess water. Coarsely chop the cooked spinach and return it to the pot. In a small skillet, sauté the garlic in olive oil for a few minutes over moderate heat. Do not brown garlic. Add the cheese, bread crumbs, nutmeg, and tarragon to the garlic before adding the mixture to the spinach and tossing gently. Pour the milk or cream into the seasoned spinach and reheat briefly over low heat. Serve immediately. Serves two.

Spinach Parmesan can be used as the filling for a crustless quiche:

2	eggs	2
dash	milk	dash
pinch	pepper	pinch

Lightly oil an 8-inch (20-cm) pie pan. Spread the spinach mixture evenly in the pan. Beat eggs with the milk and pepper. Pour the egg mixture over the spinach and bake at 350°F (180°C) until the egg has puffed and browned a little, and a knife inserted into the center comes out clean. Cut the pie into wedges and serve warm or at room temperature. Serves four.

LEEKS AND WHITE BEANS VINAIGRETTE

Make the dressing by whisking together:

½ cup	olive oil	125 mL
3 tbsp	lemon juice or vinegar of choice	50 mL
1 tbsp	prepared mustard	15 mL
handful	combination of fresh herbs: basil, chives, lovage, Greek oregano, tarragon, finely minced	handful
	salt and pepper to taste	

Prepare leeks and beans salad:

4	medium-size leeks	4
4 cups	water with 1 tsp (5 mL) salt	1 L
1 14 fl. oz. can	Italian white beans, drained and rinsed	1 398 mL can
few leaves	frilly red lettuce or radicchio	few leaves
	grated carrots for garnish	

Remove roots and green tops and wash leeks thoroughly. Cut leeks crosswise into 1-inch (2.5-cm) rounds. Bring salted water to a boil. Add the leeks and simmer 5-8 minutes over medium heat until just tender. Drain leeks well, reserving the liquid for soup stock. Plunge cooked leeks in cold water and drain thoroughly.

Toss the leeks gently with the vinaigrette. Gently fold in the beans and let the salad stand for an hour or more to meld flavors. Serve on frilly red lettuce or radicchio leaves with a garnish of grated carrots. Serves four to six.

7

LETTUCE ALONE

Trendy salad greens come and go, but while radicchio and roquette or arugula have their moments, lettuce remains. After tomatoes, lettuce is the most popular home-garden vegetable; of all the leafy things growing in our garden, it is the one we most often gather. Indeed, despite shifting fads, one corn-fed neighbor of ours steadfastly maintains a preference for what he calls (at every opportunity) "a honeymoon salad — lettuce alone."

Once, our garden grew a standard romaine, a green Boston, and an ordinary leaf lettuce. But gardeners — "insatiable seekers after outlandish things," as one old book calls us — are ever on the lookout for something different. Recently, seed catalogs have sprouted a raft of red lettuces, fancy French imports, one-serving miniatures, rediscovered heirlooms, and more. One catalog lists more than fifty cultivars, some described in such living color — "pale pink on cream in the blanched hearts and burgundy on exposed leaf surfaces" — you'd think they were flowers. All have sterling features to recommend them: heat or frost tolerance, exceptional taste or texture, sheer beauty.

Our solution to the dilemma of choice is to grow three or four tried-and-true types each year, and experiment with as many more unfamiliar lettuces. Since a fine new (to us) variety can move

It is amazing how much can be grown in a fairly small space. Peas, romaine lettuce, onions, and carrots share a 4-foot (120-cm) bed.

to the must-grow list in a season, the band of old faithfuls is a revolving lot — a summer in the garden, a hiatus, around again. To sort out the confusion of cultivars, it is helpful to group lettuces according to shape and habit of growth.

• LOOSELEAF: Plants are V-shaped with loosely opened centers. Shades of green or red, leaves may be smooth or curly. For early salads nothing is quicker than lime-green "Black-Seeded Simpson" or the darker "Salad Bowl," the kinds so often grown in crowded rows. "Oakleaf" is an older variety that has found a new audience for its light green, lobed foliage that fans out in flattish bunches. Last year we grew "Lollo Rossa," a frilly red lettuce better suited as a garnish or a leafy bowl for tabouli or potato salad. "Red Sails" is a big, easy, dramatically curled and colored lettuce with flaccid, slightly bitter leaves, more impressive in the garden than in the salad bowl.

Although these are all described as leaf lettuces, given space — 10 to 12 inches (25 to 30 cm) apart — they will surprise you by developing full hearts much tastier than the coarse outer leaves. For an extended harvest we pick outside leaves before they grow too big, leaving the centers to develop.

• BUTTERHEAD: Also known as bibb or Boston, soft-textured leaves fold over into squashy, flat-topped heads. We always include "Buttercrunch," a sweet, easy lettuce that deserves its popularity. For a marbled row we interplant with either "Red Boston" or a truly marvelous red

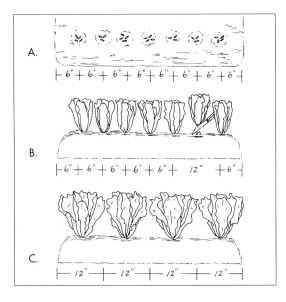

*Seeding lettuce with some precision makes the
inevitable thinning much simpler later on.
A) Make a shallow thumbprint indentation
every 6 inches (15 cm) along a row or across
a bed. Into each drop three or four seeds.
As seedlings develop, thin to the sturdiest
one in each place. B) When lettuces are
about half grown, begin to cut every other
one for early salads. C) Leave the rest to fill
out a foot (30 cm) apart.*

butterhead call "Merveille de Quatre Saisons," or
"Four Seasons." Lovely to look at, with reddish-
bronze outer leaves wrapped around pink and
butter-yellow hearts, "Four Seasons" is a treat to
munch. If we have salad loving company, I like to
serve each person a small butterhead, the separated leaves arranged on the plate as they grew; a
drizzle of vinaigrette laced with fresh herbs makes
a simple, perfect salad. Other notable butterheads
are "Esmeralda" and "Kagran Summer."

• CRISPHEAD or, simply, head lettuce: Mainstay of supermarkets, iceberg or head lettuce gets
a lot of bad press from garden writers — "bland,"
"watery," "hard to grow . . . needs muckland." I
happen to like it, but for years we were dissuaded from trying it, until we read about "Ithaca
M.I.," a head lettuce said to be "excellent for

transplanting on sandy land." And so it proved.
"Ithaca" now finds a perennial place in our garden; some of the fun of harvesting head lettuce
comes from proving the naysayers wrong.

• ROMAINE or COS: Familiar in Caesar salad,
crisp sturdy romaine grows into upright cylindrical heads. In the past we grew the standard
"Valmaine Cos," a big, dark green lettuce that is
quite good if cut early, before heat prompts the
start of a seedy core. Recently we've added "Little
Gem," a small lettuce also called "Sugar Cos."
Ideal for intensive beds, the diminutive heads can
stand 8 inches (20 cm) apart in all directions.
Here is a crop that almost lives up to the catalog's
pitch: "the best tasting and most troublefree lettuce you can grow."

• INTERMEDIATES: Sometimes called French
Crisp or Batavia, these lettuces (many of them
European imports) combine the qualities of head
and leaf lettuce or romaine and Boston. After a
one-season trial, "Canasta" jumped from experimental to old-favorite status. Its waved and glossy
outer leaves are shaded from apple green to pur-
ple-red at the edges, while the hearts have creamy
leaves; the texture is crisp but tender. For color
contrast we plant a mixed row of "Canasta" and
"Victoria," an all-green counterpart. Tight, conical
heads grow from seed of "Green Ice," one of the
crunchiest lettuces I know.

A good seed catalog tells you which varieties
must have cool weather, and which thrive or flag
under the summer sun. By making an informed
selection, and sowing at intervals throughout the
season, it is possible to keep a supply of lettuce
coming from May to October.

HEAD START

Lettuces of all kinds mature best under cooler
conditions of air and soil. With that in mind, we
get a jump on summer by seeding lettuce indoors
in late March or early April. After that we try to
get around to additional sowings, either in pots or
directly in the ground, at three-week intervals.

We start with 2-inch (5 cm) pots filled with
dampened seedling mix, then sow 3 or 4 seeds,

¼ inch (5 mm) deep, in each pot. Given warmth and moisture, seeds sprout practically overnight. After a week or two in a sunny window, seedlings are thinned to the strongest pair per pot, before being shifted into a cold frame. The frame cover is adequate to deflect frost, but there is always the possibility of stressing the small-fry in an over-heated box. We pay particular attention to watering and ventilating on hot days. A shading cover of lathing or snow-fencing (in place of glass) keeps seedlings comfortably cool.

The first seedlings are ready for the open garden by mid-May, several weeks before the last expected frost. At transplanting time we dig a helping of sifted compost or old manure into the lettuce patch, if we haven't done so the fall before, and sometimes even if we have. If such organics are in short supply, it would be better to concentrate them where needed: a few trowelfuls stirred into the soil for each seedling will create an adequate zone of fertility. Seedlings are planted at the same level they were growing, or slightly deeper to steady spindly stems.

If you want fat, full lettuces, give them room to stretch — set the small transplants a foot apart. But given a generous organic diet and steady moisture, they soon fill the gaps.

A tip: If you have a lot of extra seedlings, transplant them a measured 6 inches (15 cm) apart at first. Then, as they grow, harvest every other one for early salads, leaving the rest to fill out at the right spacing.

With transplants in, we sculpt a saucer shape around each plant before pouring in fish emulsion mixed to half the usual strength; this settles the soil and provides a fast flush of plant foods. The saucers remain to funnel rain water to the roots; failing rain, we aim the watering can into them at least once a week. Since lettuces thrive on readily available nitrogen, they receive a full-strength dose of fish emulsion twice during their stay in the garden.

Not all vegetables benefit equally from mulch, but lettuce appreciates it. A thin layer of straw, old hay, or grass clippings keeps the earth cool and moist. Lacking these, make sure that the soil surface is cultivated shallowly — or you will injure surface roots — to form what is called a dust mulch, a layer of dryish pulverized earth that keeps moisture from wicking up and away from beneath. This is especially important on clay soils that tend to harden and crack.

While the earliest salads grow from transplants, lettuce seed sown directly in the ground provides a follow-up harvest. Again, don't wait until the traditional "putting-in-the-garden" date — sow the seeds as soon as the ground is workable. Hardy lettuce seed will simply sit in the ground, waiting for the first warm nudge.

I like to be precise about spacing lettuce seeds; a bit of measuring now saves a lot of finicky thinning later on. Once the ground is fertilized, raked, and smooth, lay a measuring tape along the row, then with fingers or a trowel handle make small shallow imprints at 6-inch (15-cm) intervals. Into each little dip drop 3 to 5 seeds, close together but not on top of each other. Cover seeds lightly, pat to firm, water, and wait. Sprouts soon appear in nicely spaced clusters that are thinned to the strongest seedling in each spot. As the young lettuces stretch and touch, harvest every other one for salads, leaving the rest to fill out a foot apart. This method need not be limited to single row planting; double rows or wider beds can be seeded on a 6-inch grid as well.

COLORFUL HARVEST

Waved, puckered, or frilly; lime-green, emerald, bronze, or burgundy; lettuce is as decorative as any garden vegetable. If only the plants remained low and leafy all summer, they would be perfect for landscaping — an edible border for flowerbeds. However, eventually they bolt to seed, leaving you with a patch of shabby stalks. It is possible to enjoy their leafy aesthetics for a month or so. Every spring we plant a row of alternating reds and greens, "Simpson" and "Red Sails" or red and green butterheads. What a feast for the eyes and a colorful feature for the garden!

Lettuce ought to be picked in its prime, in the cool of the morning. A quick wash-and-dry, then cold storage in a closed container keeps it garden-fresh until mealtime.

8

CULTIVATED COLES
Growing Cabbages and Kin

"I give up," a neighbor said, waving a dismissive hand toward her vegetable garden. "If it isn't one thing, it's another with those wretched plants — just look at them." The plants in question were a shabby assortment of young cabbages, broccoli, and Brussels sprouts. Anemic, stunted, and bug-ridden, her band of brassicas did, indeed, look wretched. They also looked familiar, facsimiles of those that once grew at Larkwhistle. We could sympathize with her frustration: there is no doubt that the cole family can tax any gardener's skill and patience.

What do we mean by "brassicas" and "coles"? Botanically speaking, a number of food plants belong to the genus Brassica. Chinese cabbage is Brassica chinensis. Kale, kohlrabi, Brussels sprouts, cauliflower, broccoli, and cabbage are all variations on one brassica species, probably the wild sea kale native to Britain. When brassicas go underground, they become turnips and rutabagas.

"Coleworts" is an old English moniker for the whole group. The word survives today in cole-eflower, broc-cole-i, cole-rabi, kale (also known as borecole) and, of course, that ubiquitous fast-food sidekick, coleslaw.

What makes cole crops so tricky to grow? In a word, and at every stage: bugs. First, cutworms prey on seedlings, either mowing them down or eating the tender centers — hearts of cole prove

Curly kale is one of the most decorative edibles from June to November. Its leaves are packed with nutrition.

irresistible to cutworms. Next come root maggots, larvae of a fly that lays eggs at soil level around brassicas; once hatched, larvae tunnel into roots with withering results.

If coles survive these pests, they face an onslaught of hungry green caterpillars that hatch from the eggs of white cabbage butterflies. Slugs and earwigs also enter the picture. Add the various diseases that affect cabbages and kin, and you have a recipe for frustration. It is easy to grow an uninspired cabbage patch, but, if our experience holds true, it is possible to do much better.

Why cultivate cabbages when they are so cheap and abundant at the market? Taste and see. Every gardener knows how good vine-ripened tomatoes and fresh peas and corn can be, but one of the vegetables we wait for most eagerly is cabbage; not just any cabbage but a succulent cultivar called "Salarite." The crinkle-leaved (semi-savoy) heads make a delicious coleslaw — as far from boiled cabbage as you can get. Maturing midsummer, "Salarite" keeps us in salads after the first wave of lettuce has turned bitter and seedy, and before September's endive, Chinese cabbage, and late lettuces are ready.

"Early Jersey Wakefield," an heirloom variety, is also exceptionally delicious. Some cabbages, though, can be long on fiber and short on flavor; "Stonehead," a "high-quality shipper," matures as hard as a rock and is just about as tasty.

Broccoli is the other stand-out in the brassica bed, and for good reasons: first, the plants are capable of yielding a nutritious green vegetable for many weeks, often from July into September if adequately fed and watered. "Emperor" is a popular broccoli that grows a succession of side shoots after the big central head is cut; the same is true for the early "Green Comet" and later "Cruiser." Crossed with an Oriental brassica, "Paragon" is notable not only for fine heads, but also for sweet and tender stems all the way down.

My first attempt to grow broccoli started with skinny nursery plants. After wrenching the tangled roots apart, I set the transplants (with high hopes) a few inches apart in the fresh-dug ground of a shady city yard. They soon broke into sprays of yellow flowers, while I wondered when and where the heads would appear. Little did I know that the broccolis had come and gone, flowers following barely visible buds — that was the anticipated harvest — all the feeble plants could muster in an effort to survive.

Live and learn. All cole crops respond to the same basic conditions. The steps here apply equally to cabbages, cauliflower, kale, and Brussels sprouts. Timing of seeding and transplanting depends on whether you want a summer or fall harvest (or both) of cabbages and broccoli. Hardy and slow-growing, kale and Brussels sprouts are seeded once, in late spring, for a harvest that extends into early winter.

COLE CROP CALENDAR

• Early cabbages and broccoli: For a summer harvest, seed indoors six to eight weeks before your average last expected spring frost; set young plants in the garden about two weeks before that date. Once accustomed to the outdoors, seedlings can withstand several degrees of frost, and it is not difficult to protect small plants if necessary.
• Late cabbages and broccoli: For fall picking, seed indoors (or in a cold frame) around your frost-free date and transplant four to six weeks later. We use the same varieties for both early and late, often with the addition of a fall red or savoy cabbage. For storage cabbage, choose suitable "winterkeeper" types.
• Cauliflower: Seed into small pots a week or so before the frost-free date, and transplant a month

later; older plants do not establish as well. Sensitive to sudden temperature changes, cauliflower does remarkably well for us under a floating row cover. A June seeding and July transplanting brings cauliflower to maturity during September's cooler days.
• Brussels sprouts: Seed and transplant this slow-poke cole as for late cabbage; harvest in fall. Keep fed, watered, and mulched for steady growth.
• Kale: Extremely frost-hardy, kale is seeded like late cabbage for a summer/fall harvest; flavor is better after frost. We've had good success with "Winterbor," "Blue Surf," and "Westlandse." Kale, the vegetable, is just as decorative (if less colorful) as the so-called flowering kale.
• Kohlrabi: Start indoors two or three weeks before the last spring frost; transplant a month later, spacing seedlings 4 inches (10 cm) apart. Like beets, kohlrabi may also be seeded directly in the ground from spring to midsummer for a continuous supply.

STEP-BY-STEP COLE CULTURE

For Starters

'Tis a brave gardener who tries to seed most coles directly in the open garden, where the young plants fall easy prey to flea beetles, drought, deluge, and neglect. Brassicas do much better when started indoors or in the shelter of a cold frame, and then transplanted to the garden at the month-old stage. If you are buying nursery plants, look for those growing in "cell-paks" so you will not have to pull their roots apart.

Coles can be started in flats, but for easier transplanting, seed into 2- or 3-inch pots (or equivalent) filled with a sterile soil mix. Some local gardeners sow cabbages and other coles in a cold frame a few weeks before the last spring frost. For details of growing seedlings in the house or cold frame refer to Chapter 4.

Thin seedlings in flats to at least 2 inches (5 cm) apart; in pots, thin to the strongest single one. If grown on a windowsill or under lights, seedlings need gradual exposure to outdoor conditions. Cool growing conditions produce stocky seedlings; our coles live in a cold frame from the second-leaf stage until they are ready for the garden. In the meantime, we prepare a bed for them.

Soil Food

Brassicas are the garden's gourmands; the earth can hardly be too rich for their taste. Even though we turn a generous dressing of manure or compost into the bed the fall before, we often prepare an enriched zone for each plant prior to transplanting. To do so, blend a batch of organic matter and natural fertilizers. Our recipe calls for equal parts of crumbly manure (store-bought is fine) and compost sifted to a fine texture. To each wheelbarrow of the mix, add a spadeful of bone meal or phosphate rock, half that amount of blood meal (or a spadeful of 50/50 blood and bone meal), a few handfuls of wood ashes if available, and perhaps the same amount of kelp meal. The mix can be stored for future transplanting or top-dressing. For mixing in a bucket, use a trowel rather than a spade for measuring fertilizers. If your soil is already well supplied with organic matter, stirring a measured amount of a balanced natural fertilizer into each transplanting hole may be all you need to do.

Fertile Zones

Once the bed is raked smooth and level, we measure and mark off the transplanting locations, then dig out a shovelful of earth from each spot. Put a heaping shovel of the manure/compost mix into each hole and stir thoroughly into the surrounding soil. Step into the hole to gently firm the ground and you are ready to transplant.

Another approach is to spread compost and manure over the bed, broadcast some natural fertilizer, and dig everything under. The "zone of fertility" method just described is especially recommended if organic matter is in short supply, or if you are transplanting in a new garden where the soil is not up to par.

Transplanting

Young brassicas are set in the ground deeper than they were growing, up to their two lowest leaves. Firm the soil carefully around roots to ensure good contact with the earth. Around each plant we sculpt a shallow water-catching depression, dinner-plate diameter, to funnel water to the roots. New transplants are watered thoroughly to settle the soil and wash out air pockets. If you are working with flat-grown seedlings, some root damage is inevitable and plants may wilt; a shade cap of newspaper or an inverted flower pot helps for a day or two.

Move Them Around

The surest prevention for brassica diseases is rotation, more easily accomplished if brassicas share a bed. The taller broccolis (or Brussels sprouts) go 18 inches (45 cm) behind the cabbages in a 3-foot-wide (90-cm-wide) intensive bed, both spaced 18 inches apart in their rows. No cole crops are planted here again for at least three years.

Pest Control

Now what about those bugs? Prevention is always better than cure. Lively organic soil gives plants the vigor to withstand some insect damage, but there are other measures that can make a difference between bug-ridden brassicas and a clean crop.

Cutworms can be foiled at planting time by surrounding each plant with tarpaper or cardboard stapled to form a cylindrical collar that extends an inch into the ground and several inches above; make sure there is no cutworm conveniently trapped inside. Lately we've been using 5-inch-diameter (12-cm-diameter) fiber pots with the bottoms cut out as an effective cutworm barrier; they last for many seasons and are then compostable, the inverted pots are "screwed" down into the soil, one over each brassica.

The next step, mulching, is critical. If your coles are thriving one day and wilting the next, their roots are probably riddled with small white maggots. Once you see such signs above ground, the damage below is irreversible. I have salvaged some maggoty coles by heaping compost or topsoil around their stems to induce new roots to sprout, but plants are never the same. A thick mulch — 4 or 5 inches (10 or 12 cm) is not too much — of hay, straw, grass, or leaves laid

Snap off lower leaves where they join the stalks to give Brussels sprouts room to expand.

around transplants, and snugged right up to their little necks, has proven to be an effective barrier. Then the root maggot fly cannot get through to the base of the brassicas to lay eggs.

Floating spun-fiber row covers improve chances for bug-free broccoli and cabbage. Laid loosely over the bed, the gauzy fabric excludes root maggot flies, cabbage butterflies, and flea beetles. Providing some degree of frost protection, the cloth also creates a gentle nurturing environment that young brassicas thrive in.

Most gardeners have brought a dish of broccoli to the table with the extra garnish of hidden green worms. Summer brings a wave of white butterflies to the garden in search of the only food — our beleaguered brassicas — that sustains their caterpillar stage, small worms as green as the leaves they eat. This camouflage makes them hard to spot, even though their droppings litter the chewed leaves. If worms are few, you can do a search-and-squash tour. Before they get out of hand, however, we bring out a sprayer full of *Bacillus thuringiensis* (BT), a

biodegradable bacterium that kills cabbage worms and other larvae of moths and butterflies.

BT keeps coles worm-free, but slugs and earwigs may crawl out from under the mulch to feed after dark. Insecticidal soap is the only organic control I know for earwigs, but the pincered pest must be hit directly with the spray. ("At least they die clean," quipped a visitor.) Several times a week in early summer we inspect the garden around midnight, flashlight and soap spray in hand. If small earwigs are cleaned up early in the season, they don't spawn another batch. On the same rounds, slugs are sprinkled with salt for a quick end.

Vigorous vegetables can usually withstand some insect grazing. Cole crops are watered deeply into that earth "soup bowl" once a week if rainfall is not enough. At least twice in their garden life, they are treated to a drink of fish emulsion; you can practically see a spurt of growth after such a feed. For full broccoli heads, pour on the nitrogen-rich fertilizer when you see small broccoli "buds" nestled in the broad, blue-green leaves.

Side-dressing is a further inducement to growth. Dust a palmful of blood meal around each brassica after they have been in the garden for a month or so. On top of that spread a ring of very old manure or compost from stem to leaf edges. Don't be stingy; lay it on thick. Your brassicas will show their approval by extending new roots into the organic stuff. Pull back the mulch to side-dress.

HARVEST

Cabbages

Cabbages are ready when they feel firm, but we start the harvest a week or two earlier before heads have filled out completely. Those first few are especially tender and mild. Even after cabbages have attained full size, they keep on packing leaves into their centers until finally, after a heavy rain, some may burst open from the outward pressure. Twisting the whole plant around once or twice, or slicing into the ground beside it with a spade, breaks enough roots to slow growth and prevent splitting.

Broccoli

Broccoli comes to the table when heads have expanded and the individual buds are still tightly closed. With its central stalk cut, all of the plant's juices go into smaller side spears. When the bite-sized shoots taper off, it's time to haul plants to the compost heap. Early broccoli can be conveniently followed by fall endive or lettuce; late broccoli is usually followed by snow.

Brussels Sprouts

As much as we enjoy Brussels sprouts in the fall, we do not grow this long-season cole every year since the bulky plants take up a lot of space for the yield. As the stalks lengthen, snap off leaves, starting at the bottom, to give sprouts room to develop. Soon after the first fall frost, pinch out plant tops to direct energies into the mini-cabbages. The best sprouts come from plants that are heavily fed and consistently watered all summer long; top-dressing and mulch help.

Cauliflower

To form proper pale curds, cauliflower must be "blanched" by tying the leaves together over developing heads. "Self-blanching" types grow broad upright leaves, shielding heads from sunlight. Last summer we had an excellent crop from plants growing under a floating fabric row cover from transplanting time to harvest day. On occasion we lifted the cover to check on their progress, as well as to mulch, water, and feed. No insects invaded the gradually rising tent.

Kale

Curled, leafy, and non-heading, kale is the most primitive cole grown today, likely a form that ancient Greek and Roman gardeners grew. It makes sense that a plant so close to its wild roots would be a rich mine of vitamins and minerals. Kale is the most nutritious vegetable you can grow and eat, containing ten times the vitamin A of an equal weight of lettuce, up to three times the vitamin C as the same amount of orange juice, more B vitamins than whole wheat bread, and more calcium than milk.

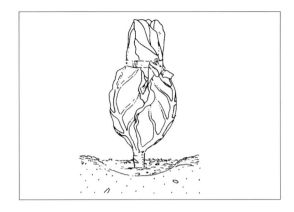

The broad outer leaves of cauliflower must be tied over the developing head to exclude light and blanch the curds.

Apparently insects couldn't care less about nutrition. Kale is usually untouched by the bugs that bother other brassicas. We like to feature kale's decorative (unchewed) foliage by planting it in a prominent corner of the garden with a group of red and green Swiss chard for company. Such an arrangement would work nicely in a flowerbed, sunny shrub border, or a large container.

Too coarse for salads, kale is a fine addition to robust fall soups after a touch of frost has sweetened the leaves. Snapping off the tough bottom leaves seems to encourage tender new growth.

Kohlrabi

Also rich in calcium and vitamin C, kohlrabi looks like a green or purple turnip growing above ground. Here is a vegetable that must be harvested small and tender, about tennis-ball size. Large bulbs are tough and tasteless. Raw young kohlrabi is as crisp and full of juice as an apple, a refreshing change on a plate of vegetables and dip.

Cole crops provide an abundance of flavor and nutrition over many months; we wouldn't know what to grow in their place. More difficult than lettuce or zucchini, they reward a gardener willing to prepare a fertile place and take timely steps to keep the bugs at bay. After a season or two, you catch on and frustration in the brassica bed becomes a thing of the past.

9

THE ROOT OF THE MATTER

Carrots, Parsnips, Beets, Radishes, and Potatoes

At potato-digging time, children love to play prospector, rooting around after spuds, sifting through the loose earth to find stray tubers. They love to yank at carrot tops and come up with a fistful of feathery greens dangling long orange roots. I know the feeling: the excitement of a treasure hunt, wondering what is hidden underground, the surprise when you bring to light a perfect golden beet, monster carrot, prize parsnip, or cache of potatoes. You can watch your tomatoes grow and color and see peas pass from flowers to pods, but roots remain a mystery until harvest.

Considering that the word "mundane" means "of this earth," root crops can be called the most mundane of vegetables. Everybody eats them; nobody gets too thrilled about them. But once you grow roots, you know that there is nothing dull about a popsicle-crisp carrot — pulled, rinsed, and eaten Bugs Bunny style. There is nothing boring about new potatoes, boiled, buttered, herbed, and served with the last of the green peas. Roasted parsnips or a subtle parsnip soup made from roots sweetened by a winter in the ground are very different from the same vegetable simply boiled and dished.

A dense living mulch of leafy carrot and parsnip tops shades the bed, leaving no room for weeds. A deep weekly drink may be all the care this intensive patch needs once it is established.

CARROTS AND PARSNIPS

Both carrots and parsnips are umbrella-makers, or members of the botanical family Umbelliferae, all of which send up umbels of tiny flowers arrayed at the ends of spoke-like stems. Dill's yellow-green parasols show its connection, and when parsley goes to seed you see the resemblance; caraway, lovage, fennel, anise, and sweet cicely are herbs that also belong. Wild umbelliferous plants include hemlock, cow parsnip, fool's parsley — you'd be a fool to eat this poisonous parsley — and the ubiquitous Queen Anne's lace, wild parent of garden carrots.

Root Rationale

Considering that carrots are abundant and cost so little, a new gardener might assume (as I once did) that they practically grow themselves. You soon learn that they don't, at least not during their fragile early stages. Why bother growing such a cheap, abundant vegetable? First, for the space they occupy, carrots return a lot of food. Shelling peas may yield for three weeks or so; the same garden space, however, can supply carrots for up to ten months, from the first picking in July until the last root, perhaps stored right in the ground, is pulled next April.

Then there is the carrot's versatility in everything from soup to cake. But what keeps us growing carrots is the aromatic sweetness and juicy

Even a fairly small bed will grow a surprising amount of food. Carrots, beets, and parsnips are natural bedfellows that are planted at the same time and thrive in loose, humusy soil.

crispness of home-grown roots — supermarket carrots seldom compare. As often happens, the gardener has access to varieties that may never make it to market. Over the seasons we have experimented with many carrot cultivars. Trials continue, but so far the standouts for flavor include: "Ingot" and "A-Plus," both with "super-sweet genes" and a boosted vitamin-A content; "Touchon Deluxe," "Rumba," and "Rondino" are a trio of Nantes carrots, a type identified by blunt rather than tapered roots. Consensus has it that the best-tasting carrots are found under the Nantes heading, but according to one expert, "Nantes are rarely found in supermarkets because their blunt shape is . . . less than 'classic carrot'. And their crisp texture makes them too brittle for mechanical harvesting."

Given proper care and feeding, long, straight carrots thrive in Larkwhistle's loose, sandy loam. Shorter varieties such as "Minicor" and "Short-and-Sweet," or the small round "Parmex" and "Planet," may be the ones for shallow or heavy clay soils, at least until you build up raised beds of fluffy organic soil.

No such variety choice exists among parsnips, a vegetable pretty much summed up by "Harris Model" and "Hollow Crown Improved." Only a parsnip connoisseur, if such a one exists, could tell the difference anyway.

Whatever varieties you choose, it is important that seeds of both carrots and parsnip be absolutely fresh. In common with other umbelliferous plants, seeds lose their spark quickly, especially if badly stored. There is no point preparing the earth carefully and then planting last year's seeds.

Root-friendly Earth

At Larkwhistle we are fine in the sand and no-stones department, not bad for weeds, but often short of moisture and plagued by earwigs. Here are the steps to prepare a bed for carrots and parsnips:

• Loosen earth down 9 inches (23 cm) or so. In some gardens this may mean shoveling out top-soil, breaking up the hard subsoil, and returning topsoil — a classic double-dig. If you can plunge a spading fork into the ground to its full length to stir the ground, that's deep enough. A raised bed, built as described in Chapter 3, provides a greater depth.

• Remove stones as you dig. If a burrowing tap root hits a rock, you get a forked carrot.

• Incorporate a helping of fine-textured, sifted (not rough or bulky) compost into the topsoil — a 2-inch (5-cm) layer is not too much. In a clay garden, a dressing of sharp sand (the kind used for concrete) or thoroughly decayed sawdust opens the soil for better root growth.

• Apply an organic fertilizer high in potash, such as wood ashes or kelp meal. Compost is usually all we use. Manure is fine if it is rotted down to the crumbly, dark-earth stage; anything approaching fresh invites rough, sappy roots.

Better Late

Books and seed packets urge you to plant carrot and parsnip seeds "as soon as the ground can be worked in spring," but don't. Their seeds and seedlings are sensitive to both cold and temperature swings. In our experience, earwigs mow down sprouts that get off to a slow start. Nothing is gained by sowing too early.

When the tulips are in bloom — mid-May here, or around the average frost-free date — it is time to sow parsnips and the first round of carrots. A second batch of carrots, seeded four to six weeks later, around the summer solstice, should fatten up nicely for fall meals and storage. If you want to get cosmic about it, hold off seeding until the moon is on the wane; the darkening lunar phase is said to favor root vegetables.

Weak Seed, Delicate Seedlings

Compared to the seeds of cucumbers, corn, or beans, carrot and parsnip seeds are frail and slow, hardly able to break through dry, crusty ground. Ideally, sowing will be followed by two weeks of warmth and showers, but why take a chance on weather when you can lend nature a helping hand? Once the soil is prepared, we draw out a series of shallow furrows, 8 to 10 inches (20 to 25 cm) apart, across the bed; we then sprinkle in seeds fairly thickly by hand. Here's the dilemma: sown thickly, both carrots and parsnips always need thinning, a job that is either painstaking or meditative, depending on outlook. Sown thinly, seeds may sprout unevenly, and earwigs may thin them further; you're faced with resowing, which is frustrating and time-consuming. We opt for thick sowing and meditative thinning. An old saw on the subject runs: "Sow thick, thin quick."

With seed sown, we cover the furrows with a scant ½ inch of sandy soil. In heavier ground, a covering of sifted compost or pure sand presents less of an obstacle to wispy seed leaves than a crust of clay.

Steps must be taken to keep a newly seeded bed moist until germination. If rain is sparse, we shower the rows every day or two. Lately we've been covering the patch with burlap sacks and watering through them; the bags hold moisture and prevent seeds from washing out. Some gardeners lay boards over seeded rows or cover them with spun-bonded garden fabric; even a scattering of straw will reduce evaporation but may shelter earwigs. Check covered seeds daily after a week or so, and lift the board or burlap at the first sign of green. The fabric can stay.

Earwigs

In our garden, the earwigs head directly for tiny carrots, parsnips, and beets. One day there is an unbroken green thread along the rows; the next morning there are gaps and bare patches, but no sign of bugs. Earwigs, like vampires, hide from the sun and come out to feed at night. Ignore the damage and the green line may vanish completely in a week.

Our environment-friendly solution is to use a spray of insecticidal soap, or 1 teaspoon of 99-percent-pure dishwashing soap mixed in a quart of water, which dispatches earwigs cleanly if they are hit directly. Simply spraying foliage may leave the insects foaming at the mouth, but alive and chewing. A midnight flashlit tour brings earwigs to light and a quick end. Running a hand over the feather-tops dislodges earwigs that are hard to see; as they scatter, you spray. Spiders stalk their own catch of earwigs for a midnight supper; I try to shoo these helpers away before spraying. A tip: Earwigs seem to prefer wilted carrot and beet leaves to fresh and growing ones. Little piles of thinnings left here and there will often be crawling with the beasties that night. A few squirts of soap spray gets the lot.

Thinning

"Never thinned a carr't in my life," a neighbor informed us — in these parts, "carrot" rhymes with "part" — as he watched us squinting into a tangled forest of seedlings, carefully plucking first one, then another. To thin or not to thin: in his rocky, clay garden, never-thin Ed grew fine carrots, odd sizes and some twined around each other, but bags enough to store in his cold cellar all winter and has plenty to give away. So much for fussy soil preparation and careful thinning. But Ed had space for long rows; what his parsnips and carrots lacked in uniform quality, they made up in quantity. However, at Larkwhistle, as in many home gardens, every root counts.

When carrot and parsnip tops reach 2 or 3 inches (5 or 8 cm) high, we get down on hands and knees and thin. Parsnips are thinned once to their final 2-inch (5-cm) spacing. The strongest seedlings stay, others between them are gingerly plucked. The goal is to leave young carrots close but not touching. The first carrot thinnings are fit only for earwig lures or compost, but about three weeks later we start to pick small roots for the table. Our goal is to leave the rest barely rubbing shoulders at maturity — about 2 inches (5 cm) apart. It's advisable to water a dry root bed before and after thinning.

Home Stretch

Thinning accomplished, we have only to see that our roots are kept weeded and nicely moist; a deep weekly watering is preferable to a daily light shower, especially once taproots have stretched deep in search of food and moisture. After every rain or watering, I run a pronged cultivator between the rows to loosen the top layer of soil; this crumbly "dust-mulch" impedes moisture from wicking up from below and evaporating. If carrots and parsnips are planted in close rows, their tops eventually form a dense canopy, a living mulch that shades the ground, inhibits weeds, and holds moisture. A top-dressing also helps; once thinned roots are tall enough, we often spread an inch of sifted compost between them.

There is no urgency about picking carrots. Peas and corn may rush past their prime, but carrots can stay in the ground for weeks — even months — beyond their official sixty or seventy "days to maturity." A deep orange color is the clearest sign of readiness and full flavor. Says one expert, "As long as the carrot is pale, its flavour will be pale and its nutritional value low . . . color is a strong indicator of vitamin A content. The deeper the orange the more beta carotene the root contains."

A May seeding gives you carrots to shred into coleslaw with early cabbages. Seed sown in early summer yields roots for hearty fall minestrones,

carrot soups, energizing juice, or simple steamed carrots seasoned with fresh tarragon, sesame seeds, and sautéed shallots.

Parsnips tend to be bland and boring in fall; by spring, after cold weather has changed their starch to sugar, they are a whole new vegetable. Parsnips can be stored in the ground all winter. Once the snow goes, the harvest lasts for a few weeks before new leaf growth saps the roots and spoils their texture. We also leave a few rows of carrots in the ground over winter. Protected from freezing by armloads of leaves or hay and, later, snow, the roots stay sweet and fresh until April. Digging carrots and parsnips from the cool, dark earth in spring, we pause to remember that the Earth is generous with her gifts — all we need for life — at all seasons.

BEETS

In winter, I find it curious that market shelves are laden with broccoli, cucumbers, tomatoes, and fancy lettuces — summer food — trucked in from afar, while locally grown roots often sit shriveled and overlooked in out-of-the-way corners. Among the ranks of unappreciated roots are rutabaga (big yellow "Swede" turnips), parsnips, "Purple-Top White Globe" turnips, and beets. I know several people who will eat any vegetable but beets. "Too earthy," says one. A fourteen-year-old friend is more blunt, "Beets, ugh — taste like dirt." A long-time beet grower tells me that some varieties tend to "take on the taste of soil, but not Early Flat Egyptian." I can't say I've ever noticed a "dirt" taste in garden grown beets.

The beet varieties we favor at Larkwhistle include:

• "Burbee's Golden Beets": Pleasantly mild, tawny orange roots. Marble-sized thinnings can be steamed, with their yellow-stemmed tops, for a vegetable dish that tastes more like spinach or chard. Small golden beets are lovely cooked whole, sliced and marinated; slivered for stir-frys, they taste almost like corn.

• "Chiogga": an Italian "heirloom" beet showing red-and-white "candy" striping when cut; the sweet roots are less prone to bleeding than all-red beets.

• "Formanova": The name means "new form," but engravings from the last century show that long cylindrical beets have been around for a while. Perfect for slicing, the fat carrot-shaped roots cook faster than the round ones. Growing best in the deep, loose soil that favors carrots, "Formanova" beets can stand closer together than round beets.

• "Albina Veredun": As round and white as a summer turnip, but the resemblance ends there. Wonderfully sweet, with none of the earthiness of some red roots, this beet does not bleed when cut or cooked. Highly recommended.

• "Winter Keeper" or "Long Season": A storage beet that keeps getting larger, without losing a trace of sweetness, until late fall. A mid-June (or later) planting keeps roots from growing monstrous. Because they take a long time to boil, we put "Winter Keeper" beets in the oven while other things are baking; over the next few days, slices are used in salads or warmed in butter with a few drops of cider vinegar as a side dressing.

In Europe beets — fresh, not canned — are sold already cooked, a treat for travelers who picnic. Beets are anything but a convenience food. "I never cook them," says a friend, "too messy, and they take so long." But the same woman told me that, when she was pregnant, she often ate a salad of grated raw beets and apples dressed with lemon juice and herbed salt, "for the iron." Beet root is a mine not only of iron but of calcium and phosphorus as well.

Wonderful fall and winter food, such a salad could be elaborated with grated carrot and Chinese radish (or daikon), endive, and Chinese cabbage, all discussed in Chapter 13. Add a handful of minced fresh parsley, tarragon, lovage, and chives for both flavor and nutrition. However you dress it — oil and lemon, seasoned yogurt or mayonnaise — the salad turns pink as you toss.

Big but still tender and sweet, "Winterkeeper" beets will store for several months in a cold, slightly damp place.

Best Beets

The same rich, deep, stone-free earth that suits carrots also grows the best beets. Adequate amounts of potash (from kelp meal or wood ashes applied with a light hand) and phosphorus (from bone meal or phosphate rock) go toward smooth, properly sized roots, while a whopping dose of nitrogen from blood meal or fresh manure rushes to beet tops and may leave roots stunted and oddly shaped.

Same soil, same schedule: we seed our first beets with the early carrots at tulip time, then sow the "Winter Keepers" a month later in mid-June. In all but the hottest regions beets can also be seeded in July, following early lettuce or peas, for a batch of young roots in fall.

Some seasons in April, about a month before we would normally sow outdoors, we start beets indoors in a fairly deep flat or in small pots; seedlings are thinned to an inch or so between them. Then, one misty May afternoon, about the time the lilacs are out, we transplant them into the garden.

The "sow thick, thin quick" rule applies to beets as to carrots, only more so. What you sow as beet "seed" is actually a fruit husk holding two or more true seeds. No matter how precisely you space the seeds, sprouts come up in clusters that must be thinned. In an intensive bed, sow beets in rows 8 to 12 inches (20 to 30 cm) apart, farther depending on how you will cultivate. Drop seed into furrows (½ to 1 inch deep), spacing them about an inch apart; cover and pat soil lightly. In heavy soil cover seeds with fluffy compost or lighter ground.

When seedlings start to crowd each other, we thin carefully to give each plant a few inches of space, room enough to develop small globes. Subsequent thinning, which may last for weeks, counts as a harvest as we gradually pull golfball beets, leaving the rest about 5 inches (12 cm) apart. Bulky "Winter Keepers" need 6 or 8 inches (15 or 20 cm) between them. Fast growth makes for tender sweet beets and, all else being equal, nothing slows a root crop like dry soil. In dry weather, a morning soaking twice a week or so is preferable to an evening shower, which may encourage fungus to infect damp foliage overnight.

With beets, and throughout our kitchen garden generally, the story of pests and diseases is soon told. As Stokes's seed catalog says, "Since pests and diseases are not major concerns, beets are relatively easy to grow." Just as seedlings emerge we keep a sharp eye out for earwig damage and pounce with the soap spray after dark. Various skin scabs, interior white zoning, and brown patches all point to a soil out of balance, a problem best remedied by consistent applications of compost, old manure, and organic fertilizers.

Cool Roots

Beets for storage are left in the ground until quite late in fall — early light frosts leave them unharmed. Cut or twist tops off before squirreling away roots in a very cold but not freezing place. We routinely bury a sack of various roots — beets, carrots, rutabagas, Chinese radishes, and the like — in a hay-lined pit covered with more hay and earth, where they are stored until March and beyond.

RADISHES

In the beginning we assumed that, if we could grow anything, we could grow radishes. Seed catalogs proclaimed them "very easy," and articles recommended them for a child's first garden.

Fifteen years later we are still surprised if we bring in a decent crop. Planted in cool April — "as early as the soil can be worked" is the usual advice — radishes poke along and mostly feed flea beetles, tiny black jumpers that leave foliage riddled with holes. Planted a month later, radishes may play unwilling host to root maggots — end of harvest. During dry, hot weather, summertime radishes turn pungent and pithy, and by fall we should be picking foot-long Oriental radishes seeded in midsummer.

What's a gardener to do? "Quick in, quick out" is the rule for radishes, which often serve as a spring "catch crop" in a space reserved for tomatoes or peppers. Since our peppers grow in a frame that usually sits empty until mid-May or later, we wondered if this could be the answer for radishes, too. Why waste that warm sheltered space for six weeks in spring?

Last April we sowed the ground in the frame with "French Breakfast" radishes. Before sowing, we turned in some fine compost; radishes need relatively small amounts of plant food accessible in the top 6 inches (15 cm) of soil. In the loose earth it was easy to draw ½-inch-deep (1-cm-deep) furrows, spaced 4 inches (10 cm) apart, with a finger. Seeds were dropped in an inch apart, covered, and watered. With its glass top in place, the frame captured and held the spring warmth, prompting sprouts in two days — a good start. The frame had to be watered by hand, almost every day. Adequate moisture means quick, mild roots. After sprouts had grown a few leaves, we thinned to 2 inches (5 cm) apart; crowded radishes may be all leaves and no roots. Untouched by flea beetles or frost, the pampered radishes were ready by mid-May, a colorful addition to the first salads of spinach, green onions, lettuce, and wild greens. Even the slightly bristly radish tops went into the salad bowl. The framed radishes had been our best crop yet — and about time.

An Array of Radishes

Although some types are naturally hotter than others, variety in radishes has more to do with shape and color than taste. The aptly named "White Icicle" grows salad-quality greens and mild tapered roots. Round and colorful, "Easter Egg" radishes pop up red, white, rose, and purple. Maturing in three weeks under ideal conditions, round, red "Cherry Belle" and "Champion" are the quickest of a quick crop. "Sparkler" is red and white and round; "French Breakfast," red and white, long, and tapered.

Pests

If grown in the open air, radishes may need some protection from beetles and maggots. Stirring a thin layer of wood ashes into the soil should ward off maggots; more ashes can be dusted around young radishes as a further deterrent. Also avoid planting radishes where broccoli and/or cabbages grew the previous season. Both are radish relatives bothered by the same bugs. A garlic spray may scare away flea beetles; rotenone and diatomaceous earth should kill them. No cure is as effective as physically shutting out the tiny shiny-black hoppers with glass or fabric.

If radishes do come along, you can soon get too many. Roots left for even a few days past their prime grow hot and corky. Better to sow another short row of radishes every ten days and eat them young, tender, and mild. If they are getting ahead of you, radishes keep better in the refrigerator — up to two weeks — than in the ground.

A sunburned potato turns green, bitter, and mildly toxic. To keep tubers in the dark underground, cover potato plants with earth or spread a layer of organic mulch—we usually do both.

POTATOES

I think of potatoes as two vegetables: big, mature tubers for fall and winter eating, and new potatoes, mouthwatering morsels for summer. Potatoes new and old can be had from the same plants at different times. A few weeks after our bushes have flowered we feel around in the loose soil and under the hay mulch, and steal a few meals of small spuds, leaving the rest to size up. In August, well before green tops have withered, we pull up several whole plants to get at the cache of odd-sized new potatoes underneath. Even if garden space were limited, we would still grow a few plants for the wonderful taste and texture of young tubers.

Family Ties

Considering that potatoes have been cultivated in their native South America since at least 2000

B.C., and that they are the one vegetable that everyone eats today, I find it surprising that they were not grown to any extent in England until the 1800s. In an 1833 gardening book, Englishman William Cobbett wrote of the potato that it "shouldn't be used as a substitute for bread . . . I never eat of it myself, finding so many things far preferable."

The potato's family ties may explain the long-standing reluctance to "eat of it." Tubers of *Solanum tuberosum*, wild mother of all potatoes, are both bitter and toxic, characteristics shared by the green leafy parts of tomatoes, eggplant, and peppers, all related to potatoes under the family name Solanaceae — the ominous-sounding Nightshade. I shy away from green peppers and green tomatoes, and never eat a green potato, whether from the store or the garden, unless it is peeled deeply. Left to green up from exposure to light, potatoes become harsh-tasting, indigestible, and mildly toxic.

Colorful Cultivars

Before we pick a growing method, we need to choose our tubers. Until I began to garden, I had no notion that potatoes were anything but tan outside, white inside — no-name spuds. Variety in potatoes had to do with how you fixed them and what you put on them, not with the tubers themselves. A trip to the local feed-store to pick up potato "seeds" for our first patch taught us that potatoes do have names — at least four were available — and they can be red-skinned as well as tan. And that was just the start.

Our tuberous adventures really began when a visitor brought a sack of potatoes shaped like pudgy toes: "German Fingerlings," he called them, "the favorite in the old country for potato salad." Since then we have saved a handful of tubers every fall to replant in spring; a few "Fingerling" plants usually pop up on their own — "volunteers" a neighbor calls them — from tubers missed during last year's harvest. Rarely growing bigger than thumb-sized, the waxy, yellow-fleshed potatoes hold together when tossed warm with a herbed yogurt or a mayonnaise dressing. While not a mainstay for winter use, this heirloom, often sold as "Banana" potato, is a summer treat. A good choice for a small kitchen garden, the compact, small-leaved plants can be spaced a mere 8 to 10 inches (20 to 25 cm) apart.

In their native Peru, potatoes crop up in surprising shades: red, tan, purple, rose, russet, yellow, and blue. A blue potato? Every year we try an exotic potato or two, but unusual color is not all we look for as we go through the list of cultivars. First priority is scab resistance, since in our sweet (alkaline) soil potatoes are very scab-prone, less so when we turn a quantity of pH-reducing leaves into the potato bed the fall before. Good flavor, too, is important. Early maturity is desirable in a short-season area, and any potato described as "drought tolerant" and "an excellent storer" is worth a trial.

Of the fifteen or more potato varieties we have grown, a handful stand out for good yield, good health, and good taste — what more could you ask for? Good looks, perhaps: "Pink Pearl" is elegantly oval and rose-colored, while "Urgenta," a European favorite for years, is a lovely combination of pink-orange skin and yellow flesh. From Newfoundland comes "Brigus," with bluish-purple skin over yellow interiors. Yellow inside and out, the trendy "Yukon Gold" deserves its popularity as one of the tastiest potatoes. "Rose Gold" describes itself, and "Caribe" is purple-skinned and white inside. A bevy of beautiful tubers, and not a tan-skin among them — no need for boredom in the 'tatie bed.

What, When, and How to Plant

To grow potatoes, you plant a potato. You could plant sprouting store-bought spuds — assuming that they do sprout, since most have been sprayed with a growth-inhibiting chemical — but it's not a good idea. Specially grown seed potatoes look exactly like eating potatoes, but there is a healthy difference: potatoes for planting have been inspected and certified to be free of virus and disease, a boon to all gardeners. Under ideal conditions a pound of planting stock may yield 14 pounds (6 kg) of food.

Traditionally, preparation for planting begins the day before, when whole seed potatoes are cut into chunky egg-sized pieces, each with at least one, but not more than three, sprouting "eyes." Cut pieces are left exposed to the air overnight to form a callus over the cut surfaces and are often dusted with a fungicide, rendering them less likely to rot in cool spring ground.

This is one tradition we abandoned years ago. Instead we plant whole potatoes, the size of an egg, and certified free of fungi and diseases. With no cut surfaces, the chances of rotting are virtually nil (unless the soil is cold and wet). Pick or rub off any eyes clustered together at the ends of a whole potato, leaving all the juice to flow to the remaining two or three sprouts. The consensus is that whole potatoes give rise to vigorous plants less prone to various potato ailments.

Recently we have experimented with potato "sets," melon-ball pieces scooped from whole potatoes. Sets have been carefully dried and callused. In early May, we hoe open three trenches, 4 inches (10 cm) deep and 18 inches (45 cm) apart, across a 5-foot-wide (1.5-m-wide) intensive bed; the two outside rows are a foot in from the bed's edges. Single sets or small whole potatoes, spaced 10 inches (25 cm) apart, are snugged into the loose soil, eyes up, in the bottom of the trench. We then back-fill with earth, leaving sets 3 inches (8 cm) under. As tops grow, we hoe earth up along each side of the rows. At this close spacing we cannot hill too high without dehilling the adjacent row. Nor do we need to, since soon after a soaking June rain, we'll lay a thick layer of hay over the entire potato patch. If enough rain falls thereafter, our work may be done for the season. If not, we try to soak the bed at least once every couple of weeks, especially as the plants are coming into flower and after.

While potato tubers themselves are fairly cold-tolerant, tops are withered by the lightest frost. The solution is to plant potatoes two or three weeks before the last expected spring frost. By the time leaves emerge, the danger is usually past. If an unseasonable frost is predicted, we cover foliage with old blankets, or simply heap earth over each plant, burying leaves completely; new growth shows through in a few days.

We have an old friend who loves to figure out how to grow things in a garden that is mostly limestone outcroppings, deep fissures, and boulders of all sizes. One summer, our friend picked and shoveled a deep and wide rectangular pit where, over the years, he dumped masses of maple, birch, and poplar leaves. Digging into the pit one spring, he came up with handfuls of leaf mold, so dark and fine he decided to bury some leftover seed potatoes in the stuff as an experiment. If they grew, fine; if not, no loss. Planting was all he did. Come fall, to his surprise, he retrieved a heavy crop of well-formed, thin-skinned tubers, so clean they needed only a quick rinse. Growing in leaves alone, the impromptu potato patch had been an unqualified success. No doubt the slight acidity of the leaf pile had kept his spuds scab-free; a pH hovering around 5.5 inhibits potato-scab organisms.

Newfoundland gardeners tell of laying their seed potatoes directly on flat rock and heaping seaweed over them. Other growers set chunks of potato on the soil surface and lay on a foot of hay or straw; green tops push through the mulch and tubers form underneath. Another approach involves piling leaves, sappy green stuff, unseedy weeds, manure, and the like to a depth of a foot or two over a garden bed in fall, in essence building a long, low compost heap that will rot and settle somewhat by spring. At potato planting time you nestle seed pieces into the deep mulch and, again, cover with 6 to 10 inches (15 to 25 cm) of straw, hay, or loose leaves. If any tubers show through, you cover them with more mulch. Reports say that potatoes so grown are less prone to bug damage and diseases — worth a try.

Bugged Spuds

Other than earwigs, which can turn young potato leaves into lace, our spuds have not been bothered much. Many gardens, however, attract the black-and-yellow striped Colorado potato beetle (alias potato bug). Handpicking the orange eggs, larvae, and adult beetles is the safest control, but time-consuming in a big, badly infested patch. Marigolds and garlic are said to repel, and a deep mulch impedes movement. Horseradish is another repellant, but we've had more than enough trouble trying to get rid of this invasive herb — no thanks. Potato bugs, apparently, will eat bran sprinkled on damp leaves, swell up, and explode. Toads eat potato bugs. Old-time gardeners used to boil up cedar boughs until the water turned to weak tea for a foliar spray. Finally, from the garden center come two organic dusts, rotenone and pyrethrum, which should prove effective, as a last resort.

Treasure Trove

Potatoes are ready to dig when their green tops have yellowed and withered. A spading fork is the tool of choice for the job. What fun to turn up a hill, uncovering a treasure trove of colorful tubers. Some spuds come up attached to the roots. Others hide in the soil and have to be ferreted out by hand; you could use the fork, but it's more fun to find potatoes with your fingers and you avoid shish-kebabing them on the tines.

To prepare them for storage, we spread potatoes out in a single layer in a dry, airy, shaded place for a day to set their skins; clods of soil are brushed off beforehand and tubers turned several times to cure evenly. Any small or damaged tubers are set aside for immediate use. Potatoes are stored in a cool, airy place in open boxes or paper (not plastic) bags. It is important that the storage locale be absolutely dark; otherwise all that careful hilling and mulching is quickly undone as the tubers turn green and bitter.

Usually considered a field crop, potatoes are often left out of smaller gardens. True, the plants are bulky, but they occupy less space than the home gardener's top crop, tomatoes. Like vine-ripened tomatoes, home-grown potatoes are one of the kitchen garden's most delicious gifts. When so much of the garden's output is green and leafy like lettuce, or succulent and juicy like cucumbers, there is something comforting about being able to provide what a Caribbean friend refers to as "food" — a starchy staple that you could almost live on exclusively if need be.

LEEK AND POTATO SOUP

This is a hearty, warming fall soup that makes a meal with an endive-and-carrot salad and crusty bread.

4	leeks (the white part and an inch of green)	4
1 tsp	curry powder	5 mL
2	bay leaves	2
pinch	cayenne pepper	pinch
pinch	fresh nutmeg	pinch
3	medium-size potatoes, peeled and cubed	3
4 cups	water or stock	1 L
1½ tsp	salt	7 mL
handful	celery or lovage leaves	handful
1 cup	milk or cream	250 mL
	salt and pepper to taste	

Thinly slice the leeks crosswise. (Be sure that all sand and grit has been rinsed from between the leaves.) Sauté leeks in butter or oil until soft, about 5 minutes. Add the curry powder, bay-leaves, cayenne pepper, and nutmeg to the leeks and stir. Add the cubed potatoes and stir to coat with seasonings. Add the water, salt, and celery or lovage leaves. Bring soup to boil, then immediately reduce heat and simmer gently until potatoes are quite soft. Use a potato masher to purée the potatoes right in the soup pot. Stir in the milk or cream. Add salt and freshly ground pepper. Serves four.

MARINATED BEETS

The quantities for this recipe are flexible according to servings required.

	medium-size beets
	olive oil
	vinegar (cider or other)
	fresh tarragon, basil, and parsley, minced
	Spanish onion, sliced
	salt and pepper to taste

Boil whole beets until tender, leaving the taproots and tops intact to prevent bleeding and flavor loss. Let beets cool, then peel and slice or cube. For the dressing, mix together 3 parts olive oil, 1 part vinegar, the herbs, Spanish onion, adding salt and pepper to taste. Toss beets in dressing. Chill dressed beets for several hours or overnight.

PASTA PRIMAVERA

A simple, sustaining dish of noodles and fresh vegetables. Ingredients are as variable as the garden's seasonal abundance; quantities depend on number of servings to be required.

garlic cloves, crushed and chopped
carrots, thinly sliced
turnips, julienned
leeks and/or parsnips, thinly sliced
broccoli, cut in small florets
cauliflower, cut in small florets
"Sugar Snap" or snow peas
Swiss chard or spinach leaves, torn
summer squash, cut in rounds
salt and pepper to taste
nutmeg, freshly grated
cream
fresh chervil, basil, and/or tarragon, minced
fettuccini noodles
grated Parmesan cheese

Using a wok or large skillet, sauté a few cloves of garlic, crushed and chopped, in olive oil for a few minutes. Add the melange of vegetables (except for Swiss chard or spinach leaves and summer squash) to the garlic and sauté until the broccoli is just fork-tender. Add greens and summer squash and sauté for a few minutes longer. Season with salt, pepper, and a dusting of freshly grated nutmeg. Pour in enough cream to coat the vegetables and toss thoroughly. At the last minute, sprinkle in a handful of minced fresh chervil, basil, and/or tarragon. Serve over fettuccine noodles, and pass the Parmesan cheese.

NEW POTATO SALAD WITH HERBED DRESSING

This is a salad that works especially well with firm, waxy "German Fingerling" (or "Banana") potatoes. Quantities have not been given because they are flexible, so the salad can be prepared for a picnic for two or a family get-together of twenty.

potatoes
red onions or scallions, chopped
celery, chopped
red peppers, chopped

Boil potatoes in salted water until cooked through but not mushy. Drain well and set aside to cool. When cool, combine potatoes in a big mixing bowl with chopped red onions (or scallions), celery, and red peppers.

For the dressing:

plain yogurt
mayonnaise
A combination of fresh herbs (in quantity): parsley, chervil, tarragon, and/or basil; in lesser amounts: lovage, chives, and/or spearmint
garlic cloves, pressed
salt
pepper
dry mustard
vinegar
sugar to taste
frilly red lettuce or radicchio leaves

Whisk together equal parts of plain yogurt and mayonnaise. Finely chop the herbs. Add the herbs and pressed garlic to the dressing. Season with salt, pepper, and perhaps a little mustard, vinegar, and sugar to taste. Pour the dressing over the potatoes and mix gently but well. Let the salad stand for an hour or so. Serve on a bed of frilly red lettuce or radicchio leaves.

10

TROPICAL FRUITS
Tomatoes, Peppers, and Eggplant

"After you taste them ripe from the garden," commented a visitor, "you're just not interested in out-of-season tomatoes from the store — there's no comparison." Anyone who has ever harvested his or her own tomatoes probably seconds the sentiment. Tomatoes are the most popular home-grown food.

When tomatoes are ripening, we eat them every day in many ways. There is no better start to a summer meal than sliced tomatoes dressed with olive oil, rings of Spanish onion or slabs of mozzarella cheese, and minced fresh basil. Simple and refreshing, such a salad reminds us of why we do the work of seeding, planting, weeding, and watering.

It is no coincidence that tomatoes, peppers, and eggplant are ready together. Botanically related, the three belong to the Solanaceae, or Nightshade, family. Included in the group are such familiar annual flowers as petunias, nicotiana, salpiglossis, and datura, as well as noxious weeds like nightshade, jimson, and tobacco; potatoes are an underground Solanaceae.

Wild tomatoes survive year round on lush mountain slopes in equatorial Peru, where temperatures seldom dip below 50°F (10°C). In Mexico, peppers stretch into perennial shrubs the size of lilacs, and the eggplant's ancestors still grow

From two mini greenhouses made of cast-off storm windows come plump purple eggplant ripe for grilling, baking, or ratatouille and sweet red peppers ready for roasting.

wild in torrid India. The three need similar growing conditions. Given their tropical origins, they respond to plentiful heat and sun, and all are understandably touchy on the subject of frost.

You can't expect to sow a row of pepper, tomato, or eggplant seeds and hope for a harvest. These tropical fruits call for (and are certainly worth) some extra effort. Like many gardeners, we have devised ways of making the southerners at home in a north-country garden: fancy frost protectors, custom-made soil, special supports. The reward is plump, ripe fruit that graces the table with tropical colors — red, yellow, orange, purple — wonderful flavor and more nutrition than any pill can pack.

All of these how-to-grow details apply equally to tomatoes, peppers, and eggplant. Here are the steps:

• Choose early varieties if your season is short and/or cool, and look for built-in resistance to disease.
• Six to nine weeks before your average last spring frost date, start seeds indoors in 4- or 6-inch (10- or 15-cm) pots, sowing four or five seeds in each.
• Germinate in a warm environment and set container in the sunniest window as soon as seeds sprout.
• Thin small plants as they grow to the strongest single one per pot.
• Water as necessary to keep soil moist but not soggy, allowing soil to dry somewhat between

A dense living mulch of leafy carrot and parsnip tops shades the bed, leaving no room for weeds. A deep weekly drink may be all the care this intensive patch needs once it is established.

waterings to foster strong roots.

• If starting extra early, shift seedlings to 6- or 8-inch (15- or 20-cm) containers (or equivalent) about halfway through their windowsill life.

• Accustom plants gradually to unfiltered sun and drying winds by exposing them to outdoor conditions for a longer time each day over a week before transplanting.

• When frosts are past, set transplants in full sun, in earth naturally enriched with compost, old manure, and organic fertilizers high in phosphorus such as bone meal and rock phosphate.

• Foil cutworms with a protective tarpaper or cardboard collar around stems.

• Protect from flea beetles with a rotenone-based

dust or a translucent covering of cloth or plastic.

• Water deeply once a week, soaking the soil not the plant.

• Avoid working around plants when foliage is wet to prevent the spread of fungus.

• Mulch after the soil is thoroughly warm to retain moisture and suppress weeds.

No amount of careful culture, we've discovered, compensates for a lack of heat, the factor that makes the difference between a meager harvest of immature fruit and a bumper crop ripe on the bushes. Unripe fruit has a disagreeable harshness. Given time and warmth all peppers will turn red, yellow, orange, or purple, losing sharpness as they sweeten deliciously. They also grow more nutritious: reds have nearly twice the vitamin-C content of greens.

TOMATOES

Last spring my friend and I were away from the garden in early April, the time we normally start tomato plants indoors. During the winter we had sent tomato seeds to a friend, with a request that she start them for us at the appropriate time, which she did — a month before our usual schedule. We were expecting to pick up nice little seedlings in late April. Instead, Sandy presented us with hefty 10-inchers, six weeks old, almost on the verge of flowering. "What'll we do with them," John lamented on the way home, "we can't put them in the garden for a month or more — they'll be huge!"

Since the seedlings were outgrowing their 3-inch (8-cm) pots, we repotted them in deep 8-inch (20-cm) containers filled with sandy garden soil, sifted compost, and bone meal. Plants were shifted daily with the sun from a southeast to a southwest window and watered as necessary. We were careful to let the surface soil dry between drinks. The plants were fed once with half-strength fish emulsion, as if they needed the extra push.

During the third week of May we set two long cold frames over garden beds, after turning a hefty 4 inches (10 cm) of compost and a dusting of natural fertilizer into the soil. Every 2 feet (60 cm) within the frame we dug a hole deep enough to take the flowering tomato plants up to their bottom leaves. Two reasons for the deep planting: first, tomatoes will root out from the buried stem; and second, we had to get our big babies down low enough so that their tops would not be crushed by the frames' storm-window covering. Before planting we stirred a cupful of bone meal into each hole; afterwards we watered thoroughly to settle soil and wash out air pockets.

By early June, when frost-danger was over, leaves were pushing at the glass for headroom. Off came the windows and away went the plants. June visitors wondered at the thigh-high bushes already sporting sizable fruit — and so did we. Thanks to Sandy we had learned a lesson about starting tomatoes extra early indoors and giving them plenty of root room. Next year we will move our seeding date back to mid-March, about eight or nine weeks before we expect to transplant, and shift seedlings into 8-inch pots before they are too far along.

When to transplant tomatoes is a gardener's perennial dilemma, as spring moves two steps forward and one potentially fatal step back. Like all seedlings, tomatoes need to be hardened to the elements for a week before transplanting. Even so, they do not tolerate a hint of frost, and it's a shame to lose plants overnight when a slight covering would see them through. There are many ways to deflect the "silver sting." We use flower pots ample enough to cover without crushing; light bedsheets or other cloths draped over seedlings; or paper grocery bags anchored with soil or stones.

Choose and Pick

A fruitful summer starts in winter when we select tomato varieties. Everyone hankers after the first ripe tomatoes, and earliness is a further virtue where frost often wraps things up in September. Remember, too, that bigger is not always tastier — some of the bite-sized cherry tomatoes are packed with flavor — and taste is sometimes sacrificed for earliness.

Our list of standbys includes:

- "Early Cascade VFN": These tennis-ball tomatoes in heavy clusters are usually the first to color. The flavorful tomatoes are firm when picked but mellow after a few days in the house. This year we'll leave fruit on the vine past what growers call the "firm ripe stage."
- "Early Girl": Ripening first and continuing into fall, this older hybrid lacks the built-in disease resistance that is crucial in some areas. Here it remains healthy.
- "Ultra Girl VFN": This plant is resistant to several tomato afflictions later in the season. Round, firm fruit weigh in at 7 to 9 ounces (250 g).
- "Sweet Million" and "Sweet 100": These sugary cherry tomatoes grow in profuse clusters, like grapes, on vines that, according to one gardener, can reach the roof of a two-story house — we've managed 6 feet (1.8 m), which is tall enough, thank you. "Sweet Million" trades a touch of sweetness for disease resistance.
- "Park's Whopper VFNT": Even a northern gardener longs for big meaty tomatoes oozing juice and flavor. With an early start, this disease-resistant hybrid brings in Beefsteak-style fruit about seventy days after transplanting.
- "Lemon Boy": These are big and bright yellow and less acidic than most reds.

Since we are growing in a short-season area, the list is limited to tomatoes that will ripen here. What works for us may bomb elsewhere, and you may have wonderful luck with some of the delicious late-season tomatoes that stay green and boring here. Part of the fun of food gardening comes from trying something new. Experimentation eventually leads to tomatoes that suit a gardener's needs, space, soil, and climate.

Degrees of Health

Under certain conditions tomatoes are notoriously prone to various wilts and blights. The initials after a tomato's name refer to a specific disease or pest that the plant is genetically able to resist. Give us a V for vanquished verticillium wilt; an F for forgotten fusarium; an N for no nematodes. Pile on the letters as thickly as the compost we heap on the beds, and the tomatoes are likely to be a picture of health and vigor. If possible, we choose cultivars with the horticultural equivalent of a degree in health.

Disease problems can be further minimized by:

- planting in lively organic soil fed with a balanced diet of compost, manure, mulch, and natural fertilizers;
- situating plants in an open sunny spot;
- pruning to open vines to breezes that dry up fungus spores;
- rooting out wild nightshade vines from around the garden;
- ensuring uninterrupted growth with adequate water and a few drinks of liquid fertilizer;
- soaking the soil, not the plants, and forgoing the hose in the evening for fear of fungus;
- not planting tomatoes in ground used for potatoes, eggplant, and/or peppers the year before;
- adopting a no-smoking policy in the tomato patch because tobacco is a sister (not to say sinister) plant that may harbor tomato-afflicting viruses.

Octopus or Espalier

Whether starting from seed or buying nursery plants, pay attention to whether the variety is determinate or indeterminate because the two are grown quite differently. Determinate or bush tomatoes branch freely, but the length of each stem is fixed or "determinate." After it has produced a flower cluster, a branch ends. Determinate types are usually left to ramble at will without pruning or staking. The result is a low, sprawling octopus of a plant loaded with tomatoes that tend to ripen all at once. Inevitably, some are out of sight under foliage, or lying on the ground where they may rot in wet weather. A straw (or other dry) mulch cushions fruit above the damp earth. Because they need so little attention, determinates may be the tomato of choice if you have more space than time.

If indeterminate, or vining, tomatoes are left to find their own way, each branch and side shoot continues to grow until checked by frost or a gardener's pinch. More shrub than octopus, an unpruned indeterminate tomato can become a confused tangle. Classically, indeterminate tomatoes are trained to one, two, or three stems, each tied to its own stake, to form a one-season espalier.

Of Suckers and Stakes

At Larkwhistle we grow indeterminate tomatoes because they take up a lot less space than the sprawlers. They also take more tending than bushes, but we enjoy pottering in the tomato bed, pushing in the crooked tree branches for stakes, plucking suckers, tying the hairy stems with strips of old bedsheets, watching the fruit swell from week to week, then blush and finally turn red.

Aiming for a triple-branched plant, we leave the main stem to grow, plus the first two side branches. Any shoots that sprout from the place where leaves attach to the three chosen stems are pinched out before they get too long. You'd be surprised how quickly side shoots, or suckers, appear at the height of growth. If plants are not "suckered" once a week, a lot of useless greenery saps juice that could be plumping up fruit.

Tomato stakes must be tall and strong enough to support the weight of a fruit-laden branch. We use sturdy branches cut from dead trees in the woods across the way. Old broom or rake handles, snapped hockey sticks, and the like are fine, as are 6-foot (1.8-m) lengths of one-by-two, or stout bamboo canes. Position stakes close enough to plants so that branches can be easily tied, but not so close that you rip through roots in the process. With stakes along the north side of the row, the three-armed plants are open to the sunny south. Wire tomato cages have their followers but the plants seem so hard to work with when caged up like that. Soft cloth or old nylon stockings are better for securing branches than choking twine.

Earthing Up

Here's a trick picked up from my tomato-growing grandad: when plants are half-grown, heap fertile earth, fine compost, or extra-old manure thickly — 6 to 8 inches (15 to 20 cm) is not too much — around their base. You'll be surprised how quickly new roots sprout to take up nutrients.

Bugs, Cracks, and Cat-facing

Our tale of tomato bugs is thankfully soon told. One menace is the yellow-striped green hornworm, a creature so perfectly camouflaged you might not see it. I can't say I've ever seen one, nor the ragged foliage and droppings it leaves behind.

Hornworms can be handpicked, but I would be reluctant to step on them underfoot; the sphinx moth is a pleasure to watch and it must do its share of pollinating. How about a free trip down the road, along with the live-trapped raccoons?

If Colorado potato beetles threaten to reduce tomatoes to skeletons, and there are too many to handpick, a dusting or two of rotenone should halt their progress.

Tomato plants work hardest during July and August, months that are often plagued by drought. Vines may not show signs of dry-weather stress, but a dry spell followed by a heavy rain can spoil fruit with blossom-end rot, a dark, scabby patch that starts at the base or the blossom end and spreads. A deep weekly drink staves off the affliction, as does the removal of any affected fruit. Mulch laid down after the first fruits have formed maintains even moisture. The same steps may prevent fissures, or cat-facing, from appearing in the tops of tomatoes, a breeding place for fungus. Some varieties are listed as crack-resistant.

Tomato Juice

What is there to say about harvesting tomatoes: let them ripen thoroughly, let every drop of green chlorophyll transform to "a red carotenoid called lycopene" — believe me, it tastes much better than it sounds. Pick your tomatoes at their peak and let the juice run down your chin.

Protection from Frost

It's late September or October. Your tomatoes are laden with red and ripening fruit. Suddenly the wind shifts into the north and the temperature drops; by evening winds are calm but a new air mass, clear and chill, has rolled in from the Arctic. Frost tonight — tomorrow all of the fair-weather crops may be reduced to limp black flags mourning summer's unofficial but very real end, unless you take steps.

Here are the options:

• Pick all red tomatoes, any that are barely blushing, and everything in between; pick them all if you plan green-tomato anything. Left on counters and windowsills, half-ripe fruit will slowly turn; others can be wrapped in newspaper and stowed away in drawers or boxes, the greenest at the bottom, those approaching ripeness on top. Tomatoes have an uncanny ability to turn vaguely red and soft off the vine, which accounts for those bland pink billiard balls pawned off as tomatoes in winter. Those you ripen indoors can only be an improvement.

• Toss big blankets over the vines to deflect frost; some gardeners lay vines on the ground, the better to cover them. Chances are there will be some summery days or weeks after the first frost.

• Pull up your tomato vines, roots and all, and hang them upside-down in a warm shed or garage.

PEPPERS AND EGGPLANT

For years we gave peppers and eggplant the same treatment we gave the tomatoes. We'd start with early maturing peppers such as "Gypsy," "Stokes Early Hybrid," "Early Sweet Banana," and "Crimson Hot"; early eggplants "Dusky" and "Early Bird." Then we'd follow the steps.

June often flirts with both spring and summer here, a warm "growthy" spell, followed by cool days and downright chilly nights. While peas run up their chicken wire and lettuces grow plump, peppers and eggplant sit still, waiting for heat. If it doesn't arrive until July, they've lost a month. The result is a ho-hum harvest of green peppers and small eggplant hardly worth the work and garden space. The problem was how to coax these tropical fruits to succulent maturity within the deadlines of our season.

Framed Fruit

Enter the pepper and eggplant frames, homemade variations on a cold frame that make quite a difference. One chilly June day it was clear that our miserable peppers and eggplant would be

Easy to tend, this homemade glass enclosure creates a protective environment that brings peppers and eggplant to maturity in our cold garden.

better off in a frame, not a traditional sloped frame, but one tall enough so that they would not hit the roof before outgrowing their need for contained warmth. "What if we stood storm windows on their sides and built a special little greenhouse to hold peppers and eggplant all season," my friend mused. "After all, we grow only six of each." It was worth a try.

Rooting through a stack of old storm windows we found two matched pairs, one set longer than the other. It was a simple matter to nail the four windows together, the pairs opposite each other, to form a 2½-foot-high (75-cm-high) rectangular glass box with no top or bottom. We were careful to wield the hammer with a light hand for fear of shattering the glass. Wood screws would have

been better for the job than nails, but when the hardware store is 12 miles away and enthusiasm keen, you use what you have. With a fifth window sitting on top, the prototype pepper frame was set for a trial run in the garden.

The new frame did everything we hoped it would: by August it was filled with bushy plants loaded with ripening fruit. This simple construction adds six to eight weeks to our pepper and eggplant growing season.

The tropical fruit frames sit neatly and permanently at the end of two vegetable beds. Maintenance consists of removing the top window for winter storage. The frame itself stays in place. When the putty falls out, we secure the window with metal glazing points. Once in a while we scrape the peeling paint onto a drop sheet — lead paint and soil don't mix. The bare wood will eventually weather a neutral gray.

Each spring we turn some old cow manure, Larkwhistle's staple fertilizer, into the earth within the frame, along with a dusting of bone meal or rock phosphate, fertilizers high in phosphorus, to spur fruiting. A neighbor fed her framed peppers only blood meal (concentrated nitrogen), and had lush leafy plants barren of fruit. With the organic stuff dug in, soil is tamped down lightly and leveled.

Pepper and eggplant seedlings are transplanted into the frames during the third week in May. There they stay for the whole season. The frame is not a temporary shelter but a little pocket of tropicana in the north. Transplants are set about 16 inches (40 cm) apart and watered thoroughly.

With the top window on, the glass walls are soon misty with condensation, a sign that the enclosure is suitably steamy. Like any cold frame, these glass houses buffer chilly breezes, warm both soil and air, and create a tropical microclimate. The peppers and eggplants never miss a beat; stretching roots into the fertile soil, they grow apace whatever the weather outside. Inside temperatures may push 90°F (32°C). On hot days we slide the lid aside; there are lots of gaps in the glass box anyway.

Peppers and eggplant flowers are self-pollinating. Every little breeze shakes pollen from stamen to pistil within each flower. Sheltered frame plants may need a gardener's helping hand. Every few days when plants are in flower we reach in and give them a jostle.

By mid-July, as plants reach the top of the box, we take off the lid, leaving the frame in place for extra protection. A pail or two of sun-warmed water is poured into the frame twice a week; a compost mulch does weed-and-feed duty.

Growing steadily without setbacks, seldom bothered by bugs, framed peppers and eggplant tend to be healthy and fruitful. Through August and September peppers gradually ripen red or golden, a treat for stir-frys, salads, sauces, and antipastos. When the weather turns cool, we replace the window lid; no matter that leaves are squashed a bit at this stage. Fruit keeps maturing under these conditions long after the tender plants would have been blackened by frost in the open.

RED ONION, RED PEPPER, AND ROQUEFORT PIZZA

2	red onions (or leeks)	2
4	long red peppers	4
1 or 2	small hot peppers (optional)	1 or 2
⅓ cup	olive oil	75 mL
2 tsp	balsamic vinegar	10 mL
pinch	salt and freshly ground pepper	pinch
1 tbsp	fresh oregano, finely chopped	15 mL
2 leaves	fresh sage, finely chopped	2 leaves
1	prepared pizza crust	1
	crumbled Roquefort (or other blue cheese)	

Thinly slice onions and peppers. Sauté in olive oil until quite soft (about 7 minutes) but not brown. Add the vinegar, salt, pepper, and herbs, and cook for another minute. Spread the onion and pepper mixture over the prepared pizza crust and top with crumbled Roquefort cheese. Bake the pizza at 375°F (190°C) for 15 to 20 minutes. Serves four.

EGGPLANT TERRINE

1	eggplant	1
1 or more	garlic cloves, pressed or minced	1 or more
3	eggs	3
1½ cups	milk	375 mL
handful	a combination of fresh herbs (use up to five in quantity: basil, tarragon, fennel leaves, chervil, parsley, dillweed, lemon thyme; in smaller amounts: oregano, rosemary, marjoram, lovage, thyme, coriander, crushed cumin)	handful
1 cup	dry bread crumbs	250 mL
2 tbsp	grated Parmesan cheese	25 mL
	salt and pepper to taste	

Slice a medium-size eggplant into rounds, then dice the slabs. Using a light olive oil (or your preference) sauté the diced eggplant in batches until it is brown and soft. Eggplant soaks up oil like a sponge; if this sounds too greasy for you, toss the eggplant with just enough oil to coat and spread it thinly in a roasting pan; roast in a moderate oven until soft. Also sauté the garlic (or oven-roast it with the eggplant if you go that route).

Whip together the eggs, milk, and fresh herbs. Stir the egg mixture into the cooked eggplant and, stirring well, add the bread crumbs, grated Parmesan cheese, and salt and pepper to taste.

Spoon the mixture into an oiled terrine dish, spring mold, or loaf pan. Bake, uncovered, for 30 minutes at 350°F (180°C), then reduce heat to 300°F (150°C), and continue baking the terrine for another 30 to 40 minutes, or until a knife or toothpick poked in the center comes out clean.

Serve slices of the terrine warm or cool, sprinkled with one of the fresh herbs, with some bread and a green or tomato salad.

Note: A young fresh eggplant should not need the salting and draining that removes some of the strong flavor from a tough older fruit, and you can leave a garden-grown eggplant unpeeled. Serves six to eight.

11

THREE SISTERS OF LIFE
Corn, Squash, and Beans

The original inhabitants of "this Turtle Island," later renamed North America, knew themselves to be "one strand in the web of life." Out of such an understanding grows the wisdom of Native Chief Seattle: "Whatever we do to the web, we do to ourselves." Now, more than ever, we need to remember that we are vitally connected, for better or worse, to the Earth. This is not some vague romanticism, but a truth to keep in mind and heart as if our lives depended on it. They do.

For Native people, "all our relatives" encompasses not only family, but also "the perfumed flowers . . . the bear, the deer, the great eagle" — all aspects of creation. A special respect is due to the plants and animals that provide food — the direct, day-to-day links between human life and the Earth. "If your philosophy doesn't grow corn," an Elder once said to me, "I don't want to hear about it," which is to say that a view that neglects the lively bonds between the land and its people is not only incomplete but dangerous to the health and well-being of both.

For indigenous people, corn, squash, and beans are the Three Sisters of Life — foods you can live on — sustaining staples that grow out of the harmonious interaction between another triad — humans, humus, and Manitou, the Great Spirit. As often happens, science eventually catches up with traditional knowledge. Nutritionists tell us that

Snap beans, whether yellow, purple, or green, are prolific and easy to grow in average soil.

corn and beans complement each other to provide complete protein; the sweet yellow squash gives a wealth of vitamins A, B, and C; iron; calcium; phosphorus; and energizing sugars.

CORN

Once, in an outdoor market in Guatemala, I watched a Mayan woman gathering up some dried corn she had spilled. On hands and knees, she slowly picked the kernels from the cobblestoned square until she had retrieved every last one. Before coming south, I had worked in a Vancouver restaurant where I routinely scraped perfectly good food into the garbage can. What a contrast between that careless waste and this demonstration of a healthy appreciation for the stuff and staff of life. I trust that the lesson in true economics — meeting the needs of a household with thrift and care — sank in. As an old neighbor of ours says, "A willful waste makes a woeful want."

To Native people, corn is more than nutrition, it is a gift to be cherished and shared. Often called Sacred Mother, corn stands for fertility, renewal, and power — the "fire in the belly." When the new crop comes in, it is a time of celebration and thanksgiving.

Eating and gardening are perhaps the two activities that most clearly remind us that our physical life-line is tied to the Earth. More than food grows in a garden. Plant a corn seed, pick an armload of cobs for dinner, and in the moment's quiet your awareness of the source may deepen.

Coming originally from Central and South America, corn is a member of the Gramineae or grass family. As early as the eighth century, the Aztecs cultivated dry corn for grinding into nutritious cornmeal, a year-round staple. Specialty seed catalogs continue to list heirloom dry corn for gardeners interested in following in traditional footsteps. Most of us, however, grow sweet corn-on-the-cob, a gift of the gods if ever there was one. Corn lovers have their own harvest rituals: get the water boiling; pick the corn and rush it into the kitchen; three minutes in the pot, butter and salt it. For me, a "feed o' corn," as everyone around here says, always feels like a special occasion — rolling the cobs in the communal butter, eating with your fingers, the delicious mess of it all. No wonder outdoor corn roasts and boils — open-fire, seething kettle — mark summer celebrations, family picnics, and community get-togethers.

Corn Varieties

When the lilacs are in bloom, usually during the last week in May, we seed corn. With a view to harvesting cobs over a number of weeks, we sow two varieties, one early maturing and one late, both at the same time. Every spring we mull over which varieties to plant. With one catalog listing more than sixty cultivars, choosing can be confusing. The selection has become more complicated with the recent addition of "sugar enhanced" and "supersweet" types to the list of "normal" corn.

Let's sort through the distinctions. Traditional sweet corn — now called "sugary normal" to distinguish it from the newer kinds — begins to convert its sugar to starch quickly after harvest, or if cobs are left unpicked for a few days past their prime. These regular, "old-fashioned" corn varieties are identified by "(su)" after their names.

Working with corn genes, breeders have modified the sugar-to-starch trait, giving rise to corn that remains sweeter longer, either on or off the plant. Called "sugar enhanced" corn, such varieties are followed by "(se)" in seed catalogs. They may also be tagged "EH," denoting an extended harvest. Because enhanced corn holds

it good-eating quality for a longer time, there is no rush to pick the corn all at once, before it gets past its best, or to cook it within minutes.

Between normal and enhanced corn are "all sweets," or high sugar normal types "(su)," regular corn with a higher sugar content than normal, but with the same rapid loss of sweetness.

Then there are "supersweet" corn cultivars, bred to stay sweet for hours, even days, after harvest. The code "(sh2)" refers to the "shrunken" gene responsible for the slow change of sucrose to starch (with a fructose stage on the way), and to the shrunken appearance of the dry seed. Supersweet corn has a rather crisp texture, even when cooked, unlike the nice chewiness of both normal and enhanced corn. Because the seeds are very sensitive to soil temperature, supersweets should not be planted until the soil has warmed to at least 65°F (18°C), usually a week or two after the spring frost-free date. Another quirk: Supersweet corn must be kept well away from other types or the flavor and texture of all will suffer. Either separate supersweet corn from other types by 25 feet (7.5 m) or more, or, if space is limited, choose a supersweet type that matures at least ten days earlier or later than the rest.

A range of good sweet corn cultivars includes: "Earlivee II," an all-sweet version of a popular extra-early yellow; "Sugar Buns (se)," tender, sweet, and the next to ripen; "Tuxedo (se)," a midseason yellow gaining in popularity for its good taste and adaptability; "Double Treat (se)," tall, late bicolor to plant with "Earlivee" for a successive harvest; "Platinum Lady (se)" and "Silver Queen (su)" are delicious white corns, midseason and late, respectively.

Seeding and Planting

At one time, we assumed that corn took up too much room for a home garden. True, the plants are tall and bulky, but in fertile soil they can stand fairly close together, making corn as suitable for intensive beds as broccoli or tomatoes. What it takes is some precision at seeding time. At Larkwhistle, we plant corn, like most of our food crops, in a 4- to 6-foot wide (1.2- to 1.8-m-wide) bed. Once the soil is fertilized, dug, and raked smooth, we use a foot-long stick to mark out a grid of planting spots along and across the bed. A 4-foot-wide bed accommodates four rows, a foot apart, with outside rows 6 inches (15 cm) from either edge. Every foot along the rows we plant three seeds, in a close cluster, about an inch apart. Seeds are covered with 1½ inches (4 cm) of earth, roughly the distance between fingertip and knuckle. If the earth is soft, we simply push the seeds in with a finger. The adjacent row is the same, except that the groups of seeds are not directly opposite but staggered. Although this one-foot grid-planting saves space, I'll admit that corn grows rather better and is much easier to tend if you can spare 18 inches or 2 feet (45 or 60 cm) between the rows, while retaining the 1 foot in-row spacing.

You are advised never to plant a single, long row of corn, but rather three or more rows side by side. Corn is wind-pollinated; pollen grains shaken by breezes from the tassels atop the stalks rain down on the silks protruding from the immature ears. Planting in an intensive block ensures that most cobs will be filled to the tip with kernels, a sign of good pollination.

Whatever the starting distance, the next step, thinning, cannot be skipped. Once seedlings have grown 3 or 4 inches (8 or 10 cm) tall, we remove all but the strongest one from each spot. Pulling up a lusty young plant is not easy — the instinct is to leave everything that grows — but steel yourself. Three corn stalks growing on top of one another will not amount to much.

Raising Corn

Like other grasses, corn is a strong, self-sufficient plant that will make the best of a range of soils and sites. For tall stalks and fat cobs, three elements are needed: full sun, adequate water, and deep, rich organic soil. Nothing creates the last two conditions — moisture and fertility — as well as a thick layer of manure or compost turned into the corn patch in fall or early spring.

Several summers ago, in the middle of a hot, dry spell, our corn stopped growing and leaves began to curl. Like fields all around, our patch looked stunted and shriveled. Watering helped,

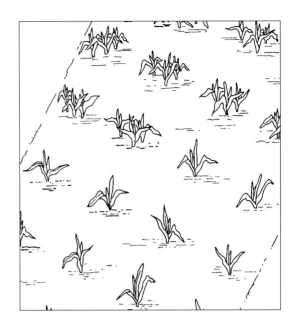

Where space is at a premium, corn can be intensively planted on a grid. Mark off rows 12 inches (30 cm) apart and sow a cluster of three seeds the same distance apart along the rows. When seedlings begin to crowd each other, thin to the strongest single corn plant in each spot.

but in a few days the ground was dusty again. Our instinct was to pile a thick mulch of half-decayed, strawy manure around the base of stalks. We then poured on buckets of water, which carried a quick shot of manure "tea" as it filtered through. What a dramatic difference! Almost overnight, leaves turned green and turgid again; growth resumed. Before long the corn was sinking new roots into the dark, damp manure. Visitors, having traveled through fields of suffering corn, wondered at the tall, thriving stalks, a result of the necessary care at the right time.

Whenever possible, we situate our corn where a load of manure has been dumped the year before. Last year we sowed seed in what appeared to be half-manure, half-soil. With natural ingredients, you'd be hard-pressed to overfeed corn. Fresh manure, of course, needs to mellow for a few months either in a heap or in the soil.

Insects, Diseases, and Corn Bandits

Most corn diseases are better prevented than cured. As always, plant disease-resistant types, clean up the corn patch in fall, and (if possible) move corn around the garden from one year to the next. If corn earworms pose a threat, a spray of *Bacillus thuringiensis* (BT) is the remedy, but it must be used before larvae have burrowed into ears. Corn borers are harder to control without chemicals. To paraphrase Joni Mitchell, give me borers in my corn, but leave me the birds and the bees. Cut away the bored parts and be glad for organic cobs.

One of the (many) strikes against chemical pesticides is that they kill insects indiscriminately, friend and foe alike. "Insect friends?" you ask. Any organic garden is home to a host of helpful insects — tachina flies and trichogramma wasps are two — that prey on an array of potential pests.

The wasps, for example, lay their eggs in the eggs of a corn earworm; little wasps hatch, earworms don't. The flowers of several umbelliferous plants — dill, parsley, Queen Anne's lace — provide the nectar that trichogramma wasps need if they are to stay in the garden. I've noticed that flowering lovage, a green giant among aromatic herbs, is always humming with a bevy of these nonstinging insects, welcome helpers in pest control. Nature teaches gardeners that diversity is one of the hallmarks of a healthy balance.

As the harvest approaches, gardeners are not the only ones sniffing around the corn patch for signs of ripeness. Wily raccoons pay an early visit, maul a cob or two, make a mental note, and return when the corn is prime. How many times have we anticipated a lovely feed the next day, only to find chaos in the corn patch: torn-down, ripped-up stalks and half-chewed cobs strewn around. A raccoon is one messy eater. Some gardeners swear by a chicken-wire fence, with the mesh fastened to its supports only halfway up; the raccoon climbs the wobbly wire, which then bends backward with the weight, landing the creature on its ear — end of raid. How about a radio, tuned to an all-night rock station, set under a bucket in the corn patch? I hear it works, but our garden is too close to bedroom windows for such a noisy scheme.

So far we've had reasonable luck live-trapping raccoons and taking them for a ride into the woods. Rather than waiting for signs of damage, we bait the trap with apple halves or melon rinds soon after we plant the corn. If we capture the local bandits early enough, there will be none around to steal the corn — we hope. As the cobs reach ripeness we may drop a chunk of fish skin into the trap, muttering all the while "Some nice, smelly old fish for you, Mr. Coon? Much tastier than corn, you know . . ."

The Harvest

Everyone agrees: harvest corn when it is at a peak of tender sweetness. We look for signs: silk that is light brown, dry but not altogether withered; ears that are rounded at the ends rather than pointed; firm but not hard. If this sounds too mysterious, you can pull back the husk a bit and puncture a kernel with a fingernail; if the sap is milky, as opposed to watery, pick the corn. Be warned, though: peeled corn may attract birds and raccoons.

SQUASH

With their boisterous growth, lush leaves, and abundant fruit, squash seems to stand for the exuberance of summer. The Native name for gourds, *ascutasquash*, has come into English as *squash*, a term that, like the plants themselves, covers a lot of ground from tiny courgettes to big, knobbly blue Hubbards, from curious crooknecks to giant pumpkins that tip the scales at 400 pounds plus.

Summer and Winter

For a gardener the most useful distinction is between summer and winter squash, and their variations. Summer squash includes green and yellow zucchini, round pattypan or scallop squash (also green or golden), several pale-green Lebanese and Italian types, vegetable marrows,

Started in individual 4-inch (10-cm) containers about a month before their transplanting date (a week after spring's last frost), squash, zucchini, cucumbers, and melons need all the indoor sunlight you can give them—at least seven hours a day.

and knobbly crookneck squash. The differences between them are mostly skin-deep; shape and color aside, all summer squash tend to be rather bland-tasting, a sponge for the herbs, garlic, onions, tomatoes, and chilies often cooked with them. Of those we've sampled unadorned, the old-fashioned yellow crookneck has the most taste and substance. All are picked while still immature, a few days after pollination. If a thumbnail pierces the skin easily, a summer squash is still fit for the table, but smaller is better.

Winter squash, in contrast, must stay on the vine as long as possible; as fruits mature, they develop their full flavor potential. In early October, the day before frost threatens, we search for the rock-hard fruit hidden in the leafy tangle. Only those with a firm, tough shell and a rather dull finish are worth taking; shiny, soft skin is the mark of insipid, half-grown fruit that will not

keep well. We use rose pruners to cut squash from the vines with an inch or so of stem intact.

There is something comforting about this end-of-summer ritual: piling the fruit carefully in a wheelbarrow, laying them out in a single layer in a patch of sun on the living-room floor. The same instinct that prompts chipmunks to bury acorns and bears to put on weight in fall is satisfied by the sight of squash spread out to cure indoors. Colorful Indian corn and a sheaf of dried grasses complete an autumn still-life, a wistful reminder of summer's glory as the sun heads south and cold grips the garden. By November, the squash have been squirreled away, perhaps under the bed if all the storage shelves are full. Once a mainstay in pioneer gardens, winter squash keeps for months in a cool (45° to 60°F; 7° to 15.5°C), dry locale. An hour in the oven melts the hard flesh, releasing the stored, sun-ripened sweetness.

Winter Varieties

Like related cucumbers and melons, squashes interbreed easily, a trait responsible for their many shapes, sizes, and colors. Gourds are nothing more than weird, wonderful, and inedible squashes. A varied selection of winter squashes includes:

• Acorn or Pepper squash: Usually dark green, the acorn-shaped, hard-skinned fruit may also be orange or white. All tend to be moist, fibrous, nutty, and only mildly sweet when baked.

• Sweet potato squash: "Delicata" and "Sweet Dumpling" are two that show the characteristic pale yellow skin striped with dark green; the first is cylindrical, the other is rounder. Ideal for one or two servings, these smaller, orange-fleshed fruits bake up sweet and moist.

• Butternut squash: Shaped like a fat cylinder with a bulbous base, butternuts have beige or light tan skin and orange flesh. Excellent for storage, they are moderately sweet and moist when cooked. "Waltham Butternut," a garden classic, yields four or five hefty fruits on a ranging vine, while the "semi-bush" vines of "Early Butternut Hybrid," an All America Winner, need only half the space. Because their vines are almost solid compared to the hollow stems of other squash, butternuts are less susceptible to the destructive squash vine borer.

• Buttercup squash: Characterized by smooth, blocky, dark green fruits striped with gray, buttercups are our favorite for their wonderfully sweet taste and dry texture — if you like sweet potatoes, you'll enjoy buttercup squash. We often grow the Burgess strain, long-keeping, 3- or 4-pound (1- or 2-kg) fruits with a gray-green button or turban at their base; vines ramble far and wide, scaling a split-rail fence, climbing into a pear tree — strange fruit hanging from the pear boughs — or ramping into the tall grass. "Sweet Mama," a turbanless buttercup, develops smaller, paler fruits on more restrained 4-foot (120-cm) vines. One of the sweetest, the well-named "Honey Delight," improves over the weeks in storage.

• Spaghetti squash: Nice idea, a vegetable spaghetti; you're supposed to bake or boil the whole fruit, scoop out the strands, and "top with your favorite sauce." The strands, however, lack both taste and texture — no match for real pasta at all. The vine takes up a lot of space in return for a few bland fruits.

• Naked-seeded squash: This novelty, in contrast, is a sterling snack food, tasty and nutritious. Resembling a small jack o' lantern, the fruit is filled with hull-less seeds. Kids might enjoy the messy job of separating the seeds from the slippery membranes. Spread the rinsed, lightly salted seeds in a single layer on a cookie sheet and toast in the oven until dry and crunchy — home-grown pepitas.

• Hubbard squash: Weighing in at 10 to 20 pounds (4.5 to 9 kg), Hubbards are blue-gray or golden, hard-shelled, knobbly squash for long storage. The oversized fruits are more impressive for fall fairs than practical for a small family.

• Oriental squash: From Japan come two intriguing squash, "Green Hokkaido" and "Red Kuri," described in seed catalogs as "excellent for soups and pies" and "dry . . . buttery and sweet" when baked. One vine yields two or three round to teardrop-shaped fruit, weighing in at 4 to 7 pounds (2 to 3 kg).

Of Hills and Compost Heaps

Given their prolific growth, squash makes good use of all the compost and manure you can spare. For summer squash, we concentrate the nutrients in a fertile zone or "hill." Here's how: Mark off a circle of ground 2 to 3 feet (60 to 90 cm) across. Dig out the top 6 or 8 inches (15 or 20 cm) of soil and pile it to one side. Into the shallow pit, dump a half-bushel (two or three pails) or more of compost or old manure and a handful of all-purpose natural fertilizer. Stir the organics into the soil, trying not to bring up subsoil, and top the hill with the reserved soil. Flatten the top of the mound with a rake or by hand, and sculpt the earth to form a rim or lip around a slightly concave circle.

Planted atop the compost pile in late May, squash vines crawl over and through the snow fence enclosure and climb over anything within reach.

Against a warm southwest wall, summer squash thrives under a mulch of strawy, aged manure. Every time it rains, the vines receive a shot of plant food.

Such a space will accommodate three summer-squash plants. Two such hills, spaced 4 feet (1.2 m) from center to center, should provide an overflow crop of zucchini, pattypans, and others.

Occasionally, we seed summer squash directly in the ground outdoors, a few days after spring's average frost-free date, when the soil feels warm to the touch. In that case, we poke eight or ten of the big seeds into the loose earth of the hill, covering with an inch of soil. Seeds are spaced a hand-span apart. As seedlings sprout and grow, we thin them to the sturdiest three per hill, preferably choosing plants that stand at least a foot apart. Eventually the three entwine and look like one robust bush.

Most seasons, however, we start both summer and winter squash indoors on precisely the same schedule and in the same way as described for melons and cucumbers (see Chapter 12); that is, seeding in early May, in 3- or 4-inch (8- or 10-cm) pots, transplanting no more than a month later or about a week after the last spring frost. An early start is especially important for winter squash in northerly areas where fruit might otherwise not mature before frost blasts the vines. If possible, with an ear to the long-range forecast, we time transplanting to coincide with the onset of a warm spell. A covering of translucent garden fabric keeps the young plants cozy for a few weeks; when the first fruiting blossoms appear, the veil should be lifted to admit the bees.

Like zucchini, winter squash can also be seeded outdoors in somewhat larger hills, two or three plants in each, the hills spaced at least 5 feet (1.5 m) apart. Remember that most squash vines range for yards in every direction. In recent years we have come up with a way to satisfy the plants' prodigious appetite while curbing their enthusiastic spread.

Noting that volunteer vines often grow with great vigor from the compost heap, we decided to locate the pile where we wanted the squash. The process begins the fall before, during cleanup in the food and flower gardens, as we gather wheelbarrow loads of compostable material — everything from seedy lettuces to frosted tomato plants, to armloads of stems from perennials we are cutting back at this time. Some seasons we build a long mound of compost directly over one of the wide vegetable beds. Alternatively, a big, squarish heap rises in an open grassy spot on the garden's perimeter; a base layer of cardboard (boxes opened out and flattened) discourages grass from creeping into the compost. Because the pile is destined to be growing space next year, we make the effort to chop bulky stalks and leaves into smaller pieces with a machete. The pile begins with a bulky, foot-high layer of garden residues. As we stomp and chop, the rough green stuff subsides to 6 inches (15 cm) or so of finer material. This layer is topped with several inches of the freshest manure we can get — fresh, because we want the pile to heat up quickly and cook as long as possible into the fall. Lacking manure, we might use topsoil or last year's compost sprinkled with blood meal to boost the activating nitrogen. Green and brown, the grand heap rises in layers to about 3 feet (90 cm) high. It is then topped with a few inches of earth over the last manure layer. If we are making compost over a garden bed, we rake away some topsoil before we start and reserve it for "icing" the finished pile.

Come spring, the compost warms quickly; the manure layers hold moisture. In early June, we transplant our winter squash seedlings, 2 feet (60 cm) apart, right into the pile. If the material looks too coarse as we trowel out transplanting holes, we "line" each with fine soil that is also used to fill in around roots. The squash plants soon sink roots into the damp fertility and on down to the ground beneath. Before long they are off and running. At this point we surround the pile with snow-fencing, a barrier that provides some support for the climbing vines, and more or less contains them; if space is tight, stray shoots can be tucked back into the enclosure.

After the harvest, when the frosted vines have been hauled away to a new pile, the compost is ready for spreading around the garden, a year after it was put together. I like to think that the squash roots have helped to break it down, saving us the back-breaking job of turning. Needless to say, the place where the pile stood will be much more fertile than before.

The compost-as-growing-space technique can be modified to fit into any sized garden and would be suitable for cucumbers and bush (unstaked) tomatoes, too. The essentials are: build the heap in the fall; chop the ingredients; use generous layers of manure or soil throughout; top with earth.

Trouble

The same insects and afflictions that menace cucumbers and melons affect squash as well. The remedies are also the same. Sheer garden cloth goes a long way to keeping young plants out of the reach of various borers and beetles; older plants are generally safer. A heavy mulch prevents moths

from reaching the soil where they lay eggs that hatch into squash vine borers. Lacking the cloth or mulch, dust the base of vines with rotenone, ashes, or black pepper if borers have been problematic in the past. Once in, borers can be gingerly hooked out with a hairpin or wire; cover the wound in the vine with a mound of earth and/or compost to induce new roots. Several sanitation steps discourage a buggy population boom: clear away and compost all squash residues in fall; keep garden borders mowed; dig or till a conventional squash patch in spring. So far (knock on wood), our squash plants have enjoyed the best of health, whether due to the spring excavation or the compost planting, the diversity of our kitchen garden — some people don't see the vegetables for the tangle of flowers and herbs — or simply our northerly location.

BEANS

Beans are a home gardener's crop insurance. If the melon vines wilt and raccoons get the corn, we can usually count on beans to provide food faithfully for eight weeks or more. As they are feeding us, the plants feed the soil: on their roots are little bumps or nodules, colonies of bacteria that work to change nitrogen from the air into nitrates, free fertilizer for plant use. Gardeners can stimulate this process by dusting damp bean seed, prior to planting, with "legume inoculant," a dry black powder containing the nitrogen-fixing bacteria. As one catalog notes, "It's a natural, simple process that takes just a moment, but pays benefits all season long." After beans have been rotated throughout the garden, you can stop powdering seeds because the organisms remain in the soil and attach themselves to the roots of any legumes — peas, beans, favas, even clover — you might plant.

Although I am intrigued by the possibility of growing dried beans for the winter, their cultivation and threshing take up more space and time than we can spare. Like most gardeners, we focus on snap beans for fresh summer use. Snap beans, your old string beans minus the strings, grow on either branching, knee-high bushes or tall, twining, climbing plants that need the support of poles, strings, netting, or wire fencing. Pole beans may take a week or two longer to bear, but they grow more food in less space than bush beans; some say that the flavor of a pole bean is "superior to even the best bush bean." In our cool locale, pole beans do not thrive as well as their bushy counterparts, but we keep trying.

A Bevy of Beans

Seed catalogs insist that certain snap beans (i.e., the ones they list) have "exceptional taste," "rich, beany flavor," "superior eating quality." To test the claims, we try a new bean or two every year. Frankly, I find the flavor nuances so subtle that an extra minute on the stove seems to make more difference than which bean is in the pot, and yet, we have our favorites. "Green Crop" we grow every year for its abundant flat, wide pods that are easy to sliver for cooking. The newer "Derby," an All America Award winner in 1990 (and the first bean to receive the honor in more than twenty-five years), yields round, green beans that are long on taste and short on fiber and stay tender for days as the seeds develop slowly in the pods; after a heavy first flush, it continues to flower and fruit for weeks. Like "Derby," "Provider," a popular early green bean, resists several common diseases. "Bush Blue Lake," a short version of classic pole beans, needs more space than others.

"Beurre de Rocquefort" is a long-bearing, yellow bush bean from France that takes to cool northern summers and can be planted earlier than others. "Rocdor" and "Cherokee Wax" are also fine wax beans with some disease tolerance. Next year we'll try "Dragon Tongue," a flat, bronze-mottled yellow bean said to be "one of the tastiest beans around," and "Dutch Stringless" for "real bean taste" — the search goes on.

From France come skinny "filet" beans that are picked young and served whole. "Triomphe de Farcy" and "Marbel" are universally praised for earliness and fine flavor, but the purple-streaked green pods must be picked when very thin, almost every day at their height. Once they attain snap-bean size, filets lose their appeal, growing tough and stringy. Filets are not for freezing.

"Royal Burgundy" and "Royalty Purple Pod" are choices for a sunny corner of ornamental edibles. Give the bushes a foot between them and they'll fill out gracefully with lilac flowers, followed by dangling wine-purple beans. After two minutes in boiling water, the purple turns to green, telling you when the beans are blanched for freezing.

The Bean Bean

Coming originally from Central and South America, beans of all kinds respond to warm soil and air; a whisper of frost is enough to kill them. In cool soil the seeds tend to rot, and any that do sprout lack vigor. Although beans may be started indoors — two seeds in a 2-inch (5-cm) pot, thinning to one — a few weeks ahead of time, most gardeners sow them outdoors a week after spring's last frost. When the maple trees are in full leaf and the soil is warm to the touch, our beans go in. A second and third planting, at two- or three-week intervals, gives a steady supply until frost. Because the plants bear fairly heavily over several weeks, a succession of smaller seedings is the only way to go if you want beans for fresh eating rather than freezing.

Beans need a place in full sun and earth lightened and enriched with compost or leaf mold, but not clogged with nitrogen-rich manure; excessive nitrogen pushes foliage at the expense of fruit. Pole beans need relatively more nutrients to support their vigorous growth and heavy fruiting. Here, we turn an inch of compost, sometimes augmented with a dusting of bone and kelp meal, into the bean bed a few days before planting. The goal is to boost the potash and phosphorus levels. But since beans prefer a slightly acidic ground, wood ashes, a potent source of both potash and alkalinity, tends to raise soil pH above the comfort level.

My grandmother grows fine pole beans in a tiny city garden that has never seen manure, "real" compost, or chemical fertilizer. All she does

Basking in the rooftop sun, this giant pumpkin originates from a wooden half-barrel filled with fertile soil and compost.

is bury her garden leftovers — frosted plants, leaves from the peach tree, spent bean vines — in the ground, along with residues from canning. In many gardens, beans prosper without fussy soil preparation — just dig, rake, and plant. You'll know in a season whether the earth is out of balance or deficient; if beans fail to thrive, you have some soil-building to do.

Our bush beans grow in an intensive bed, which is one way of saying they get mighty crowded sometimes. Beans are one plant we never thin, although we usually wish we had at harvest time as we hunt for pods in the tangle. The recommended distance between bean plants in a row is 6 to 8 inches (15 to cm); traditional methods would put the rows 18 inches (45 cm) or more apart. One principle of intensive gardening says that the distance between rows can be the same as the space between plants in a row. With that in mind, we hoe open bean furrows, 1 inch (2.5 cm) deep, 6 to 8 inches (15 to 20 cm) apart, across the width of a 4-foot (120-cm) bed. Fine so far. We then plant one seed every 2 inches (5 cm), reasoning that some may not sprout and earwigs may chew off a few more. In clay soil, it is advisable to cover the seeds with sifted compost or lighter ground; beans have a hard time hoisting their hefty seed leaves through crusty ground. If germination is good and earwigs few, we're left with a crowded, hard-to-pick forest of beans. Old habits die hard, but, be it resolved: next year we thin the beans. Close planting has one benefit: weeds don't stand a chance once the bushes have closed ranks.

Giving beans room to breathe not only make for easier picking, it also fosters better health as circulating breezes dry foliage, inhibiting the spread of fungal diseases. On one point all experts agree: Working among wet bean plants can spread disease.

To grow pole beans, first set up supports. Traditionally, slender 10-foot (3-m) saplings, with bark left on, are pushed firmly into the ground at 18-inch (45-cm) intervals. A crowbar is handy to loosen the earth first. At the base of each pole sow eight to ten beans — big beans are easy for little hands to plant — thinning later to four to six plants. Variations on the method are possible. Three or more poles, lashed together at the top, teepee style, make an interesting feature in a sunny corner of the garden. Make it bigger and the kids can hide out in its leafy shade. One teepee may be all you need; otherwise, space them on 4-foot (120-cm) centers. Beans will climb special nylon netting or tall, wide-mesh chicken wire. One grower recommends two tall, sturdy posts set in firmly, 8 feet (2.4 m) apart, with a cross piece between them, top and bottom. On this frame you weave a grid of untreated twine. At season's end, twine and vines come down together for composting. As an annual climber, pole beans, and especially the striking "Scarlet Runners," can decorate trellis work, porch front, or chain-link fence.

Plants take in nutrients from both roots and leaves. Last summer, we gave the bean patch a foliar feed of seaweed emulsion, a dark green liquid mixed into a concentrate from powder and further diluted for use. The results were dramatic as leaves turned noticeably greener during the ensuing spurt of growth.

Bean Bugs

Beans are one of the healthiest, most insect-free crops we grow. In the cause of prevention we shift the patch around the garden so that they grow in the same place only once in three years. We also bury spent plants either in the ground or in an active compost pile in fall, and remove any ailing bushes as soon as trouble appears. The Mexican bean beetle is almost a dead-ringer for the beneficial ladybug, except that the beetle is more orange than reddish, has no spots on the segment between head and body, and turns bean leaves to lace. Handpick both beetles and their tiny yellow, spiny larvae; clusters of orange eggs can be crushed in the process. Planting beans next to potatoes is a time-honored way of deterring both bean beetles and potato bugs. As always, a mix of flowers and aromatic herbs — specifically savory, garlic, nasturtium, hyssop, sage, and petunias — adds to the bug-baffling diversity that helps protect the beans. Our kitchen garden is laid out in permanent plots that are worked by hand, an arrangement that allows for groups of perennial herbs at the ends of beds. Hardy annual flowers such as alyssum, California poppies, calendulas, borage, and Shirley poppies self-sow freely along pathways and among the vegetables to create a colorful jumble that must be more confusing to insects than a large tract of their favorite food.

Pick of the Pods

When beans are at their peak, we pick them every few days, before the pods are lumpy with developing seeds. Even if they end up as compost, all mature beans should be picked so that pods will continue to form.

Here is a favorite and very simple way to serve snap beans: Cut the beans, on a sharp slant, into thin strips and place in a heavy-bottomed pot with water just covering the bottom. Add a few whole sprigs of summer savory — the German *Bonenkraut* or bean herb. Cook on medium heat, shaking the pot to redistribute the beans. If water starts to evaporate, add a little more. Cook until tender, but not mushy, to bring out their natural sweetness. There should be almost no water left when the beans are done.

Leaving the beans in the pot over low heat, dress them with olive oil or butter, a pressed clove or two of garlic, lemon juice, salt and pepper to taste, and a generous sprinkling of fresh summer savory. Stir beans and seasonings together briefly to melt the garlic and meld the flavors. If beans look watery, thicken the juice with a touch of cornstarch before serving.

Full of flavor and nutrition, fresh beans are a natural for any kitchen garden. Easy to grow and always prolific, they return a lot of food for relatively little attention. Every gardener needs at least one crop like that.

WINTER SQUASH AND KALE PASTA SAUCE

Tarragon, ginger, and Indian spices complement the sweetness of winter squash in a creamy sauce that teams two fall vegetables.

1 cup	winter squash, cubed	250 mL
1	medium onion, chopped	1
2	garlic cloves, minced	2
1 tsp	fresh ginger, minced	5 mL
¼ cup	cooking oil	50 mL
1 tsp	fresh tarragon, minced	5 mL
½ tsp	garam masala (sold in Indian spice shops)	2 mL
½ tsp	curry	2 mL
pinch	cayenne pepper	pinch
3 or 4	small to medium kale leaves, coarsely chopped	3 or 4
1¼ cups	plain soya milk (sold in health food stores)	300 mL
⅓ cup	water	75 mL
1 tsp	tamari soy sauce	5 mL
	or	
	freshly ground pepper to taste	
	cooked pasta spirals, shells, or penne noodles	

In a heavy skillet over medium-low heat, sauté squash, onions, garlic, and ginger until onions are translucent, about 5 minutes. Add tarragon, garam masala, curry, and cayenne, and sauté for a few minutes more. Add kale and stir to coat leaves with spices. Add soya milk, water, and tamari, and simmer over medium-low heat until the squash begins to disintegrate and thicken the sauce. Stir occasionally, adding more water if sauce becomes too thick. Season with freshly ground pepper and serve over pasta spirals, shells, or penne noodles. Serves four.

12

FRUIT OF THE VINE
Melons and Cucumbers

CANTALOUPES AND WATERMELONS

In August, if all goes well, melons begin to ripen, one by one. Then, the rising sun finds us crouched among the vines, searching for fragrant cantaloupes ready to "slip"; listening for watermelons that answer our rapping and tapping with a low-pitched echo of maturity. Melons, according to Mark Twain, are "the proper food of angels." At least two earthbound gardeners agree: nothing could be finer for a summertime breakfast than a ripe melon taken from the vine in the dewy cool of the morning.

Pollen Exchange
Melon plants, botanists tell us, are "highly polymorphic," meaning the various species are rather free and easy about swapping pollen. This exchange, whether spontaneous in nature or planned in breeders' fields, has given rise to an array of shapes, sizes, and colors. But round or oblong, smooth-skinned or roughly pebbled, orange-, yellow-, or red-fleshed, home-grown melons are bound to be ambrosial.

A sweet dream of garden melons begins in winter when we send for seed. Those big Texas blimps that need 100 hot days to mature are not

Sending cucumber vines up strings attached to a wall frees up space in front for a planting of Florence fennel and chicory that follows an earlier crop of snow peas.

for us, nor are exotic honeydew, casaba, or Crenshaw melons. Instead, we look for quick cantaloupes (or muskmelons) and "icebox" watermelons seldom larger than a volleyball. What we want are melons that will make it to maturity within the deadlines of our season.

Fortunately for gardeners, the folks who juggle melon genes have come up with varieties whose very names promise to extend the borders of cultivation into cooler short-season areas. So far we have had good success with "Quick Sweet," "Earlisweet," "Alaska," and "Earligold" cantaloupes. "Minnesota Midget" ripens a vineload of softball-sized muskmelons.

The watermelon cultivar we keep coming back to is "Yellow Baby," a green-and-cream mottled melon that grows to coconut size. A delicious spiciness underlies the sweetness of its bright lemon-yellow flesh. "Sweet Favorite," a red watermelon, ripens in the traditional oblong shape, but earlier than most. "Sunshine," a medium-sized yellow watermelon growing on compact vines, is on our list for a trial, as is "Passport," a green-fleshed melon, recently bred in New Hampshire and said to be "widely adapted."

Southern gardeners may get away with seeding melons directly outdoors, but the rest of us must be prepared to coax them along if we hope for a worthwhile return. Their tropical origins give us clues about making the heat-lovers at home in cooler climes. For healthy and fruitful growth, melons require dawn-to-dusk sun, warm soil, steady moisture, and enough time to ripen.

Indoors and Out

To get a head start, we seed melons indoors sometime during the first ten days of May, about a month before we plan to transplant outdoors; this brings the transplanting date to a week or so after our frost-free date. Some plants are forgiving about being crowded together at the start and then wrenched apart for planting; lettuce, for instance, bounces back from such a trauma. Melons, however, are so sensitive to root stress that they may "up and die on you" in response to the disturbance. The solution is to sow seeds in individual containers, three seeds in a 4-inch (10-cm) pot.

Melon seeds need the extra warmth provided by heating cables, a radiator, or proximity to the stove during a baking session; ordinary room temperatures leave them cold and dormant. On sunny days our seeded pots, covered with clear plastic or a glass pane, sit in front of a south-facing window. The covering traps the sun's heat like a greenhouse. Once the seeds have sprouted, melons continue to have priority sun-space by the windows. At this late date we have room to spare — early lettuces and broccoli are already in the ground and tomato seedlings are "hardening" in the cold frame.

When the young vines are working on a second leaf, we snip away all but the strongest one per pot. Pulling up unwanted seedlings may damage roots of the one left to grow.

Turn Up the Heat

Melons are the most cold-sensitive crop we grow. With an ear to the long range forecast, we delay transplanting until summery weather has settled in for sure, usually a week or two after tomatoes and peppers are in the ground. A chilly spell may stress the vines beyond recovery.

The ideal melon soil is light, warm, well drained, and fertile. Sandy loam is a good start; all that may be needed is a generous dressing of compost and/or extra-old manure. Whenever possible, we add these soil amendments in fall and again in early spring. A balance of natural fertilizer, turned in before transplanting, keeps the hungry vines well fed. Kelp meal or greensand supplies potash; bone meal or phosphate rock adds phosphorus. Soil that tests below 6.5 on the pH scale needs a measured amount of ground limestone to sweeten it to 7 plus.

Many melon growers resort to artificial means to boost the soil and air temperature. Very effective is the bottom-sheet, top-sheet method: Cover the melon bed with a sheet of dark or clear plastic anchored with sticks, soil, or stones; transplant melons carefully through X-slits cut in the plastic at 2-foot (60-cm) intervals; cover plants with a top-sheet of translucent spun-fiber garden fabric. Vines run riot under the cloth, which must be lifted when yellow blossoms appear to let in pollinators.

On sandy soil, a plastic bottom cover may be redundant — we're glad to avoid it, in any case, because it soon becomes bulky garbage. If I gardened on clay I would experiment with a surface layer of heat-holding sand spread on a melon bed, in addition to the sand turned under. Remember how hot a beach can be underfoot.

Most seasons we grow our melons in two long cold frames that sit over prepared raised beds. Sometime in late May or early June, seedlings are transplanted, 2 feet (60 cm) apart, in the middle of the frame. With recycled storm windows fitted on top, the frames create a tropical microclimate as June bounces between spring and summer. By July, when melon leaves are pushing at the glass, we remove the windows; the liberated vines soon trail over the frame sides, and, before long, flowers appear.

Sex Among Melons

Melon flowers are either male or female. Female flowers are backed by a small swelling, a tiny embryonic fruit; male flowers are attached to the vine by a thin stem. Melons will develop only if pollen is transferred from male to female, a task usually performed by bees and other flying insects. In short-season areas it is important that the first female flowers are, in fact, pollinated, since these will be the melons most likely to ripen before frost. Flowers stay open for only one day, and if no bees happen by, you can say farewell to that fruit.

Enter the gardener in the guise of matchmaker. We use a small watercolor brush — the kind that comes with a child's paintbox set — to transfer pollen. A random flight with the brush from the heart of male to female blossoms should do it, even though melon pollen is so fine you may wonder if you are accomplishing anything at all. Bees usually discover the flowering vines after a few days and then return on a daily pollen run. When that happens we let nature take its course.

Once pollinated, the little pea-sized melons begin to swell quickly under the summer sun. Thirsty melon vines need a lot of water to plump their fruit. A deep weekly drink is better than frequent shallow showers; sun-warmed water preferable to icy cold. To reduce the risk of fungus, we water in the morning so that vines are dry by nightfall. Melons are one crop we never mulch; a moisture-holding layer of hay or grass may keep the earth too cool for them. Vine growth is usually dense enough to shade the ground from the sun's full drying force.

Trouble

Both watermelon and cantaloupe vines sometimes fall prey to various wilts, blight, and fungae. Fusarium wilt, a disease spread by the yellow-and-black striped cucumber beetle, can cause vines to collapse almost overnight. That warming garden fabric does double duty now by excluding beetles from young plants; the pests are less interested in older vines.

Catnip and nasturtiums are said to deter cucumber beetles, as are onion skins strewn through the patch. Whenever I pull onions or garlic for the kitchen in summer, I twist off the unusable green tops and toss them around the garden, among the melon vines or over the cabbages. Handpicking beetles is always a possibility, and a selective dusting of rotenone may be a last resort, but I'd worry about killing bees.

As always, prevention is better than cure. Gardeners can be grateful that breeders have not overlooked the health of melon vines. Look for cultivars with built-in tolerance or resistance to one or more maladies — anthracnose, fusarium wilt, powdery and downy mildew. If any plants

In short season areas, melon plants must be started indoors about three weeks before spring's frost-free date and set in the garden about a week afterward when the weather is warm and settled.

do succumb, take them up for burning, disposal, or burying in the heart of a hot compost pile. Cleaning up all debris at season's end should be standard practice, along with rotating melons around the garden from year to year. Further preventive steps: space vines at least 2, even 3, feet (60, even 90, cm) apart for good air flow and avoid watering past noon.

Where wireworm or rot spoil the undersides of melon, set each fruit on a wad of dry hay or straw or a slab of board or perch your melons on an inverted flower pot to keep them high and dry.

Slipping Cantaloupes and Inscrutable Watermelons

The harvest approaches. Ah, but when? Picked too early, melons will be less than their flavorful

Smaller icebox watermelons, such as "Yellow Baby," are the choice in areas where the big southern blimps may not mature.

best. Watermelons sit there, fat and inscrutable. Cantaloupes, at least, give you some clues. As it matures, a cantaloupe gradually changes from gray-green to buff-yellow. When ripe, it begins a process called "slipping," detaching itself from the vine and, one presumes, rolling off on a seed-scattering life of its own. Where stem meets melon, a circular crack appears. A gentle tug and the melon is yours. Sometimes we find melons lying there, unattached. To delay gratification is a mark of maturity, they say. A day or two indoors will bring a cantaloupe to fuller flavor and aroma. The nose will know when the melon is ready to eat.

Mark Twain, watermelon aficionado, once instructed gardeners in a game of musical melons to test for maturity. Pink, pank, punk — tapped gently, a watermelon will sing a descending scale as it ripens. Punk — low-toned, somewhat hollow — is the sound of sweetness. If you see a gardener moving along a row, bent low, tapping, listening, you know the musical harvest is on. The tone-deaf will have to use their eyes. A watermelon normally has a light-colored patch on the rind where it touches the ground. As the fruit ripens, the patch changes from white to creamy yellow. This is a sign. Or look to see if the tendril nearest the melon has shriveled and browned — another clue. If the melon's stem has withered altogether, you might as well harvest; no more juice will flow to that fruit. Some gardeners remove a sample plug from a watermelon to test for ripeness, but the gash is an invitation to ants, earwigs, and rot. As a rule: If all signs and sounds say "ripe," wait a day or two more. Watermelons, unlike bananas, apples, pears, and cantaloupes, do not manufacture a gram more sugar after they are picked.

All home-grown food is good, but garden fruit is extraordinarily good. After years of growing melons, we are still pleasantly surprised by each one that completes the race to ripeness in our frost-pocket garden. We still gather the fragrant globes with a little wonder, crack them open with the same anticipation felt that first August, grateful for the small miracle that is a melon from the garden.

CUCUMBERS

A garden links its maker in an active, cooperative way with nature's cycles. After growing vegetables and fruit for a season or two, I began to appreciate the wonderful match between season and supply. In spring, when a body needs a lift, we gather tonic greens and roots that mine the earth for minerals: spinach and dandelion leaves, spring onions, radishes, Jerusalem artichokes, and parsnips, all provide concentrated nourishment to cleanse and revitalize. Fall's apples, pears, beets, and carrots hold earth-and-sun energy for the cold days. In dark December, a golden buttercup squash, baked to melting sweetness, or a bowl of leek-and-potato soup feels like stored solar-power from the garden.

In the same way, cucumbers seem made for warm-weather eating. If lettuces start to peter out in July, we can always count on cucumbers for salads. In hot eastern lands, cooks combine cucumbers and yogurt for refreshing side-dishes: a creamy Indian raita, cumin-and-cayenne spiked, cools a fiery curry, and from Greece comes tsatziki, a tangy cucumber-and-yogurt dish redolent of garlic, olive oil, and fresh dill. A basil-flecked salad of cucumbers, tomatoes, and Spanish onions is a treat reserved for summer.

Roman Baskets

Wild cucumbers, like melons, come originally from Africa. India, however, has been a hotbed of cucumber cultivation since at least 1000 B.C. The vine trailed from east to west, meeting with an enthusiastic reception in ancient Rome. In summer, Roman gardeners grew their cucumbers in baskets rolled around from place to place to catch every drop of sun. In winter, cultivation shifted under cover, into frames or mica-glazed houses, perhaps to please the likes of Emperor Tiberius and court, who called for cucumbers every day of the year. What has changed? Even in the north today, hothouse cucumbers are available throughout the winter, catering to a taste for a vegetable second only to tomatoes in popularity.

Cucumber Cultivars

Gardeners can thank hybridists for cucumbers that are gratifyingly easy to grow. For years, geneticists have been breeding in greater disease resistance and the resulting vines are generally healthy, vigorous, and productive. Every season we grow the same two varieties. "Marketmore 80" yields a succession of dark green, 9-inch (23-cm) fruit from plants that resist four common cucumber ailments — scab, mosaic, and two mildews. Plants are described as "bitter-free," a trait that, curiously enough, makes them less palatable to cucumber beetles, spreaders of the dread wilt. Too, this cultivar's "uniform green genes" — picture it — reduce the chance of "yellow bellies," a cosmetic detail of more concern to commercial growers than to gardeners.

If we had space for only one kind of cucumber, it would probably be "Sweet Slice," a cultivar, according to one catalog, that is "tolerant to just about every disease you can think of." Now, that's what an organic gardener wants to hear! "Sweet Slice" cucumbers are long (up to 12 inches; 30 cm), straight, and thin-skinned, with a core of tiny, tender seeds. Crisp and juicy, the fruits are remarkably mild and sweet.

Cucumber Culture

Up to a point, we grow cucumbers exactly like melons, seeding both indoors in the same way, on the same day in early May. A month later, we transfer seedlings to the garden, again being extra

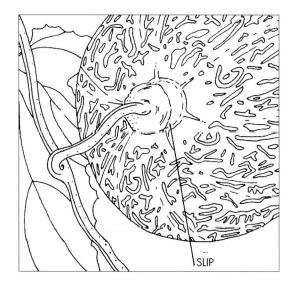

As cantaloupes approach maturity, a circular crack appears where the fruit is attached to the vine, a sign that melons are ready to "slip."

careful with their roots. In the interval, we prepare a bed of extra-fertile earth.

Our best cucumbers to date grew one summer beside a concrete water-lily pool, in soil enriched with cow manure to a depth of 18 inches (45 cm). Sprawling over a stone path, in full sun, the vines were treated to frequent floods of warmed water from the pool. You could almost see the growth. And what a crop — cucumbers "stacking up like cordwood" as a neighbor would say. That summer taught us a lesson in cucumber culture: give them manure, water, sunshine and lots of it.

Currently we grow cucumbers along the south-facing wall of a garden shed. To prepare the soil, we dig a series of holes, about 16 inches (40 cm; two hand-spans) across and 12 inches (30 cm) deep; holes are spaced at 2-foot (60-cm) intervals. Into each excavation we dump five or six heaping spades of crumbly cow manure (or finished compost) and a palmful of natural fertilizer. The amendments are topped with several spades of earth, and the mixture is turned and stirred together. After treading lightly to compress the soil/humus blend, we rake on the remaining topsoil. We then sculpt the loose soil

over each zone by hand, leaving a raised rim around a slightly concave bowl. As a neighbor once said, after watching us do this, "It's not your fault if the cukes don't grow."

A foundation of organic matter provides a reservoir of moisture and food for vines all season. In the center of each circle, we transplant one seedling. Water poured into the earth-bowls goes directly to roots. If cutworms are active, we protect young vines with collars made from 3-inch (8-cm) pressed-fiber pots with bottoms cut away. At this stage, when temperatures are apt to swing, a blanket of spun-bonded garden fabric mellows the climate underneath.

Cucumber seeds may also be sown directly in the garden, in either rows or hills. Note that hills are not necessarily mounds; indeed, in drought-prone or sandy gardens, they are best made level with the surrounding soil. Where the earth is heavy and damp, a raised area tends to be warmer and drier. Raised or level, think of a hill as a 2-foot (60-cm) circle of soil intensively and deeply enriched, in the manner just described. Gardeners with room to spare might space such hills 3 feet (90 cm) apart and mulch the ground between to hold moisture and suppress weeds. Sow six or eight seeds, a few inches apart, in each hill. As seedlings grow and touch, pinch, don't pull, all but three of the strongest.

Beetle-Proofing

The same blanket that shelters seedlings from cool spring winds offers renewed hope wherever droves of cucumber beetles appear the moment you turn your back after transplanting, or as soon as seedlings break through. Beetles and larvae not only chew vines and roots, they also spread a devastating wilt disease. If your cucumbers have been menaced by beetles, whether you seed or transplant, don't leave the patch without first tucking it under cover. Drape the cloth loosely over a bed and secure the edges against determined beetles with a perimeter of earth; we keep a bundle of warped one-by-twos on hand to batten down the cloth. When flowering starts, vines must be uncovered to let in pollinating insects. By then, however, the beetles have (let's hope) run their course, moved on for lack of food, or otherwise ceased to pose a threat. Older vines, apparently, withstand the onslaught better than fragile seedlings.

Send Them Up

When the cloth comes off, we aim vines at their supports, a network of strings tacked to the shed wall. Cucumbers will hoist themselves upward by means of strong, springy tendrils. Trained to climb, they occupy very little space; fruit will be straighter, too. Trellising can be as elaborate and permanent as chicken wire fastened to wooden frames, or as seasonal and compostable as a web of untreated twine torn down with the vines at season's end. I find it fascinating to see how the thin, fragile-looking tendrils get a quick and tenacious grip on anything thin within reach. See that supports are at least 6 feet (1.8 m) high, or vines will be waving around in the air with no place to climb. You may have to encourage cukes on their ascending journey by tying them to supports with soft cloth at the start.

Food and Water

As much as cucumber vines appreciate the sun, their roots revel in cool, moist earth. We often pack manure, compost, or other mulch into those water-catching bowls, or over the entire bed if enough material is on hand. With each rain or watering, the pampered plants get yet another helping of quickly available food. Soaking the cucumber patch every three or four days is not too often in hot dry weather. Liquid manure or fish emulsion also spurs fruitful growth.

If all this feeding sounds excessive, consider that cucumber and melon vines are stretching quickly — several inches a day — at the height of summer. Remember, too, that we are working with gentle, natural ingredients, not concentrated chemicals. It is hardly possible to overdo the humus. An organic gardener looks at the long-term view, taking care of the future in the present. Compost turned in and mulch spread now are part of the slow, steady creation of lively, balanced, fertile soil, a process that in nature never ceases. What we do for cucumbers this summer benefits the whole garden next season and the next.

It is important to pick cucumbers when they are still slim and dark green; fruit left to grow fat, pale, and seedy signal the vines to quit producing.

TSATZIKI

Cucumber and Yogurt Salad

2 cups	plain yogurt	500 mL
3 tbsp	olive oil	50 mL
3	garlic cloves, pressed	3
½ cup	fresh dillweed, minced	125 mL
1 tsp	fresh spearmint, minced	5 mL
1 tsp	fresh basil or tarragon, minced	5 mL
	cayenne pepper to taste	
3	young "Sweet Slice" cucumbers, halved lengthwise and thinly sliced	3
	salt to taste	

Stir together all ingredients except cucumbers and salt. Add the cucumber to the yogurt mixture. Let stand for half an hour in a cool place. Salt to taste just before serving. Serves eight.

13

SECOND SEASON
Midsummer Seeding for Fall Eating

In February, when seeds arrive in the mail, we gather together six or eight packets, mark them "second season," and put them away until some-time in July. These are the seeds that will renew parts of the vegetable garden in midsummer, seeds that will keep beds verdant and productive well into fall. It's a treat to see swathes of young green coming along during the season of frosts and farewells — a double treat to pick fresh salads and roots until the snow flies.

Spring's last frost-free date — May 24 or its equivalent in another region — is too early for vegetables that come into their own from September onward: Chinese cabbage, endive, turnips, rutabagas, bok choy, and Chinese radishes. All are candidates for midsummer planting and fall picking. Sown in spring, they invariably bolt to seed.

July is not a month traditionally associated with seeding and transplanting, but consider nature's rhythm. By midsummer the first phase of the kitchen garden is coming to a close. April-seeded pea vines, now thoroughly picked over, shrink from the heat. Seedy lettuces are fit only for compost. The first beets grow woodier by the day, and early cabbages are history. The season is ripe for renewal. One July morning we haul the remnants

A July seeding renews the garden in midsummer and yields a fresh fall harvest of Chinese cabbage, curled and flat-leaved endive, large white Oriental radishes and young carrots. Crisp "Russet" apples round out the fixings for a wonderful salad.

of early crops to the compost heap. That very afternoon may see their spaces filled with new seeds or fresh transplants that have been waiting in a shaded cold frame. A nice bit of synchronicity starts the garden's second phase, a phase that will continue for three months or more.

As does its spring counterpart, the midsummer garden begins with either seeds or transplants. Seeds present a challenge: In the hot, dry conditions common to July and August, they may sprout half-heartedly, if at all. The solution? First, sow a bit deeper than usual to get seeds below the dusty or crusty surface into cooler ground. Second, cover seeds with sifted compost (if you have it), a medium that stays moist and porous; this practice is especially helpful in clay gardens. Third, cover newly seeded spaces with a very light scattering of grass clippings or straw, enough to provide some shade without impeding sprouts. Finally, water every day or two — most midsummer seeds will show through in four or five days — and continue on a regular schedule until seedlings have extended roots out of drought's way.

We treat second-season transplants the same as those set out in spring. Here are the steps:

1. Prepare the soil by incorporating compost and/or old manure and natural fertilizer into the whole bed, or spot-enrich to create a zone of fertility for each transplant.
2. Transplant firmly and somewhat deeper than plants were previously growing.

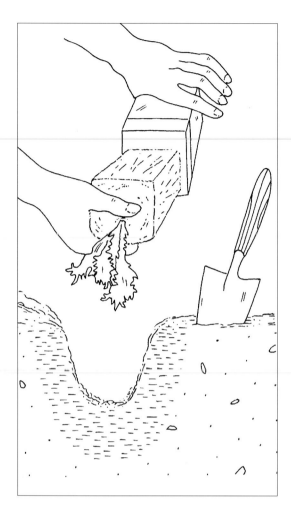

Chinese cabbage responds to root disturbance by bolting to seed. To prevent this, start seedlings in 3-inch (8-cm) pots and transplant carefully.
A spadeful of crumbly compost and a little fertilizer stirred into the soil for each plant concentrates nutrients in the root zone.

3. Sculpt the earth around each transplant to form a water-catching basin.
4. Water with dilute fish emulsion or other natural liquid fertilizer.
5. Spread a cooling, weed-suppressing layer of mulch.
6. Failing rain, water frequently during the first two weeks after transplanting.

CHINESE CABBAGE

At the head of the second-season class stands Chinese cabbage, a delicious multi-use vegetable that can sometimes challenge a gardener's skill. A member of the *Brassica* band, it is also called celery cabbage, wong bok, or pe-tsai. Mature heads may be barrel-shaped or cylindrical, depending on variety. The fat barrels are known as Napa types; the slimmer cylinders are called Michili types. We frequently grow a Chinese cabbage named simply "Lettucy Type"; tall and more open-topped than others, it is especially tender and sweet.

Moisture and Fertility

Chinese cabbage is not one of those accommodating crops that make the most of a starved, dry situation and give a decent harvest, even if crowded together in any old dirt. *Au contraire*: it asks for moisture and organic fertility. It is also rather fussy about timing.

"Do not sow before July 10," warns one seed catalog. "The gradually decreasing day length and temperatures of late summer encourage beautiful heads," says another. Under stress of long, hot days, this vegetable goes to seed before forming proper heads. A hint of root disturbance, too, is enough to trigger seeding.

All things considered, July 10 to July 25 is a useful range for starting Chinese cabbage, with the earlier date applicable to more northerly gardens and the later date to those farther south or on the mild West Coast. Individual containers make for root-friendly transplanting later on.

At Larkwhistle during the second week in July, we fill a dozen or more 3-inch (8 cm) plastic or peat pots with an equal-parts blend of sandy loam, crumbly black manure (or compost), and damp peat moss. A store-bought sterile seeding mix is an excellent alternative. Into each pot go three or four seeds, a quarter-inch deep, lightly covered. The watered pots are set in a cold frame situated in dappled shade. If the frame is in full sun, top it with a snow-fencing (or equivalent) cover for some relief from the noonday sun. Pots might also sit in the house, in front of a sunny, screened window left open to admit a breeze.

In July's heat, seedlings appear in a few days. For the next three weeks they are watered, as necessary, and given one drink of fish emulsion, mixed to half the recommended strength. If insects, such as flea beetles, menace the seedlings, place a remnant of translucent horticultural cloth, or an old window screen, over the frame. Seedlings are safer, of course, indoors.

By early August, we have taken up the shriveled pea vines, leaving a 2-foot (60-cm) band of ground open for replanting. At this point, it is worth taking time to prepare a special zone of fertility for each Chinese cabbage. A half-hour spent enriching the soil may mean the difference between mediocrity and excellence. To that end, we stir together three parts very old manure, or sifted compost, to one part damp peat moss. For each bucket of humus, we add a palmful of blood-and-bone meal, or the same amount of a complete natural fertilizer.

In the past, we used to space Chinese cabbage about a foot (30 cm) apart, reasoning that what suited romaine lettuce was about right. Not so: Chinese cabbage grows many more broad outer leaves that soon fill twice that space. Now, every 2 feet (60 cm) along the length of an intensive bed, we dig out a spadeful of earth and toss in a spadeful of the manure/peat/fertilizer mix. The organics are then stirred thoroughly into the bottom of the hole. A spading fork plunged in and turned from side to side (a washing-machine action) mixes everything without raising subsoil. After stepping lightly into the hole to compress the soil, we tip seedlings out of their containers and set them firmly in the ground. Flooding the concave earth basin around each finishes the job for now. An organic mulch, laid down when plants are taller, is a boon to this hungry, thirsty vegetable.

Given organic fertility and ample moisture, Chinese cabbage grows with astonishing speed in the heat of August. However, there may be bugs in the brassicas: slugs, cabbage worms, and flea beetles. Controls for these are detailed in Chapter 8. Earwigs, too, like to set up house in the tops of Chinese cabbage. A squirt of insecticidal soap stops them in their midnight meal.

In an earwig-infested garden, be careful where you trim up Chinese cabbage and other vegetables that may house an earwig colony. I usually bring the whole plant to the middle of a hard flat path — NOT into the house, by the compost pile, or near a garden bed — for trimming. As earwigs drop out and start to scurry away, I scrunch them underfoot or by hand — careful, they pinch! — or spray them with soap.

Fall Feast

By any name and in any shape, fresh-picked Chinese cabbage makes a favorite fall salad. Crisp and juicy, the leaves taste mildly of both cabbage and mustard greens. To the thinly sliced Chinese cabbage we add grated carrots and apples, fresh chives, lemon thyme, and tarragon; the salad is dressed with oil and cider vinegar, or yogurt, or mayonnaise, or some blend of all of the above. Grated beetroot, raw or cooked, turns everything pink. This is not a traditional use but a feast from the October garden nonetheless.

ORIENTAL RADISHES

Into a Chinese cabbage salad, I like to toss some grated daikon, a long white Japanese radish ready only in fall from a mid-July or later sowing. So popular is daikon in Japan, where it appears in soups and stir-frys, and as pickles, that it accounts for a quarter of all vegetables grown.

Thriving in loose, open soil, daikon can reach an impressive 18 inches (45 cm) long. Where heavy clay is the medium, consider making individual channels for each root. Every 10 inches (25 cm) along a row, poke a crowbar deeply into the soil and wiggle it around and back and forth to form tapered holes about 4 inches (10 cm) across at the top. Fill these with half-and-half sifted compost and lighter topsoil. A little wood ash in the mix adds potash, the root nutrient, and may deter root maggots; some rock phosphate supplies phosphorus (if needed) and the compost has enough nitrogen. How could any radish

turn up its root at such fare?

In each spot, sow five seeds, thinning to one per station before plants get too far along. All that remains is to see that the soil never goes dry. Mulch helps hold moisture and gives further protection from root maggots. Flea beetles, if numbers warrant, are dissuaded by a rotenone dust or a spun-fabric cover.

The fun comes at harvest time. Holding the radish by its "shoulders" (which usually poke out of the ground), wiggle and twist the root until it is as loose as a six-year-old's tooth, then, pop, up comes a radish that may be as big as your forearm. Like carrots, beets, and rutabaga, daikon stores nicely into winter if kept just above freezing in a fairly humid environment. Often, in fall, my friend and I dig an earth pit, lined and covered with hay, where we squirrel away leeks, cabbages, and fall roots, including a bundle of Japanese radishes for winter use.

Similar to daikon is lo bok, the Chinese white radish. The difference between the two may seem slight to some, but in the East definite preferences prevail. "Never sell daikon to Chinese chefs," one catalog advises commercial growers. Compared to pungent daikon, lo bok is sweeter, shorter, fatter, and not as tapered. Described as winter radishes, both "China Rose" and "Black Spanish" are as big and round as a softball. All mature in less than two months from a midsummer sowing and are grown like daikon.

ENDIVE AND ESCAROLE

Still close to their wild roots, endive and escarole usually display the best of health and vigor when seeded or transplanted in midsummer for fall maturity. Native to Asia and northern China, the original wild endive (*Cichorium endivia*) is closely related to the pretty blue-flowered chicory that decorates the dusty roadsides throughout Canada and the northern United States. The Asian endive has given rise to several garden-worthy variations. Broad-leaved types are commonly called escarole or Batavian endive; the variety "Full Heart Batavian" is widely available and "Nuvol" is said to be somewhat sweeter, a description to be

taken with a grain of salt when it comes to escarole. Finely cut and curled leaves characterize another endive available to gardeners as "Salad King," "Frisan," "Traviata," and others. From Europe comes *chicorée frisée* or *très fine* endive, the most frizzed, cut, and curly of all; "Tosca," "Fin des Louvier," and "Nina" are three. For the sake of simplicity, we'll refer to all three — escarole, endive, and *frisée* — as endive.

In France and Italy, endive is to salad what head lettuce is here — an everyday staple. North American palates are beginning to wake up to the pleasure of slightly bitter greens — chicory, witloof, radicchio, dandelion, escarole, and endive. If your taste in salad runs to iceberg tossed with a sweet dressing, be warned: a hint of the wild lingers in endive's pungent leaves. Their full flavor invites a hearty dressing of olive oil, balsamic or cider vinegar, garlicky croutons, fresh basil, and Parmesan cheese. With a texture that cannot be described as melt-in-the-mouth, endive also stands up to warm-salad treatment.

A hint of bitterness is welcome, but let's face it: poorly grown endive can be as tough and strong-tasting as any old lawn dandelion. The secrets to mellowing its bite are fourfold. First, provide fertile organic soil. Second, time planting so that endive comes to maturity during the cool, damp days of early fall. Third, water often for quick, steady growth. And, finally, blanch your endive by excluding light from their centers to foster pale creamy hearts that are mild and tender compared to the green outer leaves.

Endive
From Seed to Salad Bowl

Endive is an ideal follow-up crop to quick-growing spring spinach, lettuce, radishes, and green onions. In 1885, M. Vilmorin-Andrieux wrote of endive in *The Vegetable Garden*, "The gardeners about Paris . . . make successional sowings up to the end of August." Endive takes about three months to develop. Since the heads are fairly frost hardy, you are advised to determine its approximate starting date like this: add two or three weeks to the average date of your first fall frost and then count back three months. Here, where the growing season winds down by the end of October, we start seeds during the first half of July, using one of two methods.

The easiest way to grow endive is to seed directly in the ground, in a space left vacant by earlier vegetables. If sentiment or indolence deters you from the necessary job of thinning, it is better to sow seeds with some precision at the outset. Rather than sprinkling thickly in a furrow, I like to sow several seeds in a close group, every 6 inches (15 cm) or so along a row. In time, all but the strongest single young plant is removed from each group. As the adolescent endives fill out to touch each other, we take every other one for salads, leaving the rest to mature, nicely spaced about a foot (30 cm) apart.

As an alternative, when endive's future space is still occupied, we sometimes start seeds in 2- or 3-inch (5- or 8-cm) pots. Seedlings are handled in the manner described for Chinese cabbage. In the scheme of things, endive seedlings, spaced a foot apart, often replace passé pea vines. Being a legume, peas take in airborne nitrogen, essentially a free fertilizer, and return it through their roots to the soil. Being a leafy plant, endive responds to nitrogen with lush growth — a compatible succession.

The usual menu of organics prepares the earth for endive in either an entire row or individual zones. A side-dressing of blood meal sprinkled around half-grown plants boosts nitrogen, as does a mulch of decayed manure. Twice-weekly waterings in a dry spell keep endive growing, and a few drinks of fish emulsion make for fine full heads. Insects, it seems, have yet to acquire a taste for bitter greens.

There remains only blanching (literally, whitening), a process that keeps the sun from shining into the hearts of endive, which makes them light-hearted. Sunlight on leaves turns into dark green — and in endive's case, bitter — chlorophyll. Blanching takes place during the last month of maturity. Traditional methods tend to be tedious and time-consuming: placing whitewashed glass cloches over the plants or building inverted Vs of boards over them. In French markets you see broad, flat heads of creamy endives

A mulch of half-decayed hay keeps the roots of tiny endive seedlings cool and damp during hot, late summer days.

that have been blanched with weighted boards laid on top of them, a method that sounds more like setting a trap for earwigs and slugs. A simple, effective blanching technique is to gather up the outer leaves and tie them together with strips of soft cloth. The plant's centers must be dry at the time or they may rot. Endive will endure some frost, but the hearts are better protected from damage if the heads are tied.

Endive grows well in shaded places where the curled sorts are as decorative as so-called flowering kale and cabbages — and are far tastier. This is a natural for edging the edible landscape, especially in small city yards. Shallow-rooted endive can also be cultivated in containers: a box 1½ feet (45 cm) square and 1 foot (30 cm) deep will accommodate five plants on deck, balcony, or rooftop.

TURNIPS AND RUTABAGAS

Native to northern Russia and Scandinavia, turnips thrive under cool, moist conditions, and pine when it's hot and dry. Quick growth in moist soil makes for crisp, mellow roots. Turnips that poke along in dry ground grow hot and woody.

Turnip fans may want to try a spring crop, seeding two weeks before the average date of spring's last frost. Fast, steady growth, as for related radishes, is especially important in spring to keep plants from bolting to seed as days become longer and hotter. Spring turnips are often bugged beyond recovery by flea beetles and root maggots. A covering of garden fabric deters both.

All in all, fall is a better turnip season — fewer bugs, more turnip-friendly weather. Seed outdoors six to eight weeks before you anticipate fall's first frost. A little compost and natural fertilizer should be adequate to feed this spartan root vegetable. If turnips follow spring lettuce or peas in soil nicely enriched for the earlier crops, we simply scuffle and loosen the earth before seeding. Sow seeds singly, one per inch, in a furrow as deep as the distance between fingertip and first knuckle joint. Thin seedlings as they touch to stand 3 or 4 inches (8 to 10 cm) apart.

Rutabagas or swedes — essentially big yellow turnips — are planted only in midsummer for fall and winter eating. The plant's blue-green leaves, like those of broccoli, show its connection to the Brassica family. Native to Siberia, rutabagas are designed by nature to cope with cold. Fall frosts, in fact, help to sweeten your swedes. Our usual course is to start rutabagas indoors, or in a cold frame, one plant per 2-inch (5-cm) pot. The timing and treatment described for Chinese cabbage is appropriate for rutabagas as well. Seed ten weeks before fall's first expected frost and transplant three or four weeks later. Set seedlings 10 or 12 inches (25 or 30 cm) apart. With a root system that may extend down as far as 3 feet (90 cm) in search of nutrients, the big turnips usually find what they need even in less-than-ideal ground. That said, a few inches of compost or a measured amount of natural fertilizer, turned in before transplanting or seeding, helps them along.

To sow rutabagas directly in the ground — again, ten to twelve weeks before fall's first expected frost — open a furrow a scant inch deep. If the soil is dry, soak the little trench, and let water drain away before dropping seed in singly, one seed per inch (2.5 cm). Fill in the furrow about halfway with earth, tamping lightly with the back of a rake. When the small plants have a leaf or two, thin them to stand 5 inches (12 cm) apart; in a few weeks thin again, leaving roots to mature at a comfortable 10-inch (25-cm) spacing. In a dry spell, seedlings may need watering until taproots have burrowed into the ground.

Flea beetles can be murder on young rutabagas, but a light dusting of rotenone should prevent damage; the tiny, shiny black hoppers are less interested in older plants. For other cole-crop insects, refer to Chapter 8. Fall rains usually see the swedes through to harvest time. If rutabagas look rather skinny in September, don't worry. I'm always surprised how they continue to put on the pounds after most other things have stopped growing. Harvest rutabagas after a few light frosts have mellowed them, but before they are spoiled by a heavy freeze. An old-fashioned root cellar, cold and humid, is ideal for storage. Lacking that, we heap lots of leaves or hay around rutabagas in the garden. Thus protected, they keep beautifully until December and beyond.

MIDSUMMER MISCELLANY

There is no reason why the garden season should end abruptly on the night of fall's first frost. Fall is like a spring encore in reverse, and many of the early season vegetables thrive again as days grow cooler, shorter, damper. A bit of planning, and some timely seeding, keeps beds lush and full almost until the snow flies.

Candidates for resowing in July and early August for fall picking include: beets, carrots, leaf lettuce, spinach, snow peas, radishes, mustard and turnip greens, and leafy Oriental vegetables such as bok choy. All are quite quick growing and hardy enough to sail unscathed through the first round of frosts and on into Indian summer.

Gardeners soon develop an intuitive sense about when the growing season in their area winds down completely. In October, here, we revel in glorious warm interludes between spells of increasingly chilly winds and rains. By mid-November trees are bare, winds are tinged with winter, and charcoal clouds may obscure the sun for days. Hardy vegetables continue to grow until the going gets very rough, indeed; but, like a gardener, they move slower as the days turn dark and cold.

To time midsummer seeding, refer to the number of days to maturity on the seed package or in a catalog, then add a week or two to compensate for fall slowdown. Think for a moment: when is the season well and truly over? This is the time when the chrysanthemums are ashen, and "wet flurries" are in the forecast. In our area, where frost can hit in mid-September, we count back from November 1 to determine when we can seed another batch of beets, lettuce, and the rest with a reasonable chance of success.

Larkwhistle's kitchen garden is not a one-shot affair: our first outdoor seeding takes place early in April, the last in early August. Gardeners accustomed to getting everything in and over with all at once in late spring, may resist the notion of spreading the seeding and transplanting over four months or more. It takes some getting used to, some organizing of seeds, schedules, and garden space. The simplest approach would be to sow a few more seeds wherever and whenever garden space becomes free. It's a short step from there to planning a full second phase around the crops that are naturally adapted to thrive in fall. When you're cutting a fresh Chinese cabbage or nicely blanched endive on a chilly late October day, you'll be glad you made the effort to start the season over again in midsummer.

ESCAROLE

FRISEE

Endive crops up in several variations. The broad-leaved type is often called escarole; curly endive is known in France as frisée.

14

GREEN EXOTICA

Arugula, Corn Salad, Florence Fennel, Mustard Greens, Radicchio, Chicory, and Swiss Chard

Larkwhistle's kitchen garden is well stocked with the basics. But here and there, among the tomatoes, cucumbers, lettuce, carrots, beans, onions, squash, and such, are small plots and patches of oddball vegetables. Visitors scratch their heads trying to identify "that leafy plant with the red stalks — it looks like rhubarb, but not quite"; they wonder out loud why on earth we'd want to plant dandelions when they can't get rid of the darn things. As the arugula, unpicked for months, goes from peppery to incendiary, we may wonder the same thing. Perhaps an old-time writer was on to something when he described gardeners as "insatiable seekers after outlandish things."

ARUGULA

Strong and peppery, with a mustardy bite, arugula may be an acquired taste. A recent cookbook suggests getting acquainted with it by tossing "a little to start with in your next salad," adding, "You will soon find you can't do without this pungent counterpoint in your greens." The next recipe, which I mean to try once I get past the salad stage, starts with "4 cups fresh arugula leaves" as a base for a pesto sauce. An all-arugula salad is for those who appreciate the sharp flavor — one friend thinks it tastes "kind of skunky."

Among the kitchen garden's more exotic offerings are dark green arugula, red and white Swiss chard, pale Florence fennel, and the dramatic wine-and-white leaves of radicchio.

An easily grown member of the Cruciferae (or mustard) family, arugula is also known as roquette or garden rocket. Growing in loose, low rosettes, the dark-green leaves are lobed on the bottom half and spoon-shaped above, much like radish tops. Seldom found in markets, arugula is easy enough to grow, responding to the minimal attention you'd expect to give a half-wild plant. This is a cool weather green thriving best in spring and again in fall; its compact growth makes it a natural for a square-foot corner of the garden (and that may be all you need). For an ongoing harvest of tender young leaves, sow a few seeds every three weeks.

As soon as the melting snow exposes a patch of bare ground, we seed a first round of arugula, along with mustard greens and leaf lettuce, in a cold frame. The frame's storm-window lid holds spring's elusive warmth; it also excludes flea beetles, arugula's principal pest. To plant arugula, whether in a frame or in the open ground, we first open a shallow, 4-inch wide (10-cm-wide) furrow with a hand cultivator, then scatter seed thinly along the band, aiming for a seed every inch or so. A light covering of earth and a gentle watering complete the job. Thin to 2 to 3 inches (5 to 8 cm) apart. Within a month, we are picking young leaves and, soon after, cutting whole plants. If the rosettes are snipped just below the ground, they hold together for washing.

Spring sowings in the open air do better under a remnant of sheer garden cloth. Left unprotected, the leaves are often so riddled with flea-beetle bites

they lose their appeal. Arugula is naturally strong-tasting, but it can turn unpleasant if grown slowly in hot, dry soil. Frequent drinks and a light mulch help keep the leaves as tender and mild as they'll ever be.

For fall pickings, seed again one month before your anticipated first fall frost. Hardy roquette sails through light frosts and continues into Indian summer and beyond. At this season insects seldom pose a problem. Looking forward to next spring, try sowing arugula the day after your first fall frost. The ensuing small plants are tough enough to survive most winters, especially under snow. Come spring, they start to grow at the first warm nudge and are ready to pick well before anything else.

CORN SALAD

While traveling in France, we often bought a half-kilo of *mâche* in the outdoor markets; sold washed and trimmed, the small emerald rosettes became an instant salad course for a parkbench picnic of baguette, olives, and cheese. Better known as *Feldsalat* in Switzerland, lamb's lettuce in Britain, and corn salad in North America, the oval leaves are as delicate in taste and texture as arugula is robust.

In *The English Gardener* of 1883, William Cobbett wrote of *mâche*: "it is, indeed, a weed, and can be of no real use where lettuces are to be had." While I would never trade lettuce for corn salad, the little wilding is a nice touch in salads. In 1693, Scottish gardener John Reid wrote that lamb's lettuce was often teamed with cooked cooled beets; modern gardener Shepard Ogden agrees and suggests dressing such a salad with walnut oil.

As hardy as arugula, corn salad can also be sown a number of times throughout the season. Seed first in a cold frame, then in the open air around the spring frost-free date and every few weeks thereafter, ending with a late-summer seeding for fall picking — a schedule that supposes an unusual passion for this small salad plant. In hot locales, growth is better in spring and late summer. Sow in bands (4 inches [10 cm]

wide), one seed per inch, and thin plants to 3 inches (8 cm) apart. In nineteenth-century Britain, according to one writer, lamb's lettuce was rarely grown by itself, but rather as "useful things to sow between rows of more valuable crops." This interplanting treatment works as well today, with the quick-growing greens filling space between peppers or eggplant until they have stretched to shade the ground. Harvest whole plants when the rosettes are a few inches across and wash carefully to get out the grit. Greenhouse gardeners might experiment with a winter crop of corn salad. The shallow-rooted plants grow well in wooden flats filled with 3 or 4 inches (8 or 10 cm) of a fertile potting mix; seed in February, as the days are getting long enough to foster growth.

FLORENCE FENNEL

In the Italian city that gives this vegetable its name, we saw mounds of pale-green finocchio heaped high beside the fava beans, peppers, and tomatoes. A familiar vegetable in Europe, Florence fennel seems to be catching on here with cooks and gardeners who appreciate its celery crunch and mild anise flavor. Although the dill-like foliage is useful for flavoring salads and fish dishes, Florence fennel is grown mainly for its "bulb," which is formed above ground where the enlarged base of leaf-stalks overlap in a tightly clasped bunch. The plant looks like celery with a wide, flat bottom and thin stalks.

Related to celery but much easier to grow, Florence fennel thrives in moist, fertile soil. Like celery, the plants have a tendency to bolt to seed if subjected to root disturbance, the stress of temperature fluctuations, or the sudden onset of hot weather. Spring-planted fennel is especially prone to bolting, and may turn tough and fibrous during July's long, hot days. In any case, the bulbs are easily overlooked amid summer's abundance. All things considered, Florence fennel is a prime candidate for midsummer planting and fall maturity. September's cooler, damp weather encourages tender growth, and light frost poses no threat to this hardy vegetable.

We grow Florence fennel almost exactly like Chinese cabbage. Start seeds in individual 2- or 3-inch (5- or 8-cm) pots in early July, and transplant carefully to the garden about three weeks later, in ground that has been enriched with compost, old manure, and natural fertilizer. Instead of the 2 feet (60 cm) allowed between Chinese cabbage, each Florence fennel stands 8 inches (20 cm) from the next. In the scheme of things, finocchio usually follows a previous planting of snow peas, lettuce, or early cabbages.

In a dry August, we try to water the young fennel every other day, as abundant moisture translates into crisp, succulent bulbs with fewer fibers through the flesh. An occasional drink of fish emulsion and/or a side-dressing of blood meal sprinkled around the plants provide a surge of available nutrients. When bulbs are half-grown (about an inch wide) we pull loose soil up around them with a hand cultivator, or mound the row with sifted compost. This earthing-up shields bulbs from the sun for greater tenderness. In our garden, fennel seems to attract few serious predators. Earwigs invariably take a few chews out of new transplants, but, with proper care and feeding, the feathery shoots soon outgrow their unwelcome attention.

Maturing in fall, Florence fennel retains its excellent eating quality much longer than it would in summer. When the bulbs have grown to 2 to 3 inches (5 to 8 cm) across, they are ready. Pull up the whole plant; trim away most of the top growth, leaving about an inch of stalk above the bulb. Cut off roots so that the bulb remains intact with all the segments joined at the base like a bunch of celery.

Florence fennel lends a hint of licorice to many dishes, from pasta sauces to fish soups and hearty minestrones — for all three, start by sautéeing thin strips or chunks of fennel with onion and garlic until soft, and go from there. I like to feature the flavor solo in a salad or add the tender inner shoots to a plate of raw vegetables and dips.

MUSTARD GREENS

A friend of ours, who once lived in a small town on the edge of agricultural land, tells a story about

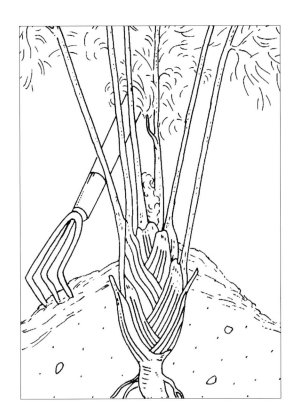

When Florence fennel is half grown, you can draw earth up over the developing bulb for greater tenderness.

the day the weed inspector came to check her garden for noxious plants that might infest neighboring fields. "Everything's fine," he said after a tour, "but you'll have to get rid of that mustard." "Get rid of it?" our friend countered. "I planted it." Which only proves the old saying: One person's weed is another's flower — or, in this case, vegetable.

Traditionally popular in the southern States as boiling greens, the various leafy mustards are much less familiar to northern gardeners, an odd state of affairs considering that they are among the most cold-tolerant of plants. One variety is actually called "Green-in-Snow."

The term "mustard greens" applies to an array of leafy plants belonging to the brassica (or cabbage) family. Most grow into loose, open-topped clusters of broad leaves with thick central ribs. "Florida Broad Leaf" is one variety. The shape,

Looking like a leafy red rose, radicchio "Giulio" gradually folds into a compact head.

month. Mustard is perhaps most appreciated in spring and fall, when there is not much competition out there in the garden. Our first pickings come from the same cold frame that was seeded with arugula, radishes, and other quick greens as early as possible in spring. Sow one seed per inch, cover lightly, and pat the earth down over the rows; thin seedlings to 4 to 6 inches (10 to 15 cm) apart, before they get too far along. The next sowing is mid-August, or about a month before we expect our first fall frost. How encouraging it is to see a stand of greens coming into their prime at a time when almost everything else is winding down.

Flea beetles find mustard irresistible; plants grown in the open air are best protected with garden fabric. Not fussy about soil, the pungent greens respond to any decent loam fed with a little manure or compost. Fast, steady growth results in much milder mustard. Mulch and moisture both help.

shade, and size of leaves vary with the type. "Green Wave" mustard is curled, frilly, and bitingly hot, with the same sinus-clearing sting as the related horseradish; a little goes a long way in salads, but cooking dampens the fire. "Osaka Purple" grows up to a foot tall; at that stage it is fine for steaming or stir-frying, but we pick the white-ribbed, purple-shaded leaves at half that size for salads. "Green-in-Snow," also known simply as "Chinese Leaf Mustard," stays in the garden until the last; pick them young for raw use, or later for cooking. Growing more outward than up, both "Tokyo Beau" and "Mizuna" are mild, exotically cut, and frilled mustards that resemble curly endive; being biennials, they rarely run to seed the first season. A friend kept a potted "Mizuna" in a sunny window indoors all winter as a splendid ornamental edible.

Still close to their wild roots, mustard greens usually display the best of health and vigor. Quick-growing, many are ready in little over a

RADICCHIO, CHICORY, AND DANDELIONS

Radicchio

Small heads of red-leaved radicchio (pronounced *rah-deek-ee-oh*) command a high price in gourmet grocers. Closely related to chicory and dandelions, radicchio shares their robust bitter taste. Sliced into thin shreds, the wine-shaded leaves add color and bite to a lettuce salad. With white veins prominent against the red, whole leaves make a beautiful bed for smoked fish, herbed potato salad, and grated carrots as a sweet counterpoint to the sharp radicchio.

In the past, radicchio was rather tricky to grow, needing careful timing, cutting back, overwintering, and indoor forcing. All that has changed with the introduction of several new cultivars bred to form heads, like any lettuce, when seeded outdoors. Sown in spring, some radicchios tend to run back to seed in the heat of summer without heading up. We wait until sometime between the third week in June and mid-July to sow a variety called "Adria." Heads are ready ten weeks later, when cool weather seems to mellow their taste.

We have had encouraging results with "Giulio,"

a slow-bolting sort developed for spring seeding. Started indoors in April, alongside lettuce and broccoli, in small pots or recycled plastic "cell-paks," this slow-poke radicchio gradually folds its burgundy leaves into grapefruit-sized heads that are ready to cut from July onward.

One seed catalog admits that the heading radicchios are not "very uniform or completely predictable" in their growth habits; another warns us to expect "only 60% marketable or firm heads." Such uneven growth may dismay commercial growers who want to bring in the whole crop all at once, but this gardener can live with 60 percent, and if some plants lag behind, so much the better. Still, we're keen to try "Medusa," a recent hybrid described as "the first nearly uniform red radicchio . . . for all cropping periods," which is to say the plants should do well spring, summer, and fall.

In May, as the lilacs are blooming, we transplant seedlings to a small bed, fertilized as for lettuces, spacing them a hand-span apart in a staggered grid. After that they are on their own, except for routine watering and weeding. If we get around to it, a top-dressing of blood meal under a mulch of compost pushes the heads to perfection, but the near-wild plants seem to thrive without the extra attention. Bugs? None. (Ah, it felt good to say that!)

Radicchio can also be directly seeded in the garden either a few weeks before the spring frost-free date, or in midsummer. Plant several seeds in a close group, spacing the clusters 8 inches (20 cm) apart. Thin to the strongest seedling in each place after a few leaves have formed. Successive sowings at three-week intervals until two months before the fall frost date ensure a steady supply. If you have been reluctant to pay the price for radicchio in the market, consider that 2 square feet (0.2 m²) of ground will grow sixteen little red heads or more.

Chicory

When I was growing up in Toronto, some of my Italian relatives would take to the city's ravines and wilder places every spring to dig cicoria for salads, soups, and pasta with greens. Nobody gave pollution a second thought then. What they were after was the same plant that just about everyone else was trying to get out of their lawns — the lowly dandelion. Since the wild-dandelion season is so short, many Italian gardeners cultivate their favorite *verdura* in the garden; I have one old relative who grows nothing else. Compared to your average lawn specimen, a cultivated dandelion is grand indeed. Look for "Catalogna Special" or "Cicoria Catalogna," a.k.a "Radichetta," "Dentarella," or simply "Italian Dandelion." All are grown like lettuce, their not-too-distant cousin, except that the dandelions are spaced 8 inches (20 cm) apart in all directions. Spring seeding or transplanting is possible, but dandelions do rather better if sown about two months before your average fall frost date. You'll have to keep your weeds weed-free, watered, and fed. And you'll improve their flavor by gathering and tying their leaves together at the top. Nothing, however, removes the bitterness altogether. Harvest any time after leaves are 4 inches (10 cm) tall by snipping individual shoots or cutting whole plants, leaving the crowns to sprout again. Left to develop, Italian dandelions can reach heights that may have the neighbors looking askance.

Very satisfying to grow and eat are the "sugar hat" chicories that grow much like romaine lettuces as upright, fairly tight, conical heads within a swirl of broad outer leaves. Their nicely blanched centers are as close as we get to those lovely pale-yellow Belgian (witloof) endives that are so expensive to buy and so hard to grow at home. We have had good success with the "Sugarlof (Pain de Sucre)" and "Greenlof" varieties. We seed these soon after the summer solstice (June 21), sowing three or four seeds, ¼ inch (5 mm) deep, in close clusters, with 8 to 12 inches (20 to 30 cm) between the groups. When seedlings are a few inches tall, we thin to the strongest one in each spot. Growing slowly all summer, the heads fill out nicely by September and store themselves in the garden through fall's first light frost. Before a hard freeze, we cut any remaining heads and store them in a cold, moderately damp place, where they'll keep for a few weeks.

A half-dozen pots of Swiss chard, both the red-stemmed "Ruby" chard and the glossy green type, start a family off on a long harvest of tasty, nutritious greens.

SWISS CHARD

I can't imagine the garden without Swiss chard, a lovely, leafy plant that is always there when you hanker for a feed of greens. A slow and steady grower, chard stands in the garden from June until late October, without turning tough and bitter, seedy, or overripe. While corn rushes past its prime and all the beans need picking at once, chard waits for you.

Still found growing wild in the Canary Islands and around the Mediterranean, chard is (as one old book notes) "the beet as it was grown by the Greeks and Romans." The ancient plant was thin-stemmed and smooth-leaved, more like today's spinach beet or perpetual spinach. Through centuries of breeding and selection, this simple green has been transformed into Swiss chard, a robust biennial distinguished by wide fleshy stalks, either white or red, and broad, dark green, crumpled leaves.

Few edibles are as ornamental as Swiss chard; few keep their looks for so long. With dark glossy leaves and brilliant stalks, red-stemmed chards such as "Ruby" and "Charlotte" are dramatic accents anywhere in the garden, all the more striking contrasted with green-and-white "Fordhook Giant" or "White King." Every spring we plant a small but prominent bed with both red and green chard next to blue-green curly kale. Once the wonderfully textured leaves have filled out, the corner remains lush and fresh-looking for the next five months or more, all the while supplying a perpetual harvest of tasty, vitamin-rich greens. A bonus: Chard is one of the few food plants that does well in light shade.

In the past, we used to seed Swiss chard in the garden, like beets and carrots, toward the end of May. The results were uneven. One year would see a thriving row, more chard than we could ever use; the next, a patch that can only be described as patchy. Earwigs, slugs, and flea beetles are all partial to newly sprouted chard. Since a half-dozen well-grown plants keep us in greens, it seemed a simple matter to add six more pots to the windowsill season.

We now start chard indoors, or in a cold frame, about a month before our spring frost-free date. Four-inch (10-cm) containers give the quick-growing roots some space to roam. An indoor start gives us hefty young plants that are much less appealing to insects. It also allows us to prepare a deep fertile zone for each one by turning under a few spadesful of compost and/or old manure boosted with natural fertilizer, a process described in detail for cabbages in Chapter 8. Because we want the plants to expand to their full decorative potential, we space them a generous foot apart.

As a leafy crop, chard responds to an extra helping of nitrogen fertilizer. This takes the form of a palmful of blood meal stirred into the soil around each plant, and a mulch of compost or strawy old manure; any mulch, however, is better than none. Fish emulsion, applied every couple of weeks, works wonders, as does a deep weekly soaking. But note: Wetting leaves in the late afternoon/evening is the surest way to encourage fungus. Chard's principal insect pest is the leaf miner, a small, squishy, pale-green maggot that burrows between a leaf's thin layers. Its tunneling shows up as squiggly white trails or blotchy areas. Unless miners arrive in great numbers, the damage may be merely cosmetic. Having trapped themselves in a leaf, miners can be crushed by hand. Look for the clusters of tiny white eggs on the undersurface of leaves at the same time. It is best to collect badly infested foliage for burning or disposal, and to shift the patch around the garden. Garden fabric or netting protects chard, but you lose its decorative value.

Often recommended for salads, raw chard has (to my taste, at least) a certain throat-catching harshness. All that changes, however, when you cook it; stalks are especially savory. Much milder than spinach or beet tops, steamed chard, seasoned simply with butter or olive oil and a touch of garlic, is our favorite dish of garden greens. Since stalks take a longer time to cook than leaves, slice them diagonally into one-inch pieces and put them on to steam for a few minutes before adding the torn leaves. A rich source of vitamins A, C, B_1, and B_2, a serving of steamed chard contains a walloping 15,000 units of vitamin A, and goodly amounts of iron, calcium, and phosphorus. Nutritious, practical, easy to grow, prolific, and ornamental: After one season, Swiss chard moved from the realms of exotica to our list of basics.

ARUGULA AND ROQUEFORT SALAD

For the salad:

2 handfuls	arugula, washed and dried	2 handfuls
	grated carrots	
	cooked new potatoes, sliced	
	beets, sliced	

For the dressing, mix together:

¾ cup	plain yogurt	175 mL
⅓ cup	olive oil	75 mL
⅓ cup	crumbled Roquefort cheese	75 mL
1	garlic clove, pressed	1
2	shallots, minced	2
	or	
1 tbsp	fresh chives, minced	15 mL
1 tsp	lemon juice	5 mL
1 tsp	honey	5 mL
1 tbsp	fresh basil, minced	15 mL
	freshly ground pepper to taste	

On a plate, arrange the arugula, carrots, potatoes, and beets. Pour on the dressing. Serves two to four.

PASTA FINOCCHIO

The tarragon enhances the licorice taste of fennel in this quick pasta sauce.

2	medium fennel bulbs	2
3 tbsp	olive oil	50 mL
3 tbsp	sweet butter	50 mL
2	garlic cloves, minced	2
3	shallots, minced (optional)	3
1 tbsp	fresh French tarragon, minced	15 mL
pinch	fresh nutmeg	pinch
3 tbsp	bread crumbs	45 mL
1 cup	whole milk	250 mL
	salt and pepper to taste	
	fusili or other pasta, freshly cooked	
	grated Parmesan cheese	
	roasted peppers, sliced in strips	

Quarter the fennel bulb and slice thinly crosswise. Sauté the fennel in oil and butter over medium heat until translucent and just soft. Add the garlic, shallots, tarragon, and nutmeg, and sauté for a few minutes longer. Stir in bread crumbs, then add milk and simmer until the sauce thickens slightly. Add salt and pepper to taste and serve the sauce over freshly cooked fusili or other pasta. Pass the grated Parmesan and garnish with strips of roasted peppers. Serves four.

15

ALL ABOUT ALLIUMS
Garlic, Shallots, Egyptian Onions, and Wild Leeks

Allium is the botanical name for a group of bulbous plants that includes not only some lovely flowering perennials, but also every cook's standby, the indispensable onion. Beyond onions there is a lot of flavor to be found in several easily grown alliums: garlic, shallots, chives, garlic chives, Egyptian onions, and wild leeks, a gift from the woods. All sprout a sheaf of flat or round leaves that gradually mature, storing food in scaly underground bulbs in the process.

GARLIC

At Larkwhistle, planting the garlic is one of fall's most enjoyable rites. Sometime in late September, we take an hour to "seed" a 4 foot (1.2 m) by 25 foot (7.5 m) kitchen-garden bed with garlic cloves. Next August, we'll pull enough full-sized bulbs, or heads, to see us through a year. I'm always surprised by garlic's generous return for so little work — plant one clove, harvest a nicely wrapped cluster of ten.

Having always associated this hot-blooded Mediterranean native with the hot south — Italy, Spain, and California, not central Canada — the first surprise was realizing that garlic would, indeed, survive and thrive in our Zone 5 frost-pocket. The assumption was shattered one

Pest-free and easy to grow, a bed of garlic starts from single cloves planted the previous fall. In less than a year, one garlic clove yields a cluster of eight or ten.

September day, when a friend arrived with a basket of big, beautiful, organic garlic that had come, not from California, but from a nearby garden. On her advice, we planted a small experimental patch the next day — and we have been reveling in the "reeking rose" ever since.

Visitors often ask if they can start a patch with store-bought garlic. I wouldn't. Commercial garlic is often sprayed with a sprout and root inhibitor that confuses its natural growth cycle; bulbs may rot before they root. Garlic from the store has probably been shipped in from the gentle south and may not be suitable for harsher climates. It would be much better to start with locally grown stock of proven hardiness.

Garlic is as hardy and easy to grow as any lily; in fact, the two are distant cousins related under the family name Liliaceae. Like lilies, garlic is one of the few kitchen garden crops best planted in the fall. Sometime in September, after frost has blackened beans, tomatoes, and peppers, we choose one of the garden beds for garlic. To prepare the earth, we whiten the surface with bone meal (or a balanced natural fertilizer) before spreading several inches of fine-textured compost or crumbly old manure. After turning in the soil amendments, we rake the ground to a fine tilth. If the garlic bed-to-be is weedy or stony, you'd do well to pick out the largest rocks and make an effort to turf out as many weed roots as possible.

Every year, at harvest time, we reserve some of our finest bulbs for replanting. When the bed is ready, we break the heads into individual cloves, being careful to retain their protective papery covering. Very small cloves are set aside for kitchen use. We then space the cloves, at 6-inch (15-cm) intervals, in short rows across the bed, with rows spaced 8 to 10 inches (20 to 25 cm) apart. In freshly dug, fluffy, sandy soil you may be able to push the cloves in by hand, as deep as your index finger is long. Otherwise, trowel out little planting holes. A warm, drawn out fall will often induce thin blades of garlic grass to emerge and continue growing until checked by severe cold. In regions where snow is here today, gone tomorrow, it is wise to mulch beds with straw, hay, or leaves in late fall to prevent freeze-and-thaw cycles from heaving the cloves out of the ground.

The fading snow uncovers a bed studded with sprouting garlic that begins to grow with remarkable vigor at the first hint of warmth. By June the arching gray-green leaves, a foot tall or more, are conspicuous in a garden full of small seedlings. More than one visitor has looked at the garlic in early summer, and wondered why the "corn" was so far ahead. The day after a June downpour, we do a once-over weeding before mulching the garlic bed with old hay to conserve moisture and suppress weeds.

After that garlic may take care of itself. In a dry season, we soak the bed occasionally and perhaps feed it once with fish emulsion. Needless to say, insects give the garlic (which has built-in insecticidal properties) a wide berth.

By midsummer, a sort of curled pigtail, topped with a little papery "bulb," emerges from the center of each plant. Peel back the thin husk and you find a tight cluster of small green garlics, ideal for use — whole, chopped, or blended — in pickles, pesto, sauces, salad dressings, and roasted dishes. Some gardeners pick off these "seed heads" in order to divert all of the plant's juice to the underground garlic. One summer, as an experiment, we snapped some off and left others on, but there was no discernible difference in the bulbs at harvest. The tops extend the fresh garlic season. We do NOT, however, plant the small bulbs, which take at least two seasons to grow to full size.

By late August, or whenever most of the leaves have withered and turned yellow, we dig the garlic. If bulbs are left in the ground much longer, especially in wet weather, they continue to fatten and may split their skins. Garlic bulbs keep much better if properly cured, a process that dries and sets their skins. To do that, we lay out the whole plants — bulbs, tops, and roots — in a single layer on a slatted bench in an airy garden shed, and roll them around once or twice over the course of a week. By then the tops are shriveled and crackling, and bulbs are encased in crisp properly papery skins. At this point, we finish the bulbs by rubbing off the caked earth and any loose flakes of husk. We then snip off roots close to the bulbs' base and cut off tops, leaving a stub of an inch or so. Any bulbs that have split their skins or are a touch moldy are put aside for immediate use. The rest are ready to store in open baskets or mesh bags, in a dry, cool, shaded spot, where they keep firm and fresh all winter. Some day we'll learn how to turn out those decorative garlic braids.

Garlic breath? Eating lots of fresh green herbs, especially lovage, parsley, and celery, with a garlic-laced dish helps mute the "sulphorous stink" that is garlic's chief virtue in the kitchen but a liability in some company. But the surest cure is to feed it to family and friends so you can all breathe easier.

Elephant Garlic

When elephant garlic suddenly appeared in catalogs a few years ago, I was suspicious. If this were such a splendid allium — "produces huge bulbs flavor is milder than regular garlic" — where had it been hiding until now? Of course, we had to try it. But after one season we knew we would never trade our patch of the real thing for this disappointing novelty. Planted next to regular garlic, the supposed giant failed to reach mammoth proportions — not that we'd know what to do with a one-pound garlic clove. Worse, a hint of bitterness underlies the mild flavor. The off-putting taste disappears with cooking, but then the bulbs are bland. We keep a small patch going perennially at one end of a vegetable bed for the sake of the handsome flat leaves and decorative pale lilac flowers.

SHALLOTS

Rosy-skinned shallots are so often linked with gourmet cooking that ordinary gardeners might reasonably assume that they are as tricky to grow as white asparagus and pale Belgian endive. Scarcity and high price adds to the illusion that shallots are for specialists. Not so: just push single bulbs up to their necks, about 6 inches (15 cm) apart, into any good garden soil. Shallots are often planted in early spring, but they are hardy enough to go into the ground in fall like garlic. Under cover of snow or a fluffy mulch, the bulbs will come through winter unscathed and begin to grow first thing in spring. One bulb turns into an aggregate of six or more by midsummer. When tops have died back, we lift the clusters, curing and storing the shallots precisely like garlic after that. The perennial part comes when we choose some of this season's bulbs for replanting, thus perpetuating our own shallots from year to year.

EGYPTIAN ONIONS

"A vegetable triffid" is how one visitor described our Egyptian onions, a gangling perennial allium that looks like it could possibly take giant steps across the garden. No other plant gets around in quite the same way. In place of flowers, this onion sports a cluster of bulblets atop a fat hollow stalk. One day the whole thing collapses from sheer weight and down comes the stalk, top onions and all. The little bulbs waste no time putting down roots where they land, often several feet from the parent, and then raising a new family that moves on from there, which is why it is also known as "walking onion."

Plant Egyptian onions where they have room to roam, and forget them. Without any intervention, this allium provides the season's first green onions. Later the bulblets can be peeled and pickled like pearl onions, popped into a summer ratatouille, or chopped for gazpacho or other soups. You can begin a perennial plantation of Egyptian onions in spring, summer, or fall — anytime a handful of bulblets comes your way. If they start to traipse too far, surplus bulbs are easily dug up and put to good use in the compost heap, where they will probably sprout.

WILD LEEKS

In his guide to wild food, Roger Tory Peterson describes wild leeks, *Allium tricoccum*, as "our best wild onion." Not only is this woodland native the only wild onion I know, it is also one of the strongest-tasting alliums, wild or tame — not even raw garlic packs such a kick. Also known as ramps, wild leeks ramp in great profusion under the maples and beech trees of our local woods, and (says Peterson) throughout southern Canada and the northeastern United States. As hepaticas and spring beauties fade and trilliums light up the forest, the wide, dark-green leek leaves emerge so thickly that they all but cover the ground in many places. We have learned to take a strong trowel along to pry leeks out of the dense, root-ridden woods soil.

To prepare this best of wild foods, wash soil from the leeks, peel back a layer or two of onion skin to reveal the clean white bulbs, pare off roots, trim the leaves, and rinse again.

There is nothing subtle about the flavor of wild leeks, but after a winter of stored vegetables, we welcome their pungency in May's robust salads along with young dandelion leaves, cold-frame-grown mustard greens and radishes, young asparagus, snippets of lovage and chives — a tonic mixture of whatever is fresh, green, and growing. A hearty, healthful soup begins with lots of chopped wild leeks sautéed in oil or butter. Add water or stock and cubed potatoes; season with fresh lovage (or celery), sorrel, caraway seed, and any other spring herbs that take your fancy. Add salt and pepper to taste, and simmer until the potatoes are tender. Serve as is, or purée the soup, adding milk or cream before reheating.

16

KITCHEN-GARDEN PERENNIALS
Asparagus, Jerusalem Artichokes, and Sorrel

ASPARAGUS

Alphabetically, and in every other way, asparagus is the pre-eminent perennial vegetable. Short season and high prices have contributed to asparagus's reputation as a gourmet vegetable. At one time I was under the impression that this must be a frail and fussy plant, a specialty crop beyond the skills of an ordinary gardener. On the contrary, those delicate spears rise from a very tough and hardy plant, one that survives winters far into the north and returns perennially for as long as most of us will ever tend a garden.

Our first asparagus bed, in ground freshly broken for the purpose, was an unqualified failure. We thought we had done everything by the book — careful trenching and fertilizing, planting two-year-old roots, but — weeds got the best of us. After three seasons, when (according to the book) we should have been cutting fat spears, only a few stringy shoots managed to push through the jungle of quack grass, goldenrod, and bindweed. Serious weeding ensued, but weeds regrew. Trying to release the asparagus from the grip of plants that had been there first proved a losing battle. In the end, we decided to start over, this time in a space that had already been cultivated for several seasons. The moral: Before you plant

Week after week, from mid-May until well into November, Larkwhistle's kitchen garden yields a marvelous bounty of fresh, lively food filled with flavor and nutrition.

any perennial vegetable (or flower), see that the roots of persistent weeds have been thoroughly turfed out.

A once-over digging may not do it. Missed roots will begin to rise again as lusty thistles or many-tentacled grasses the moment you turn your back. Tilling only multiplies the problem by chopping roots into lots of lively pieces.

There is a compelling reason for making a thorough job of the preliminary groundwork: Once planted, asparagus stays in place for decades — indeed, some well-tended plots have grown on productively for over a century. The asparagus bed should be situated in full sun, and in a place where the ferny fronds, often over 6 feet (1.8 m) high at maturity, will not cast an unwelcome shadow. With the site chosen, digging is next: a slow, deep, and careful removal of sod, rocks, and all traces of perennial weeds. This is best done in early spring. Then you wait. After the next rain, the patch will green-up again as missed roots and weed seeds, brought to the surface in the first round of digging, begin to sprout. If you can tell perennial from annual weeds, do some spot digging to round up the former, before hoeing (or tilling) the annuals. If not, you had better redig the whole patch.

At this point, you have two choices: Either repeat the digging process several times over the course of one season, or use the space for summer vegetables. Potatoes are excellent for the purpose since there is a lot of earth-moving — opening trenches, hilling-up, digging the tubers — involved

Asparagus, the garden's first vegetable, is a welcome treat. If you do the groundwork thoroughly at the start, you can expect to gather this delicious perennial every spring for decades.

weak or rotten. Mail-order sources should send stock at the right time for planting. Keep roots moist, but not sodden, in damp peat moss or earth until they go into the ground.

Asparagus for Four

With careful soil preparation, asparagus can grow much closer together than the usual recommendation — that is, roots 2 feet (60 cm) apart in rows 4 feet (120 cm) apart. Planted intensively, a 5 foot (1.5 m) by 30 foot (9 m) bed will hold forty roots — two rows of twenty — enough to provide an abundant harvest for a family of four. The following steps for creating such a bed are adaptable to any size or shape. Note, however, that the first two steps assume the bed is part of a larger cleared space. You could have an island of asparagus surrounded by lawn, if you were willing to edge it twice a year.

To Make an Asparagus Bed

1. Once the ground has been thoroughly cleared of perennial weeds and grass roots, use stakes and string to mark out the sides of the bed, 30 feet long (9 m) by 5 feet (1.5 m) wide. Use two more lengths of string to define a 2-foot (60-cm) path on either side.

2. With a shovel and/or rake (depending on soil texture), move 2 or 3 inches (5 or 8 cm) of topsoil from each path onto the bed, spreading it around evenly. Rake the bed to a fine, smooth, level surface. Level pathways with a rake, clearly defining the edges of the raised bed.

3. Measuring in 12 inches (30 cm) from either edge of the bed, reposition the strings to mark off two 12-inch-wide bands as shown in the diagram; these will be the trenches.

4. Using a square-blade spade (rather than a rounded shovel), dig out a spade's depth of soil from the marked bands, piling it carefully on either side. This layer of earth will be primarily topsoil.

5. See that the sides of the trenches are as straight as possible and then square off the bottom, scraping away soil until you see a change in color, which marks the transition to subsoil.

in their culture. The goal is a clean bed ready to receive asparagus next spring. Of course, if you are starting with a tame, relatively weedless lawn, you may get away with removing the sod in fall, and digging the patch over before planting in spring.

In most areas, April, or just as soon as the soil is workable, is the time to make a new asparagus bed.

Traditionally, roots are set in fairly deep trenches, well enriched with compost and manure. It's a tradition worth keeping. Although asparagus can be grown from seed, a much better start is made with two-year-old roots. Ours came through the mail, but they are often available at well-stocked garden centers in spring. It is a good idea to order or buy a few more roots than you need to fill a bed because some are bound to be

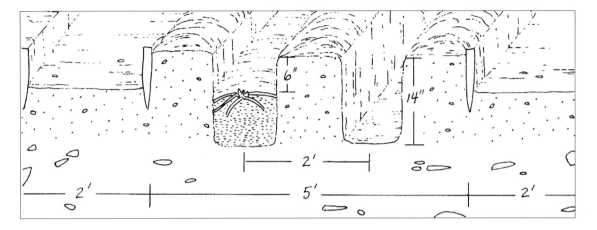

Once planted, asparagus will be in the garden for decades, so it is well worth doing the groundwork thoroughly at the start. Partially fill deep trenches with a fertile mix of compost, topsoil, and manure before setting in two-year-old roots.

6. Remove subsoil, piling it into a wheelbarrow (or buckets) as you go, until the trenches measure about 14 inches (35 cm) deep. Rich in minerals (if low in humus), the subsoil can be added in thin layers to the compost heap.

7. What is needed, at this point, is fine-textured compost, and/or crumbly aged cattle or horse manure, and/or finished leaf mold — your basic "muck," as English gardening books say. Spent mushroom compost and bagged manure come in handy, too. Shovel 4 or 5 inches (10 or 12 cm) of the organic matter into the trenches. Whiten the surface thoroughly with bone meal, phosphate rock (or a blend of the two), or other natural fertilizer high in phosphorus (the middle number).

8. Knock in a few inches of the excavated topsoil, and use a hefty hoe or spading fork to churn and stir the soil, organic matter, and fertilizer together.

9. Tamp down lightly with the back of a rake to consolidate the fluffy mixture somewhat, before adding more of the topsoil to fill trenches to 6 inches (15 cm) from the top. If you are lucky enough to have a bounteous supply of compost or decayed manure, add up to one-third by volume to this layer as well; blend and tamp.

10. Shape the soil to form a slope-sided ridge along the center of the trench. You are now ready to plant asparagus.

Planting

If roots are at all dry, soak them in lukewarm water for 10 minutes before you start. Asparagus roots are like strands of spaghetti: long, thin, and (if they're sound) off-white. It is important that they be firm and fresh-looking, not dark, moldy, mushy, or dried up — there's no point planting dead roots in that lively soil. At the top, or crown, of each clump there should be several little pointed nubs, or eyes, which will grow into shoots; be careful with them.

After trimming off any broken or extra-long strands, splay out the roots in all directions. Center the crown on the mound of earth, with roots trailing down the sides. Fill in carefully with topsoil (or a topsoil/compost mix), and tamp it gently around the roots. Cover the crowns with an inch or so of soil. Space the roots 18 inches (45 cm) apart. Plant each individually, then draw more soil into the trench between them.

Water thoroughly to settle the soil and wash out air pockets. At this stage, the trenches will be filled to within 4 or 5 inches (10 or 12 cm) from the top. Over the next weeks, as the feathery asparagus strands emerge, gradually fill in around them with the remaining topsoil, again mixed with sifted compost or fine-textured manure if you have it. Continue filling until the trench is level with the surrounding soil.

Every season, a certain amount of asparagus must be allowed to develop into feathery fronds that in turn nourish roots for next year's spears.

Wise is the gardener who keeps a sharp eye out for weeds in the asparagus patch that first summer. Hand-weed around the young plants, and stir the soil between them frequently with a three-pronged cultivator to discourage competition and keep the earth open and friable.

Like most perennials, asparagus takes a season or two to get established. The spring after planting — by now the roots are three years old — you may pick a meal or two. It is important, however, to let most of the spears grow and develop into lacy green plumes. Left until October to ripen and yellow completely, the feathery tops serve the vital function of replenishing food supplies in the roots. Vigorous roots give rise to a larger complement of thick stalks the following spring.

In the second season after planting, you can expect a more typical harvest. Even so, only the fattest spears should be taken, leaving the skinny shoots to grow and mature. Picking lasts four to six weeks from the time the first shoots appear. Since new spears appear in quick succession, especially during a spell of warm spring weather, you may have to eat asparagus every other day — such is a gardener's lot. If frost threatens, we either pick all the harvestable shoots the evening before, or throw some old blankets over the bed.

After waiting so long, it is tempting to take every last spear, but resist the impulse to keep cutting much past late June or early July. Every year, a number of stalks must be allowed to grow and mature to maintain the strength of the roots. Once you stop cutting, the patch soon becomes a lovely wall of delicate foliage as the spears shoot up and branch out.

Some folks cut asparagus spears below ground level — there is a special tool, an asparagus knife, for the purpose — but you run the risk of damaging unseen shoots. A simpler way is to go along the row, snapping spears off by hand at the point where they break easily. This way, there is no trimming to do and the whole spear will be tender; you eat what you pick.

An established asparagus bed needs very little attention. It always pays to be vigilant about weeds. In a few years, however, growth becomes so dense that most weeds don't stand a chance. In autumn we cut back the yellow asparagus tops and haul them to the compost. If possible, we blanket the bed with several inches of compost or manure, a nourishing top-dressing that is eventually digested and drawn into the soil by earthworms and other unseen creatures.

As I pick the asparagus, I often marvel that such a succulent vegetable is ready to eat at a time when the tomatoes are mere windowsill seedlings and lettuce seeds are just pushing through the cool spring earth. Having paid very little attention to the patch, I'm pleased to find more spears each year as the clumps mature. Best of all, with the work of ground clearing and planting behind us, we can rest assured that asparagus, like our peonies, phlox, day lilies, and other perennials, will rise again every spring for many years to come.

Looking like over-grown dill, asparagus fronds form a feathery hedge that blends in decoratively with the mix of vegetables, herbs, and flowers in the kitchen garden.

JERUSALEM ARTICHOKES

For centuries, North America's Native people grew Jerusalem artichokes alongside their corn, beans, and squash. In 1603, the explorer Champlain noted that the Algonquins baked cultivated tubers that reminded him of the artichokes commonly eaten in France. Jerusalem artichokes are tan-skinned tubers, like knobbly potatoes, that develop underground. Even today they remain more popular in Europe. Royal gossip has it that Queen Elizabeth's favorite soup is made from the tubers.

Related to the giant annual sunflowers beloved of gardeners, chickadees, and Van Gogh, the Jerusalem artichoke is a hardy, self-sufficient food plant that can be tucked in a sunny, out-of-the-way corner of the garden and forgotten — that is, unless it threatens to grow out of bounds. Once planted, it will be with you perennially. Our introduction to this unusual vegetable came when

a gardening friend brought us three sprouting tubers one April day. With the gift came a warning: "They're tall and they spread like crazy; plant them where they won't be in the way or shade the garden. You might enjoy them next spring when there's nothing else in the garden — just leave them in the ground until then."

The tubers were planted in an otherwise wasted space against a cedar-rail fence, between the garden shed and a mulberry bush where the compost pile used to be. Except for a leftover layer of compost, the sandy ground was unimproved. Over the summer, sturdy stalks, clothed with heart-shaped leaves typical of sunflowers, rose to 7 feet (2 m) and more — all without watering, weeding, or fussing on our part. By October the plants were blooming nicely, a flurry of yellow-petaled, sweetly scented daisies. As winter approached, we piled leaves around to protect the tubers; stalks were left standing all

One of our gardening goals is to eat fresh from the garden as early and as late in the season as possible. The first harvest — spinach, asparagus, leaf lettuce, green onions, and various herbs — are ready for the table in mid-May, the time when gardeners who follow tradition may be just getting around to planting seeds.

winter to mark the spot. When the snow began to fade in March, we pulled back the leaves and found (as hoped) soft, unfrozen earth. Digging in at the base of the stalks, we came up with six or more tubers for every one we had planted — a fair return for next to no work. Over the next few weeks, we dug 'chokes as needed until we had harvested the lot, or so we thought. In early May we replanted five reserved tubers to perpetuate the patch. By mid-June, however, a dozen or more sunflower stalks were pushing strongly out of the ground. The warning: Jerusalem artichokes have a determined ability to sprout from every fragment of broken tuber. Needless to say, if you take a rototiller ripping through the patch, you'll be coping with the scattered volunteers forever after. Even as early as 1833, one William Cobbett was complaining, "This plant . . . to the great misfortune of the human race, is everywhere but too well known." With a little care, it is not too difficult to keep a patch under control: A dig in time saves a lot of work later on. Every spring we make

an effort to dig up every last tuber. If we uncover more than we can use or give away, we dump the surplus in a back field, well away from the garden, for the wild creatures to munch. Never put Jerusalem artichokes in the compost. We still replant the usual five tubers every May, but now we're not so shocked when quite a few more pop up on their own.

There is no trick to growing Jerusalem artichokes: For an average family, three to five plants should be enough. Plant whole or cut tubers in early spring or fall, setting them 4 inches (10 cm) deep and 1 to 2 feet (30 to 60 cm) apart in a sunny spot, in reasonably good, well-drained soil. Sandy ground enables the tuber to fill out better. At over 6 feet (1.8 m) tall, the plants are well placed along the sunny side of an outbuilding or shed, where they have genuine decorative value. Harvest some tubers in fall. Mulch the patch to protect tubers over winter for another harvest in early spring. Tubers keep much better in the ground than out, so dig only what you need for a feed. Keep an eye on the patch for signs of expansionism. That done, you can count on a perennial supply of nutritious, tasty tubers just at the time they are most appreciated.

At the tail end of winter a body craves something fresh and lively; and what better spring tonic than root vegetables and greens that come straight from earth to table. Eaten raw, steamed, baked, and in soups, Jerusalem artichokes are a welcome addition to the garden's early menu of wintered-over parsnips and carrots, tangy sorrel and dandelion greens, wild leeks and watercress, asparagus, and the new shoots of perennial onions and herbs. Considered an excellent substitute for potatoes in a diabetic's diet, the tubers contain no starch; instead, they store sweetness as levulose, a form tolerated by the sugar-sensitive. As well, they are one of the few vegetable sources of vitamin B_{12}, or pantothenic acid.

The lack of starch means that an overboiled 'choke is soggy, bland, and unappealing. Steamed just to the point of tenderness, their mild nutty sweetness comes through. Raw 'chokes have a refreshing crispness reminiscent of Chinese water chestnuts. A simple spring salad combines grated carrots and artichokes with watercress and minced wild leeks (or chives); dress with a lemon-and-oil vinaigrette seasoned with sorrel, lovage, lemon thyme, or whatever garden-fresh herbs you have.

We couldn't get a hold of the Queen's recipe, but how about a sweet and creamy soup featuring a trio of spring roots — parsnips, carrots, and artichokes — with a hint of curry and toasted almonds.

SORREL

At spring's first softening, light-green, puckered sorrel leaves begin to sprout. Growing unattended for many years in the dappled shade of an open-topped apple tree, our single clump provides all the sorrel we need for six months and more.

I'm never sure whether to call this plant herb or a vegetable. Like any herb, the sharp, lemony leaves season salads, omelets, and soup. Finely minced with chives, lemon thyme, and chervil, sorrel turns plain cream cheese into a special spread. I like the suggestion of adding puréed sorrel to mayonnaise as a sauce for fish, hot or cold; and using a little chopped sorrel to season for the lack of salt in a sodium-restricted diet. Then again, like carrots or broccoli, sorrel is featured as a solo vegetable in a creamy soup. Steamed with a bit of butter, a potful of leaves cooks down like spinach; cream and garlic, grated Parmesan, and bread crumbs mellow the acidic bite. Then there is the simple pleasure of munching the refreshing vinegary leaves as you work in the garden.

Native to Britain, the original skinny-leaved sorrel, *Rumex acetosa*, was adopted by enthusiastic French cooks as *l'oseille* and transformed by French gardeners into fancy, broad-leaved cultivars such as "Blond de Lyon" and "Nobel." Seeds or small nursery plants will get you started. The surest way with seeds is to start them in early spring in 3- or 4-inch (8- or 10-cm) pots set in a sunny window or cold frame. Sow a half-dozen seeds in each container, and thin eventually to the strongest single seedling in each. Transfer the young plants to the garden when they look large enough to fend for themselves. I can't imagine any household needing more than three sorrel plants, but a single clump can be conjured into several more by dividing the roots just as new growth resumes in spring. Pry the plant out of the soil with a spading fork; bounce it a few times on the ground to shake away some of the earth, the better to see where the dividing line naturally occurs. Use a sharp knife and pruning shears to sever the ties that bind, and replant divisions.

Like all plants cultivated for their leaves, sorrel responds to moist, organically fertile soil with lush, tender growth. To that end, we turn under several shovels of compost or aged manure for each plant, and surround the clumps with a moisture-holding mulch of straw, leaves, or compost. With a preference for cooler weather, sorrel is at its tart best for weeks in spring. The long hot days around the summer solstice trigger the formation of seed stalks and tough, harsh leaves. No matter: We never miss sorrel when the garden is full of other food. Experts suggest cutting off seed stalks, but we've found that there is no way to prevent the plants from heeding nature's call sooner or later. Rather we let them go, cutting back in midsummer before seeds have had a chance to ripen and scatter. There is no point encouraging yet another self-inflicted weed. Once it is trimmed up, sorrel starts growing fresh, tender leaves again and continues well into fall. I like what one garden book has to say about pests and disease that might afflict sorrel: "None of note."

Sorrel may strike a sour note on the tongue, but, according to folk medicine, its acidic property acts as a "general tonic for the liver." I like to think that it is no coincidence that sorrel sprouts so early in spring, just when a tonic is most needed to remedy the winter blahs. What better way to take your tonic/medicine than as a hot bowl of sorrel and wild leek soup?

It's curious how the pendulum of fashion swings. Until the seventeenth century, sorrel was a popular kitchen-garden inhabitant in Britain. It then began to fall from favor, until, by the nineteenth century, it was found "only on fashionable tables." Nowadays, sorrel seems to be more trendy than commonplace, but there is no reason why this stalwart perennial shouldn't return to kitchen gardens everywhere.

17

THE FRUITFUL SEASON
Strawberries and Raspberries

Is there a gardener who doesn't yearn to grow fruit? The longing seems almost instinctive. I wonder if it has something to do with images of the mythic Eden, a peaceful paradise shaded by fruit-laden trees growing beside a sparkling stream. Bright colors, tastes bordering on the heavenly: fruit seems to be nature at her most extravagant and generous, playful almost.

When my friend and I came to the country, we looked over the wide sunny field that we hoped to transform into a down-to-earth version of paradise and, in imagination, we filled the space with fruiting plants. With the enthusiasm of new gardeners — and visions of sugar plums, peaches, pears, apricots, and cherries dancing in our heads — we cleared circles of quack grass, dug holes, and planted a dozen dwarf fruit trees. Setting out a line of dry sticks with roots along a new post-and-wire fence, we pictured the future grapevines, precisely pruned, heavy with purple, red, and green clusters. We planted brambles, currant bushes, and strawberries.

Our innocent notion that we could have fruit for the planting soon came a cropper at the hand of reality. Out in that wind-swept field, all the grapevines died the first winter. The few trees that survived failed (as they say) to thrive. Gradually, however, we discovered what tree fruit would "do" here — apples, sour cherries, certain

plums and pears — how to prune, what to spray and when. We found, too, that they fared much better within the protective bounds of the kitchen garden where we could keep an eye on them. We learned to plant grapes against a south-facing stone wall for warmth and shelter, and to bend the vines to the ground for winter protection. Fruit takes time, attention, skill, study, and patience — not to forget that unavoidable aspect of all post-paradise gardening, the "sweat of your brow," which is no reason to throw up your hands and say forget it.

STRAWBERRIES

An encouraging note in all that early fruitlessness was the strawberry patch. In June in the kitchen garden, lettuce, spinach, scallions, radishes, and other early greens are ready, but most of the beds are showing more promise than produce. With one notable exception: A heady fragrance rises from the place where strawberries — the season's first fruit and, some would say, its best — are ripening. Sunrise finds us in the patch, searching the dangling bunches for berries that have reached their ruby peak. Early botanists were so smitten with the scent of strawberries that they named the genus *Fragaria*, the fragrant ones.

Strawberries recommend themselves to home gardeners as the best choice of fruit for several reasons. First, the small plants are well suited to culture in wide, raised beds alongside the likes of lettuce, beans, and beets. Indeed, as one expert

Sweet rewards from the home garden: a bowl of perfectly ripe, pesticide-free strawberries. What could be better for a snack right in the garden?

Nursery Stock

Once started with strawberries — and assuming the patch stays healthy — a gardener can perpetuate them indefinitely by periodic renewal. First-time growers, however, must avail themselves of nursery stock, either through the mail or from a garden center. What you'll receive are tight bundles of 25 or 50 dryish small tufts with withered leaves attached to limp, pale roots — not very promising. If you cannot get plants into the ground the day they arrive, you're advised to keep the unopened bags in the refrigerator for no more than three days. To store the plants any longer, hoe open a shallow, V-shaped trench in the garden, separate the bundle into individual plants and line them out, side by side, with roots pressed flat against one side of the trench, and crowns above ground. Pull earth over the roots, covering them completely, and tamp by hand or with the back of a rake for firm root/soil contact; water well. The same process, called heeling-in, is used to hold any bare root nursery stock, from raspberries to roses, for a week or two before they are moved to a permanent home.

Ground Work

If you are breaking new ground for a strawberry bed, give yourself a full season to dig and redig the space, rounding up every scrap of quack grass, bindweed, thistle, and such as you go. Once perennial weeds have crept in among the berry plants, you'll be hard-pressed to root them out totally. The steps outlined for preparing a new asparagus bed apply here. Better yet, use an established kitchen-garden bed that has had the benefit of years of weed clearing and organic improvement.

Any soil short of dry sand or water-logged clay will grow strawberries. Keep in mind, though, that the small plants have a ravenous appetite for organic matter, and what they relish most is barnyard manure. A slightly acidic soil pH of between 5 and 6.5 is best, so lime is not needed, unless the site is very sour. New strawberries are planted in early spring, traditionally "when the deciduous trees are beginning to leaf out." I like to prepare a bed the fall before, digging or tilling in at least

Early spring is the time to set out new strawberry plants. Over the summer, runners will fill in the bare spaces with young daughter plants.

(from Britain's Royal Horticultural Society) notes, "strawberries are best grown with the vegetables" where they can be shifted from one bed to another every few years. Strawberries are quick to grow: plant dormant nursery stock in early spring and you can expect a fulsome harvest about fourteen months later; move some of your own best plants to a new bed in August, and you'll be picking next June. And they are productive: according to one study, four 25-foot (7.5-m) rows should yield "3 quarts of berries a day over a period of 3 weeks."

Strawberries are possibly the easiest of fruit to grow. Given a modicum of attention, they usually flourish — and spread. Like a green octopus, each plant sends out a criss-crossing network of wiry runners; some end in a single new tuft; others trail on to sprout a string of plants. The most puzzling aspect of strawberry culture is what to do with the surplus. Leave them alone and they eventually form a dense groundcover showing more leaves and less fruit.

3 inches (8 cm) of year-old cattle or horse manure, which continues to mellow and decay over winter, leaving the earth in fine shape by planting time. Compost, spent mushroom medium, and partially decayed leaves are excellent alternatives (or additions) to manure. Abundant organic matter translates directly into a more bountiful crop. Before planting in spring, we broadcast a measured amount of balanced natural fertilizer and scuffle it into the top few inches — strawberries are shallow rooted compared to many plants — before raking the bed level and smooth.

Planting

Having endured a trip through the mail or weeks on a garden-center shelf, strawberry plants are revived by an hour-long soak in a bucket of water prior to planting. Strawberries are extremely sensitive to the depth at which they are set in the earth. As one expert warns, "Half an inch either way will seriously restrict . . . future growth." Look for the point where leaves sprout, and position plants so that this point, the crown, is level with the soil surface. See, too, that all roots extend down into the ground without bunching or bending upward; you may have to trim the odd one. I have a pint-sized digger, halfway between a trowel and a spade, that makes short work of strawberry holes, which I excavate all at once, assembly-line style, before starting to plant. Cover roots completely, firm soil around them, and drench. Once the water has drained, go over the patch and gently ease up any plants that have been sucked too deep by the draining water. After a few hours, or the next day, scratch lightly around each plant, leaving a thin layer of loose soil.

Pinching Blossoms

Now comes the hard job. Newly set strawberry plants usually start to flower within a few weeks. For their own good, and to stimulate the growth of runners that will bear heavily next summer, we're told to nip all first-season blossoms in the bud. Note, however, that this applies only to June bearers, by far the most widely grown type of strawberry. If you have planted everbearers or day-neutral strawberries (see below), stop pinching

An everbearing strawberry shows every stage from flowers to ripe fruit all at once.

buds toward the end of June; chances are you'll reap a modest late-summer harvest.

Mulch

No one knows for sure where the strawberry got its name, whether originally *strew-* or *stray*-berry from its wandering ways, or whether *straw* refers to the tradition of spreading barley or wheat straw beneath the plants to cushion the delicate fruit. In any case, a permanent mulch of straw, leaves, old sawdust, pine needles, even shredded cornstalks saves a fair bit of weeding and watering, and keeps the berries off the ground. In a slug-infested garden, though, I'd choose clean cultivation and traps over mulch. Weeds can soon crowd new berry plants, stealing their food, water, and sunlight. Whenever we attend to training runners, picking blossoms, or spreading mulch, we do a round of weeding. If you're the kind of gardener who thinks weeds are part of the garden's

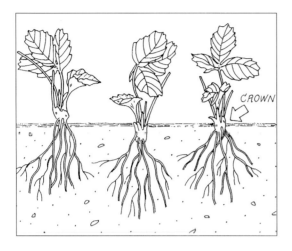

Strawberry plants are very sensitive to depth of planting. See that plants are positioned so that crowns — the point where leaves sprout — are level with the soil surface, not too high nor too deep.

natural balance, think twice before planting strawberries, or any perennial for that matter.

The Hill System

The most impressive strawberry bed I've ever seen belongs to a neighbor who sets her original plants 1 foot (30 cm) apart in compost-rich soil, mulches them heavily with maple leaves, and conscientiously cuts off all runners before they roam too far. This practice, called the hill system, sends all of the juice to the mother plants, which wax into robust clumps loaded with fruit. As soon as the last berry is picked, she shears off all of the leafy top growth, replenishes the mulch with compost or more leaves, and continues to watch for stray runners. To extend or renew the planting, she allows some runners to root down in 3-inch (8-cm) earth-filled flower pots sunk in the ground up to their rims. Rooting accomplished, she severs the cord linking mother and daughter and transplants the young one elsewhere.

Strawberry Geometry (or Spaced Matted Row)

Needing almost daily attention, this strict scheme is not for laissez-faire gardeners (or lazy-fair-

weather ones). The opposite approach, called the matted-row system, is to let all the runners root, but what you gain in time you lose in berries. We've settled, at least in theory, on a compromise between nipping every runner and total hands-off. The result is a modified or spaced matted row, once called a hedgerow.

Starting with a typical 4 foot (1.2 m) by 25 foot (7.5 m) kitchen-garden bed, we set out two rows of strawberry plants. The rows are measured 1 foot (30 cm) in from the edge of the bed, 2 feet (60 cm) apart. Within the rows, plants are spaced 2 feet apart. During their first season, we allow each mother to produce four runners. Two are trained to fill the gaps along the rows; the other two are stretched out to either side to start two more lines parallel to the original rows. The next year, as the original mothers and their daughters are fruiting, new runners are coaxed into empty spaces, leaving plants 8 to 10 inches (20 to 25 cm) apart over the whole bed. All unwanted runners are cut away. After the mother plants have fruited for a year or two, we dig them out and encourage new ones to take their place.

That's the theory. In practice, the strawberry bed usually falls into chaos and congestion after three or four years. And we are left scratching our heads, wondering "who's offa who" (as an old neighbor says when trying to sort out the family ties of folks around him), which are the mother plants, grandmothers, daughters, and how on earth we'll get rid of all that bindweed. When that happens, it's time for a fresh start, and that, alas, means tearing up the old patch.

Renewal

Rooting out and composting hundreds of healthy strawberry plants feels like the opposite of gardening, but when we remember how bounteous the patch used to be, the big luscious berries compared to the current small crop of undersized fruit, we're motivated to dig. Not, however, before we carefully pry up as many young plants as needed to start over someplace else. Keeping a ball of earth intact around their roots, we set the plants, as before, in a fresh weedless bed that has been generously enriched with compost, manure, and natural fertilizer. The job can be done anytime from July to September, always remembering that newly set plants respond to frequent waterings in the heat and drought of summer. At any season, a cooling mulch is very much to their liking, but mulch is a must for strawberries shifted in September to keep them in the ground during the coming cycles of freeze-and-thaw.

Aftercare / Renovation / Drastic Measures

When our friend shears back her plants after they have fruited, she is following the most drastic method of strawberry renovation — and, by all accounts, the most effective. Here goes: The day after you pick the last berry — time is of the essence, here — set the lawn mower to its highest cut and run it over the patch, cutting off all foliage. In a small patch use a sickle or shears. Rake up the leaves for compost. Now is the time to dig out all unwanted plants, leaving the remainder no more than a hand-span apart. Pull up overgrown older clumps rather than vigorous younger plants. You may need to position stakes and string to bring the berry patch into line; fork out any runners that have strayed beyond the boundaries of the bed or row. I always feel like an ogre tearing through the strawberries like that, but if I think of the excess plants as compost fodder, it's not so bad.

Thinning completed, spread the required amount of natural fertilizer for the size of the patch. We use either a commercial fertilizer with a balance of nutrients, or our own rich compost or rotted manure — sometimes all three! A newly renovated bed looks bald and patchy. But soak it thoroughly, spread more mulch if you have it, and you'll be pleasantly surprised at how quickly things green up. Before long, the strawberries are off and running again.

The dramatic makeover just described applies only to June-bearing strawberries, those that ripen all their fruit over a few weeks in late spring. Everbearers, which yield a light first harvest in June and a smattering of berries throughout the summer, respond nicely to the hill system of culture: set the plants a foot apart and remove the few runners that form unless they are needed to

As soon as fruiting is over, cut away all strawberry foliage, thin the patch, fertilize, and renew the mulch. The comeback will be dramatic.

increase or renew a patch. Although we grow a small bed of everbearers, we would never trade their on-again, off-again habit for the June-bearers that bring in a satisfying bumper crop at a time when garden fruit is most appreciated.

Recently another type of strawberry, the day-neutral, has been causing a stir among commercial growers and home gardeners alike. Flowering and fruiting almost non-stop from spring until fall, regardless of the changing day length that affects the others, day-neutrals such as "Tribute" and "Tristar" are said to taste better than everbearers and out-yield June-bearers. All that production and flavor, however, depends on a constant supply of plant food and moisture. Plan to pour on fish (or seaweed) emulsion or manure tea every other week, and keep the clumps top-dressed with your best compost. Day-neutral strawberries are not as hardy as the old June standbys, but they survive even a prairie winter with adequate protection.

Because new cultivars are always being introduced and some do better in one region than in another, I hesitate to recommend specific strawberry varieties. Local fruit experts, whether at a university, county extension office, or garden center, as well as current gardening magazines, make it their business to keep abreast. We make our choice from catalogs that originate in a climate zone similar to our own. What we look for can be summed up as disease resistance — no point in tempting fate — and excellent flavor. Commercial growers can have the firm, flawless beauties, all glossy red surface and little taste, that travel the continent with never a bruise. But give this gardener melt-in-the-mouth, close-your-eyes berries that ooze juice and recall the intense essence of tiny wild strawberries in the meadow beyond.

Frost Warning

Strawberries should be in the sun, and if possible, in an area where late-spring frosts are not known to settle. It happens every year: just when the strawberries are full of flowers, the wind shifts into the north, bringing a last blast of arctic air. By evening all is calm and you can almost smell the impending frost. Out come blankets, sheets, big towels, anything to throw over the blooming berry bed. It's time well spent. Frost does no harm to the plants, but it strikes at the heart of strawberry blossoms, leaving them black — and a blackened blossom means no fruit.

Strawberries of all kind fare better with some protection over winter wherever the temperature falls into the frigid digits (below 20°F/–7°C) and the snow comes and goes. The goal is to keep extreme cold from blasting the buds that are hidden in the plants' heart. Mid-November or later, after a freeze or two has triggered dormancy, is soon enough to cover the patch; the delay allows plants time to form a few extra flower buds during the warmth of Indian summer. At this point, we spread mulch not just around plants, but over them. Choose pine needles, straw, evergreen boughs, armloads of leaves, or any other fluffy organic matter laid on about 3 inches (8 cm) deep. We have a neighbor with a barn full of ten-year-old hay, free for the taking; the old stuff seems to harbor very few weed seeds compared to newly cut.

Come spring, when the first snowdrops and early crocuses are out, we rearrange the hay, snugging it around the plants and piling the leftover on the pathways. A strawberry, they say,

should be picked with its green cap attached. This is one rule we feel free to ignore as we breakfast in the strawberry bed, reclining, Roman style, on the hay-cushioned path. Decadent? Not at all. The gentle June sun, the mingled scents of hay and berries and earth, the sweet-tart taste of ripe fruit are innocent pleasures all.

RASPBERRIES

Raspberries are among the most delicate and delicious of fruit. Never abundant in markets, they are almost always expensive. Anyone considering growing their own ought to know two more things. First, while raspberries' roots are perennial, the canes — what you see above ground — are biennial. This means that, each summer, raspberries send up a number of new shoots, called primocanes; but it is not until the following year that these canes, now called floricanes, branch out, flower, and set fruit. Their mission accomplished, they gradually die back. All of this is happening at once: In a given year, some canes will be shooting upward, others fruiting, and — unless a gardener steps in with pruning shears — still others will be dying back.

The second thing to know about raspberries is that their roots have no intention of staying where you put them. In our garden, suckers routinely travel more than 5 feet (1.5 m) under a well-trodden path to get into the rich soil of a perennial flowerbed across the way. If it weren't for its berries, this prickly, invasive bramble would be classed as a bad weed.

The big pricetag on a small box of raspberries reflects not only the fragility of the fruit but also the work involved in raising the canes. Low-maintenance they are not. And yet, we persist in pruning, pulling up suckers, and protecting the canes over the winter for the pleasure of grazing on the aromatic berries for a few weeks in July.

Ground Work

The most fruitful approach to raspberry culture — thorough soil preparation — is also the most time-consuming at the start. Consider, however, that a patch may be in place for ten years or more.

A good start not only pays off handsomely in berries, it also reduces care and maintenance for years to come. As with asparagus and strawberries, it is crucial that the future raspberry bed be completely free of perennial weeds. Dig the space over once, and remove all the roots you unearth; wait a few weeks to see what sprouts, then dig again to catch the strays. Repeat.

Once the land is clean, it's time to add as much organic matter as you can spare. Raspberries thrive in slightly acidic soil (pH 6.0 to 6.7) that retains ample moisture but drains well; standing water can injure or kill roots. All soil, whether light and sandy or dense with clay, responds to an organic menu of decayed manures, compost, rotted leaves, extra-old sawdust, and such, applied with a generous hand. One expert recommends 1 to 2 tons of well-rotted manure, and a heavy application of rock phosphate, rototilled into a 4 foot (1.2 m) by 100 foot (30 m) bed.

On a smaller scale, I like the traditional English method of preparing a raspberry bed. First, mark off a 2-foot-wide (60-cm-wide) band with stakes and string. The length depends on your garden space, but consider that an established 25-foot (7.5-m) row — a mere dozen plants to start — should yield berries enough for four in a good year. Remove the soil, down to the depth of a spade, along the band and pile it to one side. Fork into the trench a 3- to 4-inch (8- to 10-cm) layer of old manure and/or compost. Whiten the surface of the organic stuff with bone meal and/or rock phosphate and stir the works into the bottom of the trench, mixing it thoroughly with the soil. Return the topsoil, mixed with additional fine-textured organic matter if you have it. Before raking, sprinkle on a measured amount of a balanced natural fertilizer. Parallel rows should be spaced 6 to 8 feet (1.8 to 3 m) apart, center to center, and should, if possible, run north and south so as not to shade each other.

Planting

New raspberry canes are best planted in early spring. Ours usually arrive in the mail looking the worse for the trip — a bundle of prickly, dead-looking sticks with a beard of dry roots. To revive them, we soak the roots in a pail of cool water for several hours prior to planting. Never leave plants lying around uncovered in the sun; one good drying could weaken roots beyond recovery. I like to dig all the holes at once, spacing them 2 feet (60 cm) apart, and making them deep and wide enough so that I can spread the roots out naturally and cover them with about 3 inches (8 cm) of earth. This slightly deeper planting is said to inhibit the rise of suckers — and raspberries can stand a little slowing down. Firm soil around roots with gloved fingers or a blunt stick, then pour on the water to saturate the root zone. Trim any long canes back to 4-inch (10-cm) stubs. Once new shoots sprout, cut these stubs right to the ground.

Mulch, and More Mulch

The next step, mulching, is the best thing you can do for a raspberry patch over the long term. See that mulch does not touch newly planted canes, but lay it on thickly as the patch gets established. A permanent deep mulch might be 5 to 10 inches (12 to 25 cm) of old straw or last fall's leaves; or half that amount of strawy manure, well-aged sawdust, shredded bark, or wood chips. Fresh wood byproducts, however, need an admixture of nitrogen; otherwise they steal more nutrients than they supply in the process of breaking down. Mix fresh sawdust with an equal amount of manure, or dust the soil with blood meal — 2 pounds (0.9 kg) per 25-foot (7.5-m) row — before applying. If all of this sounds overly complicated, bear in mind that a permanent mulch of deciduous leaves, usually abundant and always free, supplies all the nutrients that raspberries need.

Pruning
Spring and Summer

There is no way around it. Twice a year, the raspberries must be pruned, a task we approach with impenetrable gloves and strong shears. In spring, as canes are leafing out, we cut away dead canes and any winter-killed tips, as well as weak, spindly, and damaged shoots. We then thin the remainder, leaving the strongest canes standing

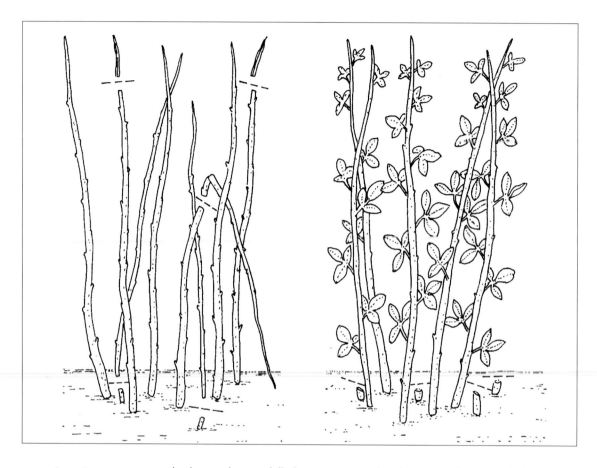

In spring, prune away broken and winter-killed canes or tips. Thin the remainder to stand about 4 inches (10 cm) apart, cutting out the weak and spindly canes. In summer, after all berries have been picked, cut at ground level all canes that have borne fruit.

about 4 inches (10 cm) apart. It's not easy to cut out fine-looking canes, but steel yourself and thin them. What we don't do is cut back the tops of live canes unless they are waving around in the air out of reach. Given enough moisture and fertility, raspberries will flower and fruit right to their tips.

The next major pruning, in July, comes immediately after the berries have been picked. This is the time to cut all canes that have finished fruiting right back to ground level; do not leave stubs, an inviting breeding ground for bugs and blights. For the health of the patch, the cut-away canes should be burned or disposed of at some distance — they are not compost material. This second pruning is crucial. Dying canes are easy targets for diseases that are then spread to the rest. Of course, suckers that have strayed beyond the allotted raspberry row must be yanked out as weeds.

Fall Pruning

Like strawberries, various raspberry cultivars bear fruit at different times. The pruning methods detailed above apply to the so-called June-bearers, which actually fruit in July in most areas. These are the most widely planted type of raspberry.

Fall-bearers, in contrast, yield a modest crop from August to October at the tops of first-year canes and more berries on the same canes next year. There are two possible approaches to pruning fall-bearing raspberries. Once they have fruited, you can cut away the tops, leaving the rest of the cane to flower and fruit the following July like a "normal" raspberry. Alternatively, treat the canes as annuals, cutting them right to the ground in late fall or early winter — there will be no prickly shoots to protect and nothing but stubble showing in the patch over winter. In spring, new canes will rise up vigorously and, by late summer, you're in the berries again. "Heritage" is a popular fall raspberry; fruiting rather late in the season, it is not suited to regions where cold summers are the rule and frost strikes in September. Both "August Red" and "Fall Red" are earlier. A lovely, sweet amber berry, "Fall Gold" is vigorous and early. In cold areas it must have winter protection; it is also apt to be slowed by viruses. As with strawberries, choose varieties that are adapted to your area. Plants from an established nursery should be certified disease-free. Avoid starting with suckers from a neighbor's patch, or propagating your own raspberries, if the canes show any signs of wilt, mold, or diseases.

Water Ways

For best yield, raspberries need a steady supply of food and water. Once the spring pruning is done, we like to rake back the mulch and spread a few inches of aged manure or rich compost in a wide band on either side of the row. Lacking that, apply a fertilizer high in phosphorus and potash before replacing the mulch.

Well-mulched raspberries may get by nicely on rainfall alone. Water is especially necessary during blossoming and fruit formation. If rains fail then, soak the ground every five days or so.

Untrained Canes

Books abound with elaborate methods of training and supporting raspberries: single or double fences, Scandinavian style, the single-post system. The various setups of posts and wire look neat and professional — and we mean to try them one of these days — but until then, we'll grow raspberries, as we have for years, without support. We have many neighbors, too, who grow long rows of freestanding canes to one side of their big farm gardens. It is our experience that raspberry canes, properly pruned and thinned, are sturdy enough to hold themselves up; if they do loll over a pathway, a temporary arrangement of stakes and strong string is enough to hold them back. Truth is, the only place I've seen those tidy trellised raspberries is in books — to which I refer you.

Down for the Winter

Where winters are bitter — and especially in places where cold drying winds howl across the land — raspberries come through in better condition if the pliable canes are bent gently as close to the ground as possible in late fall. We hold them down with lengths of two-by-four; some growers heap soil over the cane tops, or ease the canes over in bundles and secure them with stout wire hoops pushed deeply into the ground. The arched interlaced shoots catch the snow, the best insulation for any perennial. When the snow melts in March, we remove the boards and watch the canes spring back upright.

Raspberries may not be for every garden or every gardener. The canes take up a fair bit of space and, left unattended, they soon grow into a tangled briar patch. If I had but one bed for berries, I'd grow strawberries instead. But if you have the room, and the inclination to prune and train, the rewards are sweet. Most of our raspberries never make it to the kitchen.

APPENDIX
Seed Sources

Most of the sources on this list, except those indicated, will ship orders to both Canada and the U.S. Some require an IPRC (International Postal Reply Coupon), which is available at all post offices.

Abundant Life Seed Foundation
Box 772
Port Townsend, Washington 98368

Seeds grown by the foundation are certified organic. Catalog $1 U.S.

Alberta Nurseries & Seeds Ltd.
Box 20
Bowden, Alberta
T0M 0K0

Vegetables and herbs for cool gardens.

Allen, Sterling & Lothrop
191 U.S. Route 1
Falmouth, Maine 04105

Old favorites — seeds and tools. Catalog is $1, refundable with order. U.S. orders only.

W. Atlee Burpee Co.
300 Park Avenue
Warminster, Pennsylvania 18974

A free encyclopedic catalog. U.S. orders only.

Becker's Seed Potatoes
RR 1
Trout Creek, Ontario
P0H 2L0

Has "Banana" finger potatoes, "Urgenta" European potatoes with yellow flesh, and pink skin, "Blue Mac" Newfoundland potatoes with blue skin and white flesh, and about forty more, including varieties with scab resistance. Free catalog.

Bountiful Gardens
19550 Walker Road
Willits, California 95490

John Jeavons of Ecology Action is known for his ability to grow more organically in less space. The catalog is free to U.S. customers; Canadian customers should send $1.50 U.S.

D.V. Burrell Seed Growers Co.
P.O. Box 150
Ricky Ford, Colorado 81067

Sells vegetable seeds and specializes in melons. Free catalog.

Butterbrooke Farm
78 Barry Road
Oxford, Connecticut 06483

Tom Butterworth sells untreated, open-pollinated seeds grown organically on the farm. Price list is 50 cents. U.S. orders only.

Comstock, Ferre & Co.
263 Main Street
Old Wethersfield, Connecticut 06109

Heritage seeds and hybrids. Catalog is $1. U.S. orders only.

APPENDIX

The Cook's Garden
P.O. Box 535
Londonderry, Vermont 05148

Fifty lettuces, herbs, hard-to-find Asian and European greens and vegetable cultivars. Catalog is $1. U.S. orders only.

Corns
Route 1, Box 32
Turpin, Oklahoma 73950

Heritage corn cultivars. List is $1, refundable with order. U.S. orders only.

Dacha Barinka
46232 Strathcona Road
Chilliwack, British Columbia
V2P 3T2

Dacha Barinka offers Chinese vegetables and other unusual seeds. For a catalog, Canadian customers should send a business-size SASE; American customers should send an IPRC.

William Dam Seeds Ltd.
Highway 8, Box 8400
Dundas, Ontario
L9H 6M1

A dandy little catalog chockful of European varieties. All seed is untreated.

DeGiorgi Seed Company
4816 South 60th Street
Omaha, Nebraska 68117

A first-rate collection of vegetables and herbs. Catalog is $2. U.S. orders only.

Dill's Seed Company
RR 1
Windsor, Nova Scotia
B0N 2T0

The world's first pumpkinseed catalog, featuring everything from the tiny "Jack Be Little" to the huge "Atlantic Giant."

Dominion Seed House
115 Guelph Street
Georgetown, Ontario
L7G 4A2

Offers a comprehensive catalog that is free within Canada only.

Early's Farm & Garden Centre Inc.
2615 Lorne Avenue, Box 3024
Saskatoon, Saskatchewan
S7K 3S9

Has environmentally friendly fertilizers, sprays, and fungicides. Catalog is free in Saskatchewan, $2 elsewhere.

Ecogenesis Seeds
16 Jedburgh Road
Toronto, Ontario
M5M 3J6

Untreated vegetable seeds chosen for their ability to thrive in organic gardens. List is $1.

Fedco Seeds
52 Mayflower Hill Drive
Waterville, Maine 04901

A mix of heirloom vegetables selected for cold climates. Catalog is $1. U.S. orders only, minimum $25.

The Fish Lake Garlic Man
RR 2
Demorestville, Ontario
K0K 1W0

The price list is refundable: $2 and a SASE from Canada; $2 and a SAE from the U.S.

Garden City Seeds
1324 Red Crow Road
Victor, Montana 59875

A mix of old and new varieties, many grown organically, selected for northern gardens. Catalog is $2. U.S. orders only.

Gleckler's Seedmen
Metamora, Ohio 43540

Strange tomatoes and an extensive selection of heirloom squashes and melons. Free catalog.

The Good Earth Seed Co.
P.O. Box 5644
Redwood City, California 94063

Most of the Oriental standards. Free catalog.

The Gourmet Gardener
4000 West 126th Street
Leawood, Kansas 66209

Vegetable and herb seeds from around the world "selected primarily for flavor." Escarole, radicchio, corn salad, and more international salad fare. Catalog is $2 U.S., refundable.

Halifax Seed Co. Inc.
Box 8026
Halifax, Nova Scotia
B3K 5L8

One hundred twenty-five years of selling varieties based on their performance in Atlantic Canada. Free catalog.

Harmony Gardens
RR 3
Merrickville, Ontario
K0G 1N0

Garlic and shallots. Free price list.

Harris Seeds
P.O. Box 22960
Rochester, New York 14692-2960

New Yorker magazine editor Katharine White called Harris Seeds "my dream catalog." Free catalog. U.S. orders only.

Heirloom Seeds
Box 245
West Elizabeth, Pennsylvania 15088

Open-pollinated and heirloom vegetables. Catalog is $1 U.S., refundable.

Heritage Seed Program
RR 3
Uxbridge, Ontario
L0C 1K0

The program offers an exchange for old-fashioned, open-pollinated, and endangered seeds, as well as a thrice-yearly magazine, *Heritage Seed Program*. Regular membership is $10; fixed income $7; supporting $20; U.S. and foreign $15.

High Altitude Gardens
Box 4619-H
Ketchum, Idaho 83340

Has more than sixty tomatoes "of every shape and color imaginable" and other cold-tolerant seeds. Canadian customers should send $3 U.S. for a catalog; American customers should send $2.

Ed Hume Seeds
Box 1450
Kent, Washington 98035

Seeds for cool coastal gardens. Catalog is $1 U.S., refundable, to Canada; free for U.S. customers.

Island Seed Co. Ltd.
Box 4278, Station A
Victoria, British Columbia
V8X 3X8

A list of grassroots vegetables and flowers at low prices. Free price list.

Johnny's Selected Seeds
310 Foss Hill Road
Albion, Maine 04910

Offers one of our favorite seed catalogs — a treasure trove.

J.W. Jung Seed Co.
335 So. High Street
Randolph, Wisconsin 53957

Plants and seeds, ornamentals and vegetables. Free catalog. U.S. orders only.

Le Jardin du Gourmet
P.O. Box 75
St. Johnsbury Center, Vermont 05863

Catalog is 50¢.

D. Landreth Seed Co.

P.O. Box 6426
Baltimore, Maryland 21230

America's oldest seed company. Catalog is $2, refundable with order. U.S. orders only.

Liberty Seed Co.

P.O. Box 806
New Philadelphia, Ohio 44663

Vegetable varieties that "shine in adversity." Free catalog. U.S. orders only.

Lindenberg Seeds Ltd.

803 Princess Avenue
Brandon, Manitoba
R7A 0P5

Prairie and northern varieties at low prices. Free catalog within Canada; $1 to the U.S.

Long Island Seed Co.

1368 Flanders Road
Flanders, New York 11901

Catalog for a 25¢ stamp.

Mapple Farm

RR 1
Hillsborough, New Brunswick
E0A 1X0

Sells slips for short-season sweet potatoes. Send a SASE for price list; orders within Canada only.

McFayden Seed Co. Ltd.

Box 1800
Brandon, Manitoba
R7A 6N4

Free full-color catalog.

Mellingers Nursery

2328FW West South Range Road
North Lima, Ohio 44452-9731

The place to find the standards. Free catalog. U.S. orders only.

Mountain Seed

Box 9107
Moscow, Idaho 83843-1607

Vegetable and herb seeds for cool gardens. Catalog is $1 U.S.

Native Seeds/Search

2509 N. Campbell Avenue
Suite 325
Tucson, Arizona 85719

A nonprofit conservation organization specializing in food plants of the indigenous people and pioneers. Catalog is $1. U.S. orders only.

Ontario Seed Co. Ltd.

Box 144
330 Philip Street
Waterloo, Ontario
N2J 3Z9

A standby. Free catalog to Canada; $2 to the U.S.

Pacific Northwest Seed Co. Inc.

Box 461
Vernon, British Columbia
V1T 6M4

A good list of vegetables and herbs, including Oriental greens. Catalog is $1.

Park Seed Co.

Cokesbury Road
Greenwood, South Carolina 29647-0001

Excellent and comprehensive free catalog.

Peace Seeds

2385 S.E. Thompson Street
Corvallis, Oregon 97333

Melons and more. The catalog is a compendium of botanical information, and is $4 U.S. to Canada, $3.50 to the U.S.

The Pepper Gal

10536-119th Avenue N.
Largo, Florida 34643

A specialty catalog for pepper fans.

APPENDIX

Prairie Grown Garden Seeds
Box 118
Cochin, Saskatchewan
S0M 0L0

Send a business-size SASE for price list.

Rawlinson Garden Seed
269 College Road
Truro, Nova Scotia
B2N 2P6

Maritime-tested seeds. Free catalog to Canada,
$1 refundable to the U.S.

Richters
Box 26
Goodwood, Ontario
L0C 1A0

Canada's biggest herb house also stocks natural
fertilizers and pesticides. Catalog is $2.50.

Salt Spring Seeds
Box 33
Ganges, British Columbia
V0S 1E0

Eight varieties of garlic, plus lots of beans. Catalog
is $2.

Seeds Blum
Idaho City Stage
Boise, Idaho 83706

Specializes in open-pollinated and heirloom varieties. Catalog is $3, refundable with order. U.S.
orders only.

Shades of Harmony Seeds
Box 598
Kingston, Nova Scotia
B0P 1R0

Untreated seeds packaged in thematic sets: Tea
Garden, Gourmet Garden, Homestead Garden,
and more. Catalog is $2.

Shepherd Garden Seeds
6116 Highway 9
Felton, California 95018

An international collection of vegetables and
herbs. Catalog is $1.

Siberia Seeds
Box 3000
Olds, Alberta
T0M 1P0

Hardy tomatoes. Send a SASE for price list.

Stokes Seeds, Inc.
6009 Stokes Building
39 James Street
Box 10
St. Catharines, Ontario
L2R 6R6

A must! Free catalog.

T & T Seeds
Box 1710
Winnipeg, Manitoba
R3C 3P6

Short-season vegetables. Catalog is $1.

Territorial Seed Co.
Box 46225, Station G
Vancouver, British Columbia
V6R 4G5

Seeds for coastal gardens with relatively cool summers and warm winters. Free catalog.

Vesey's Seeds Ltd.
Box 9000
Charlottetown
York, Prince Edward Island
C0A 1P0

Seeds that excel in the Maritime climate. Free
catalog.

Stanley Zubrowski
Box 26
Prairie River, Saskatchewan
S0E 1J0

Offers twenty-five tomato varieties that have done
well in Saskatchewan. From Canada, send a large
SASE for price list; from the U.S., send $1.

INDEX

acidity in soil, 8, 96, 138, 143
acorn squash, 92
"Albina Veredun" beets, 71
alkalinity in soil, 8
alliums, 51, 53, 125-27
alpine strawberry, 25
Arugula, 117-l8
Arugula and Roquefort Salad, 123
ashes, 15-16, 42, 73
asparagus, 129-32
asters, 34

Bacillus thuringiensis, 43, 51,
    64, 90
bacteria in soil, 7, 14, 95
"Banana" potatoes, 74
barriers for insects, 42
Batavia lettuce, 58
beans, 95-99
bed gardening, 19-25
bees, 102-03
beets, 69, 70-72
beginning gardeners: tips for, 21
"Beurre de Rocquefort" beans, 96
bindweed, 44
"Black-seeded Simpson"
    lettuce, 57
blanching: cauliflower, 65;
    endive, 112, 113
blood meal, 13, 15, 17, 42
blossom-end rot, 83
blueberries, 8
bolting to seed, 118
bone meal, 15, 125
borers, 90, 95
brassicas, 61-65, 110, 114, 119
"Brigus" potatoes, 74

broadcasting fertilizers, 16
broccoli, 27, 28, 33, 34, 35, 36,
    43, 45, 61-62, 65
Brussels sprouts, 27, 62, 65
bulbs: Florence fennel, 118-19;
    garlic, 126; onion sets, 51-52
"Burbee's Golden" beets, 70
bush beans. *See* snap beans
"Bush Blue Lake" beans, 96
"Buttercrunch" lettuce, 57
buttercup squash, 92
butterhead lettuce, 57-58
butternut squash, 92

cabbage, 34, 35, 36, 43, 61,
    62, 64: Chinese cabbage,
    116-17
"Canasta" lettuce, 58
canes, 142-45
cantaloupes, 101-05
"Caribe" potatoes, 74
carrots, 67-70
cat-facing, 83
catnip, 103
cauliflower, 62, 65
cedar leaf spray, 43
celery, 118
chamomile tea, 29
"Champion" radishes, 73
Champlain, Samuel de, 133
chard. *See* Swiss chard
chemical fertilizers, 14
"Cherokee Wax" beans, 96
"Cherry Belle" radishes, 73
chicory, 121
Chinese cabbage, 110-11
Chinese white radishes, 112

"Chiogga" beets, 71
clay soil, 9-10, 35, 59, 98
cold frames, 33-35
cole crops, 61-65
Colorado potato beetles, 41, 43,
    75-76, 83
companion planting, 41
composting, 10-15, 17; squash,
    94-95
containers for seedlings, 28-29, 32
corn, 45, 87-90
corn salad, 118
cos lettuce, 58
cranberries, 8
crisphead lettuce, 58
Cucumber and Yogurt Salad, 107
cucumber beetles, 103, 106-07
cucumbers, 45, 105-07
cultivation, 45
curing: garlic bulbs, 126;
    onions, 52
cutworms, 36-37, 51, 61, 106

daikon, 111-12
damping-off spores, 29
dandelions, 121
day-neutral strawberries, 141
deer, 42
"Delicata" squash, 92
"Derby" beans, 96
determinate types of tomatoes, 82
diatomaceous earth, 43
diseases: beans, 98; beets, 72;
    corn, 90; cucumber, 106-07;
    melons, 103; tomatoes, 81-82
"Double Treat" corn, 88
"Dragon Tongue" beans, 96

INDEX

drought, 83
dust mulch, 59, 70

"Earlivee II" corn, 88
"Early Butternut Hybrid"
    squash, 92
"Early Cascade" tomatoes, 81
"Early Girl" tomatoes, 81
"Early Jersey Wakefield"
    cabbage, 61
earthing-up: mustard greens, 119;
    tomatoes, 82
earthworms, 13, 14, 23
earwigs, 27, 37, 42, 64, 69, 111,
    119, 122
earworms, 90
"Easter Egg" radishes, 73
Eggplant Terrine, 85
eggplants, 27, 33, 35, 79,
    83-85, 118
Egyptian onions, 127
elephant garlic, 126-27
"Emperor" broccoli, 62
endive, 112-14
escarole, 112, 115
eyes on potatoes, 75

fall: clean up, 41; composting
    process, 11-12; frost protec-
    tion for tomatoes, 83;
    midsummer seeding for
    eating in, 109-15, 118-19;
    peppers and eggplants, 85;
    planting garlic, 125; pruning
    raspberries, 144-45
"Fall Gold" raspberries, 145
Feldsalat, 118
fertility zone, 92, 111
fertilizing, 14-17
filet beans, 96
finocchio, 118-19
flats, 29-32
flea beetles, 51, 73, 111, 112, 114,
    117, 120, 122
floating row covers, 42, 64
Florence fennel, 118-19
"Florida Broad Leaf" mustard,
    119-20
flowers: melons, 102-03;
    strawberries, 139
fluorescent lights, 33
"Formanova" beets, 71
"Four Seasons" lettuce, 58

"French Breakfast" radishes, 73
French Crisp lettuce, 58
French Intensive Method, 23
frisée, 112, 115
frost proofing, 39-40; endive, 113;
    melons, 102; strawberries, 142;
    tomatoes, 83
fungus, 50, 103, 123
Fusarium wilt, 103, 106

garden fabric, 40, 95, 103, 106,
    120, 123
garlic, 125-27
garlic spray, 42-43
"German Fingerling" potatoes, 74
"Green Crop" beans, 96
"Green Hokkaido" squash, 92
"Green Ice" lettuce, 58
"Green-in-Snow" mustard,
    119, 120
greensand, 15
"Green Wave" mustard, 120
ground-up bone, 15
"Guilio" radicchio, 121

handpicking insects, 41, 98
harvesting: arugula, 118;
    asparagus, 132; beans, 99;
    broccoli, 65; Brussels sprouts,
    65; cabbages, 64-65; carrots
    and parsley, 70; cauliflower,
    65; corn, 90; corn salad, 118;
    cucumbers, 107; Florence
    fennel, 119; garlic, 125-26;
    Jerusalem artichokes, 134;
    kale, 65; kohlrabi, 65;
    leeks, 54; lettuce, 59;
    melons, 103-05; onions, 52;
    oriental radishes, 112;
    peas, 18; potatoes, 76;
    rutabagas, 114; spinach, 50-51;
    squash, 95; tomatoes, 83
Healthy Garden Handbook, 41
heat for seedlings, 32-33;
    melons, 102
heeling-in, 138
herbs, 41, 42
"Heritage" raspberries, 145
hill system: strawberries, 140
"Honey Delight" squash, 92
hornworms, 83
hubbard squash, 92
humus, 10, 44, 107

indeterminate tomatoes, 82
insecticidal soap, 37, 42, 43,
    64, 69
insects, 40-44, 113. See also pest
    control
intensive gardening, 23, 98
intermediate lettuces, 58
"Ithaca M.I." lettuce, 58

Jerusalem artichokes, 133-35

kale, 25, 35, 62, 65
kelp meal, 15, 17
kohlrabi, 35, 62, 65

lamb's lettuce, 118
leaf miners, 123
leaves: as fertilizer, 13; wilting, 45
Leek and Potato Soup, 76
leeks, 27, 34, 53-54; wild leeks, 127
Leeks and White Beans
    Vinaigrette, 55
legume inoculant, 95
"Lemon Boy" tomatoes, 81
lettuce, 27, 28, 33, 34, 35,
    36, 57-60
"Lettucy Type" Chinese cabbage,
    110
lighting for seedlings, 33
lime, 8-9
"Little Gem" lettuce, 58
live traps, 42
loam, 9-10
"Lollo Rossa" lettuce, 57
"Long Season" beets, 71
looseleaf lettuce, 57

mâche, 118
manure, 13, 89
"Marbel" beans, 96
Marinated Beets, 76-77
"Marketmore 80" cucumbers, 105
matted-row system, 140
"Medusa" radicchio, 121
melons, 27, 35, 101-05
Mexican bean beetle, 98
mignonette, 34
"Minnesota Midget" muskmelons,
    101
"Mizuna" mustard, 120
mold, 52
mulch, 44, 52, 59, 63-64, 95, 111,
    112, 123, 139, 141, 143

muskmelons, 101
mustard greens, 119-20

naked-seeded squash, 92
Nantes carrots, 68
nasturtiums, 103
natural fertilizers, 14-17
New Potato Salad with Herbed Dressing, 77
nitrogen, 13-14, 15, 71, 96, 113
nursery stock, 34; strawberries, 138
"Nuvol" escarole, 112

"Oakleaf" lettuce, 57
onions, 51-54, 103: Egyptian onions, 127; Spanish onions, 33, 51
organic gardening, 7, 10, 107
organic matter in soil, 9, 10, 139, 143
oriental radishes, 111-12
oriental squash, 92
ornamental edibles, 25
"Osaka Purple" mustard, 120

"Paragon" broccoli, 62
"Park's Whopper" tomatoes, 81
parsley, 33, 34
parsnips, 67-70
"Passport" watermelons, 101
Pasta Finocchio, 123
Pasta Primavera, 77
pathways, 22-23
peas, 47-50, 113
pepper squash, 92
peppers, 15, 27, 33, 35, 79, 83-85, 118
perennials, 129-35
pest control, 41-44: beans, 98-99; Chinese cabbage, 111; cole crops, 61, 63-64; corn, 90; melons, 103; onions, 52; potatoes, 75-76; radishes, 73; rutabagas, 114; spinach, 51; squash, 95; Swiss chard, 123; tomatoes, 83
pesticides, 43-44, 90
Peterson, Roger Tory, 127
pH level in soil, 8-9, 10
phosphorus, 8, 14, 15, 71, 96
"Pink Pearl" potatoes, 74

pit composting, 13-14
planting: arugula, 117-18; asparagus, 131-32; beans, 96, 98; beets, 71-72; carrots and parsnips, 68-69; chicory, 121; Chinese cabbage, 110-11; cole crops, 62-63; corn, 88-89; corn salad, 118; cucumbers, 105-06; endive and escarole, 112-14; Florence fennel, 119; garlic, 125-26; Jerusalem artichokes, 134; leeks, 53-54; lettuce, 58-59; melons, 101-02; midsummer, 109; mustard greens, 120; onions, 51-52; oriental radishes, 111-12; peas, 47-48; potatoes, 74-75; radicchio, 120-21; radishes, 72-73; raspberries, 143; sorrel, 135; spinach, 50; strawberries, 139; Swiss chard, 122-23; tomatoes, peppers and eggplants, 79-81, 83-85; turnips and rutabagas, 114
plastic sheeting, 39-40
"Platinum Lady" corn, 88
pole beans, 96, 98
pollen exchange, 101, 102-03
pollination of corn, 89
potash, 15, 71, 96
potassium, 14, 15
potato bugs, 41, 43, 75-76, 83, 98
potatoes, 73-76, 98, 129
pots, 28-29, 32
props. See supports
"Provider" beans, 96
pruning, 143-45
pumpkins, 90-95
pyrethrum, 43

rabbits, 42
raccoons, 42, 90
radicchio, 25, 120-21
radishes, 72-73; oriental radishes, 111-12
raised beds, 22-23
raspberries, 142-45
recipes: Arugula and Roquefort Salad, 123; Eggplant Terrine, 85; Leek and Potato Soup, 76; Leeks and White Beans Vinaigrette, 55; Marinated Beets, 76-77; New Potato Salad with

Herbed Dressing, 77; Pasta Finocchio, 123; Pasta Primavera, 77; Red Onion, Red Pepper and Roquefort Pizza, 85; Spinach Parmesan, 55; Tsatziki, 107; Winter Squash and Kale Pasta Sauce, 99
"Red Kuri" squash, 92
Red Onion, Red Pepper and Roquefort Pizza, 85
"Red Sails" lettuce, 57
Reemay, 40, 51
renewal of strawberries, 140-41
"Rocdor" beans, 96
rock phosphate, 14, 15, 16
romaine lettuce, 58
root maggots, 52, 61, 63-64, 114
rotenone, 43-44, 83
row planting, 19-20
"Royal Burgundy" beans, 96
"Royalty Purple Pod" beans, 96
rutabagas, 114

"Salad Bowl" lettuce, 57
"Salarite" cabbage, 61
sandy soil, 9-10, 47, 102, 134
scab resistance, 74
"Scarlet Runner" beans, 25, 98
scratcher, 45
seafood soup for transplants, 36
seeding, 27-35
seedlings, 28-29, 31-37
sets: onions, 51; potatoes, 75
sex among cantaloupes, 102-03
shallots, 127
shelling peas, 47, 49-50
side-dressing, 16-17
"Silver Queen" corn, 88
slipping cantaloupes, 104, 106
slugs, 41, 64, 122
snakes, 41
snap beans, 95-96, 98, 99
snapdragons, 34
snap peas, 48, 49-50
snow fence, 13
snow peas, 47, 49-50
sod-breaking, 21-22
soil, 7-10, 14, 20, 29
soil test, 7-8
sorrel, 135
sowing, 47
spacing plants in intensive beds, 23-24

INDEX

spaghetti squash, 92
Spanish onions, 33, 51
"Sparkler" radishes, 73
sphinx moth, 83
spinach, 50-51
Spinach Parmesan, 55
spores, 29
spot-enrichment, 16
sprays for insects, 42-43
spring: indoor seeding, 27-30, 32-35; outdoor seeding, 31; pruning raspberries, 143-44; sowing, 47; transplanting seedlings, 35-37
squash, 90-95
"Stonehead" cabbage, 61
storing: potatoes, 76; rutabagas, 114
strawberries, 137-42
suckers, 82, 143, 144
"Sugar Buns" corn, 88
"Sugar Cos" lettuce, 58
sugar enhanced corn, 88
"Sugar Snap" peas, 48, 49
sulfate of potash magnesium, 15
sulfur, 8-9
sulphate of potash, 14
summer: pruning raspberries, 144; seeding for fall eating, 109-15, 118
summer squash, 90-91, 92, 94
sunlight for seedlings, 33
"Sunshine" watermelons, 101
Supersweet corn, 88
supports: pea vines, 48-49; pole beans, 98; raspberries, 145; tomato stakes, 82
Swedes, 114
sweet corn, 88

"Sweet Dumpling" squash, 92
"Sweet Favorite" watermelons, 101
"Sweet Mama" squash, 92
"Sweet Million" tomatoes, 81
"Sweet 100" tomatoes, 81
"Sweet Slice" cucumbers, 105
sweet peas, 34
sweet potato squash, 92
Swiss chard, 25, 27, 31, 35, 122-23
synthetic fertilizers, 14

tapping watermelons, 104
toads, 41
"Tokyo Bean" mustard, 120
tomatoes, 15, 27, 33, 35, 36, 45, 79-83
toxins in soil, 8
transplanting: cole crops, 62-63; leeks, 53; lettuce, 59; melons, 102; peppers and eggplants, 84; radicchio, 121; rutabagas, 114; second-season, 109-10; seedlings, 35-37, squash, 94, 95; tomatoes, 81
trenches: asparagus, 130; leeks, 53
"Triomphe de Farcy" beans, 96
Tsatziki, 107
tubers: Jerusalem artichokes, 133; potatoes, 74-76
turnips, 114
"Tuxedo" corn, 88
Twain, Mark, 101, 104

"Ultra Girl" tomatoes, 81
umbelliferous plants, 67, 68
"Urgenta" potatoes, 74

"Valamaine Cos" lettuce, 58
vermiculite, 29
vines: cucumber, 106-07; melon, 102-03; pea, 48-49; squash, 94, 95; tomato, 82

"Waltham Butternut" squash, 92
wasps, 90
watering, 32, 44-45; arugula, 118; beets, 72; carrots and parsley, 69, 70; Chinese cabbage, 110; cole crops, 64; corn, 89; cucumbers, 107; endive, 113; Florence fennel, 119; lettuce, 59; melons, 103; onions, 52; peas, 49; potatoes, 75; raspberries, 145; rutabagas, 114; spinach, 50; tomatoes, 83
watermelons, 101-05
weather for transplanting, 36
weeds, 44; asparagus, 129-30, 132; strawberries, 138, 139-40 "White Icicle" radishes, 73
wilting leaves, 45
winter: raspberries in, 145
"Winter Keeper" beets, 71, 72
winter squash, 91-92, 84
Winter Squash and Kale Pasta Sauce, 99
wireworms, 102
worms, 64

"Yellow Baby" watermelons, 101
"Yukon Gold" potatoes, 74

zone of fertility, 63, 111